Facebook and Conversation Analysis

Also available from Bloomsbury:

A Critical Hypertext Analysis of Social Media, Volker Eisenlauer
Discourse and Identity on Facebook, Mariza Georgalou
Discourse of Twitter and Social Media, Michele Zappavigna

Facebook and Conversation Analysis

The Structure and Organization of Comment Threads

Matteo Farina

BLOOMSBURY ACADEMIC
LONDON • NEW YORK • OXFORD • NEW DELHI • SYDNEY

BLOOMSBURY ACADEMIC
Bloomsbury Publishing Plc

50 Bedford Square, London, WC1B 3DP, UK
1385 Broadway, New York, NY 10018, USA

BLOOMSBURY and the Diana logo are trademarks of Bloomsbury Publishing Plc

First published in Great Britain 2018

A catalogue record for this book is available from the British Library.

A catalog record for this book is available from the Library of Congress.

ISBN: HB: 978-1-3500-3828-8
ePDF: 978-1-3500-3830-1
eBook: 978-1-3500-3829-5

Typeset by Deanta Global Publishing Services, Chennai, India
Printed and bound in Great Britain

To find out more about our authors and books visit www.bloomsbury.com and sign up for our newsletters.

Contents

List of Figures

1

Introduction

Nowadays a large part of our everyday interactions takes place online. We continuously send and receive notifications, e-mails, WhatsApp messages, tweets, and so on; we also share photos, videos, and hyperlinks using smart phones, computers, tablets, and so on. In addition, almost everyone has a Facebook (FB) account. Two billion people are in fact on FB and 1.3 billion use this social network on a daily basis (Facebook, 2017). This means that a lot of social interactions take place on FB; this book focuses on these interactions. It applies the ideas of Conversation Analysis (CA) to describe the structure of comment threads, which are interactions that occur among FB users on the homepage of this website, the so-called Home. More precisely, based on a corpus of comment threads posted by speakers of Italian, it examines the comments that open these interactions and the contributions that come after them.

Conversational analytic studies have shown that in spoken conversation turns at talk do not casually follow one after the other, but they are organized in a structure (Liddicoat, 2011; Sacks, 1992; Sacks, Schegloff, and Jefferson, 1974; Schegloff, 2007). As Liddicoat (2011) claims, turns at talk are "clustered together," ordered in a meaningful way. This organization is called *sequence organization*. The idea of *sequence organization* depends on a fundamental principle of spoken conversation, which is that when a speaker utters a sentence he or she performs an action which generates another action, which in turn makes another action relevant, and so on (Liddicoat, 2011; Sacks, 1992; Schegloff, 2007). This means that by analyzing the actions performed by speakers in a conversation, it is possible to understand how an interaction is organized (Liddicoat, 2011; Sacks, 1975, 1992; Schegloff, 2007).

A request is generally followed by an acceptance or a decline, a question by an answer, a greeting by another greeting, and so on. This means that turns at talk are commonly organized in pairs, where the action performed by the first part of the pair makes the action accomplished in the second part of the pair the relevant next. The concept of *sequence organization* has thus been introduced by Sacks et al. (1974) to describe what normally happens in spoken conversation, which is that turns at talk are organized in sequences because of the actions they perform.

Several studies have pointed out that *sequence organization* is also identifiable in online contexts, especially in chats and discussion forums (Antaki et al., 2005; Garcia and Jacobs, 1998, 1999; Reed, 2001; Schönfeldt and Golato, 2003; Tudini, 2010, 2013). In other words, people tend to organize online interactions like they develop spoken conversations, for example, by using *adjacency pair sequences*.

Previous research has also shown that the affordances and constraints of the system in which an interaction occurs impact on the organization, especially if this interaction is computer mediated (Antaki et al., 2005; Garcia and Jacobs, 1998, 1999; Reed, 2001; Schönfeldt and Golato, 2003; Tudini, 2010, 2013). For example, while spoken conversation is an oral form of interaction, many forms of online communication are written. Moreover, while participants in spoken conversations, with the exception of phone conversations and similar exchanges, are normally copresent at the time of an interaction, this is not the case in online interactions, where participants are generally geographically dispersed. Finally, while spoken conversation is synchronous, which means that it occurs in real time, this is not true of many forms of online interactions, where a user may post a contribution at one point in time and another user might respond to it after several hours or even several days. Therefore, previous studies have demonstrated not only that the notion of *sequence organization* can be applied to online interactions but also that the system in which an interaction occurs may impact on the way this interaction is organized.

Although previous research has paid considerable attention to analyzing the *sequence organization* of online chats, discussion forums, e-mail exchanges, and blogs, it is interesting to consider whether this organization is also identifiable in FB comment threads. If this is the case, this study will prove that contributions do not randomly occur in FB interactions but that they are orderly and this order depends on the actions performed by FB users in comment threads. This book therefore utilizes the ideas of CA to describe the *sequence organization* of FB comment threads and it addresses the following research questions:

- Are comments within FB comment threads organized in an identifiable structure?
- If so, what is the *sequence organization* of FB comment threads?

In recent years FB has become extremely popular among scholars of different disciplines, and this has resulted in a huge amount of literature. The following section will present a brief overview of the studies that have examined FB, focusing especially on those that have analyzed this social medium from a linguistic perspective.

Previous work on Facebook

Social networks are websites that invite users to create a profile, connect with other users, and communicate with them (Boyd and Ellison, 2007; Golder, Wilkinson, and Huberman, 2007). FB is the most popular social network site of the world (Papacharissi and Mendelson, 2010; Pérez-Sabater, 2013). This popularity has attracted the attention of scholars from different disciplines, including communication (Barbulet, 2013; Baym, 2015; Boyd and Ellison, 2007; Dong, 2008; Farman, 2012; Papacharissi, 2010; Stern and Taylor, 2007; Taecharungroj and Nueangjamnong, 2015), anthropology (Lampe, Ellison, and Steinfield, 2006; Miller, 2011), sociology (Castells, 2013; Gennaro and Dutton, 2007; Golder, Wilkinson, and Huberman, 2007; Harper, 2011; Leonardi, 2009; Stutzman, 2006; Tufekci, 2008; Westlake, 2008; Zhao, Grasmuck, and Martin, 2008), education (Bugeja, 2006; Cheung, Chiu, and Lee, 2011; Davies, 2011; Hew, 2011; Hsu et al., 2012; Kitsis, 2008; Sheldon, 2008a, 2008b, 2009), and second language acquisition (Blattner and Fiori, 2009; Godwin-Jones, 2008; Kabilan, Ahmad, and Abidin, 2010; Mills, 2009). The purpose of some of these papers is beyond the scope of this book; what will be presented here is therefore a brief overview of studies which are relevant to the aim of this work, namely those which have proposed a linguistic description of FB.

Some of the linguistic studies on FB have focused on status updates, the contributions that open comment threads, which are the interactions that take place on the FB Home. For example, Bolander and Locher (2010) and Carr, Schrock, and Dauterman (2012) undertook two studies which applied speech act theory to analyze status updates, and they both found that these updates essentially consist of assertive and expressive speech acts. Status updates have also been examined by Lee (2011), Farina (2015), Georgakopoulou (2013b), Georgalou (2015b), Giaxoglou (2015a, 2015b), West (2013), Page (2010b, 2012), and Page, Harper, and Frobenius (2013). These scholars applied discourse and conversation analysis to investigate status updates; they all suggested that these messages consist of narratives, more precisely, stories (Giaxoglou, 2015a, 2015b), small stories (Georgakopoulou, 2007a, 2007b, 2013b, 2014; Georgalou, 2015b; Page, 2010b, 2012; Page, Harper, and Frobenius, 2013; West, 2013), tellings (Farina, 2015), and a form of micro-blogging (Lee, 2011).

Other linguistic studies on FB have examined the contributions that come after status updates in comment threads (Gerolimos, 2011; Hille and Bakker, 2014; Maíz-Arévalo, 2013; Pérez-Sabater, 2013; Placencia and Lower, 2013; Wang, Burke, and Kraut, 2013; West, 2015). Placencia and Lower (2013) studied contributions that were posted to respond to photos published on FB. These authors claim that the contributions that come after photographs posted on FB normally consist of compliments, and they are similar to *second pair parts* in *adjacency pair sequences* (Placencia and Lower, 2013). In addition, this work shows that FB users seem to take advantage of the affordances of the medium when they post compliments on FB. They use the *Like*[1] button, a typical feature of FB, to pay compliments on this website. This is in line with what was claimed by Maíz-Arévalo (2013), who compared responses to compliments occurring on FB and spoken conversations. This study points out that the affordances of FB, combined with its asynchronous nature, impact on the way people respond to compliments in this social networking site. In fact, FB users generally respond to compliments by using the *Like* button, or they simply leave them "unanswered, taking advantage of the social networking site's asynchronous nature" (Maíz-Arévalo, 2013).

The fact that FB users utilize the *Like* button to respond to comments posted in comment threads has also been noted by Gerolimos (2011) and Pérez-Sabater (2013) in two studies analyzing answers to comments posted on the FB pages of libraries and universities across Europe and America. These studies found that the majority of the comments posted by FB users on these webpages consisted of *Likes*. *Likes* were also investigated by West (2015), who pointed out that although they are the most common type of response to status updates, FB users seem to interpret *Likes* in different ways, including as acknowledgments, backchannels, or a form of support to initial posters.

On the other hand, Hille and Bakker (2014) made a quantitative study focusing on Dutch newspapers. They compared the number of comments posted by readers on the official FB pages of the newspapers with the number of messages readers published on the websites of these newspapers. This study found that readers tend to post more comments on the websites of the newspapers rather than on their FB pages.

Another quantitative study has investigated the impact of gender and topic choice on the number of responses received by contributions posted in comment threads (Wang, Burke, and Kraut, 2013). Findings of this study suggest that comments posted by women are more likely to secure responses than those posted by men.

Other linguistic studies on FB have focused on the language used in comment threads (Androutsopoulos, 2014a, 2014b, 2015; Barton and Lee, 2013; Dabrowska, 2012; Karrebæk, Stæhr, and Varis, 2015; Lenihan, 2011; Seargeant, Tagg, and Ngampramuan, 2012; Sharma, 2012; Sherman and Švelch, 2015; Stæhr, 2015; Tagg, 2015; Tagg and Seargeant, 2012). These studies have found that the language used by FB users in comment threads normally orients to the audience of these interactions; for example, multilingual users choose to write their comments in one language rather than in another in relation to the Friends they are addressing and the topics they are discussing in their comment threads (Androutsopoulos, 2014a, 2014b, 2015; Seargeant, Tagg, and Ngampramuan, 2012). Another feature identified by studies that have analyzed the language used by FB users in comment threads is that it normally consists of a mix of written and spoken language and it plays an important role in creating both individual and group identities (Karrebæk et al., 2015; Papacharissi, 2010; Stæhr, 2015; Tagg and Seargeant, 2012). Moreover, this language appears to be intertextual: it "refer[s] to, draw[s] upon, or reshape[s] earlier texts within the context of a latter one" (West and Trester, 2013).

Finally, Frobenius and Harper (2015) have examined the relationship between status updates and the comments that follow them in comment threads and they have claimed that these contributions are normally organized in relation to time and space. In other words, it appears that FB users rely on when a contribution has been posted on a comment thread, as well as where it has been positioned in an interaction, to tie it to the other comments that have already been published in a comment thread.

This section has presented a brief overview of the studies that have examined FB from a linguistic perspective. Some of the studies mentioned above have applied a conversation analytical approach to investigate FB and the interactions that take place in this social medium (Farina, 2015; Maíz-Arévalo, 2013; Placencia and Lower, 2013; West, 2015); the following section will explain why CA is an appropriate methodological approach to take for the investigation of FB comment threads.

Why conversation analysis?

A fundamental assumption of CA is that this methodological approach is mainly concerned with the investigation of social interaction[2] (C. Goodwin and Heritage, 1990; Heritage, 1984, 1988; Kasper, 2006; Liddicoat, 2011; Markee,

2000; Mondada, 2013a; Sacks, 1992; Sacks et al., 1974; Schegloff, 1987a, 1993, 2006, 2007; ten Have, 1999; Wooffitt, 2005).

As claimed by previous studies on FB, this website consists of social interaction (Boyd, 2006; Boyd and Ellison, 2007; Cheung, Chiu, and Lee, 2011; Golder, Wilkinson, and Huberman, 2007; Hew, 2011; Kabilan, Ahmad, and Abidin, 2010; Lampe, Ellison, and Steinfield, 2006; Leonardi, 2009; Sheldon, 2008a, 2009; Stern and Taylor, 2007; Westlake, 2008; Zhao, Grasmuck, and Martin, 2008). Golder, Wilkinson, and Huberman (2007) affirm that "since nearly everyone a college student might want to reach (i.e., other college students) can be found within Facebook, it makes Facebook a useful place to communicate with others. It also makes Facebook quite socially relevant, since it becomes the locus for much social interaction" (p. 44). The idea that FB is an instance of social interaction is also raised by Leonardi (2009), who states that "while social-networking sites (SNS) differ in goals and usage, the basic purpose of these sites remains the same, online interaction and communication" (p. 39). This is in line with what Kabilan, Ahmad, and Abidin (2010) affirm about FB: "FB with its unique features, such as feed, online games and chat encourages users to interact and engage with anyone from any parts of world in any language that they are comfortable in" (p. 180).

A second assumption of CA which is relevant to the aim of this book is that this approach is particularly useful for the investigation of the organization of social interaction. In fact, as Goodwin and Heritage (1990) state, CA "seeks to describe the underlying social organization—conceived as an institutionalized substratum of interactional rules, procedures, and conventions—through which orderly and intelligible social interaction is made possible."

A third principle of CA which indicates that this methodological approach is appropriate for studying FB interactions is that it analyzes naturally occurring interactions. In fact, Psathas (1995) claims that data for conversation analytic studies can be of any type, "the only requirement being that these [data] should be naturally occurring." Conversation analysts utilize the term *naturally occurring* to refer to interactions "that would have occurred regardless of whether the researcher had come upon the scene" (Psathas, 1995). In other words, as Liddicoat (2011) affirms, naturally occurring interactions are "interactions which would have happened anyway, not interactions which have been contrived by the researcher for the purposes of doing research," like the comment threads analyzed in this book. These interactions are in fact naturally occurring; they have not been arranged for the purpose of this book. This makes them suitable for analysis using a conversation analytical approach.

Although CA is a methodological approach which is particularly concerned with the investigation of the structure of spoken conversation, several researchers have already applied it to analyze synchronous as well as asynchronous forms of online interactions. Studies that have used CA to examine synchronous forms of online interactions found that this approach is particularly useful to investigate the organization of these interactions (Garcia and Jacobs, 1998, 1999; Negretti, 1999; Schönfeldt and Golato, 2003; Tudini, 2004, 2007, 2010, 2013; Zemel and Çakir, 1999). As Negretti (1998) states "the approach taken by Heritage (1997) to CA microanalysis was especially useful for this study, in particular the analysis of the overall structure of interaction, turn-taking organization, and lexical choice." A similar claim has been made by other researchers, in particular Garcia and Jacobs (1998, 1999), who use CA to investigate the organization of what they call Quasi Synchronous-Computer Mediated Communication (QS-CMC): "In order to discover the procedures and assumptions underlying successful interaction in QS-CMC, an understanding of its interactional organization is necessary. For this purpose we argue that an ethnomethodological conversation analytic approach provides the necessary analytical tools and conceptual framework" (Garcia and Jacobs, 1998).

In addition to its use in analyzing synchronous forms of QS-CMC, CA has also been applied to study asynchronous forms of computer-mediated communication, such as online forums, blogs, and social network sites like Twitter (Antaki et al., 2005; Gibson, 2009a, b; Lambiase, 2010; Lomicka and Lord, 2012; Reed, 2001; Stommel, 2008). As with synchronous types of computer interactions, researchers utilize CA to investigate the organization of asynchronous forms of CMC. For example, Stommel (2008) explicitly says that CA is useful to analyze the *sequence organization* of contributions in online forums: "CA investigates social action with a focus on participants' understanding of one another's conduct. This premise (language use as social action), as well as certain aspects of sequence organization, which refers to relations between turns such as adjacency pairs, can be adopted for an analysis of CMC." A similar claim has also been made by Reed (2001), Gibson (2009a), and Antaki et al. (2005), when they state that "what CA brings to these communicative environments is a perspective on people's use of interactional expectations of turn-taking, the sequential placement of messages, and their internal design."

As mentioned in the previous section, a few studies have already applied CA to examine FB interactions. Moreover, these studies have focused on the contributions that open FB comment threads (Farina, 2015), the responses that follow them (West, 2015), the relationship between status updates and the comments that come after them (Frobenius and Harper, 2015), compliments (Placencia and Lower, 2013), and responses to compliments occurring in this social network site (Maíz-Arévalo, 2013).

Despite the fact that CA has been used since the 1990s to investigate online interactions, there are still researchers who argue that this methodological approach is not suitable for investigating online data. This is because in contrast to spoken conversation, online interactions are written and persistent, typed and editable, and affected by the features of the software used for the interaction; moreover, in some cases, these interactions have an unknown audience and a nature that could potentially be both private and public (Giles et al., 2015). This skepticism has stimulated a group of researchers to establish some guidelines for developing a "digital conversation analysis," a methodological approach which is specifically suited for the investigation of conversational-like online data (Giles et al., 2015; Giles, Stommel, and Paulus, 2017). This approach would allow researchers to have a better understanding of online talk; it could be used, for example, to see how the different features of a specific platform, such as Facebook or Twitter, shape online interactions. Digital CA could also be used to investigate how online users use hyperlinks, images, and emoticons in their online interactions.

In general, therefore, CA is a methodological approach which is mainly interested in the investigation of the structure of naturally occurring social interactions. However, considering that this approach has already been used by previous studies for investigating online interactions, and more importantly that it has also been used to examine FB comment threads, all of this makes CA an appropriate approach to take for this book.

The previous sections have described the aim of this book, previous studies on FB, and the methodological approach utilized in this book. The following sections, on the other hand, will describe some features of everyday conversations relevant in discussing the structure of FB comment threads, such as the *turn-taking system*, *sequence organization*, and the telling sequence.

The *turn-taking system*

One major feature of spoken conversation is the *turn-taking system*. Although it is traditionally used to describe the organization of spoken conversations, in a sense this system seems to also apply to FB comment threads. Therefore, the aim of this section is to lay the groundwork for an exploration of the *turn-taking system* in FB comment threads, which will be discussed in Chapter 3.

What commonly occurs in ordinary conversation is that one party talks at a time (Sacks et al., 1974); in other words, speakers do not talk simultaneously: when one speaker talks another listens. Also, speaker changes occur harmoniously, with few gaps and overlaps (Liddicoat, 2011; Sacks, 1992; Sacks et al., 1974; Schegloff, 2007). The idea of the *turn-taking system* has thus been introduced to describe what normally happens in ordinary conversation, which is that conversationalists speak one at a time. When a speaker talks, he or she produces a turn at talk. A turn at talk is a single or an ensemble of pieces of talk utilized by a conversationalist to perform an action (Schegloff, 2007). These pieces of talk are called *Turn Constructional Units* (TCUs). So, TCUs are the basic units utilized by speakers to create turns at talk (Liddicoat, 2011; Sacks et al., 1974; Schegloff, 2007). A turn at talk may hence consist of one or multiple TCUs (Liddicoat, 2011; Sacks, 1992; Sacks et al., 1974; Schegloff, 2007).

When a TCU reaches its possible completion, speaker change may occur (Liddicoat, 2011; Sacks, 1992; Sacks et al., 1974; Schegloff, 2007). Points where a speaker change may occur are called *Transition Relevance Places* (TRPs) (Liddicoat, 2011; Sacks et al., 1974; Schegloff, 2007). Speaker changes generally occur "smoothly" in a conversation; in other words, a current speaker concludes his or her turn and the next speaker takes the floor. However, sometimes speaker changes may be problematic. For example, when a next speaker utters a turn before the current speaker has completed his or her turn, this generates an *overlap*. An *overlap* is a problem in the normal flow of an interaction. *Overlaps* and other problems in interaction are addressed by conversationalists with *repairs* (Liddicoat, 2011; Sacks, 1992; Schegloff, 2007).

In conclusion, the *turn-taking system* has been introduced by analysts to describe the underlying organization of speaker changes in spoken conversation. Even though FB comment threads mainly consist of written messages, "speaker" changes are also common in these interactions. It is therefore possible that despite the generally asynchronous nature of interaction, some aspects of the *turn-taking system* might impact on the organization of FB comment threads, and thus it will be important to examine how turn-taking and speaker changes occur in FB comment threads.

Sequence organization

Although conversation analysts utilize the term *sequence organization* to describe what normally occurs in spoken conversation, this can also be applied to FB comment threads. In fact, comments do not casually follow one another in a comment thread, but they are organized in sequences, similar to turns at talk in spoken conversation.

As Schegloff (2007) claims, the way turns at talk are organized in a conversation depends on the actions they perform in interaction. Moreover, each turn at talk shows how a speaker has interpreted the previous turn that had occurred in the interaction. The way in which conversationalists interpret previous turns and shape their own is an example of *sequence organization*. The *sequence organization* of spoken conversation is therefore concerned with the positioning of turns at talk in an interaction. Furthermore, this positioning depends on the actions accomplished by conversationalists in their turns at talk:

> Each turn at talk can be inspected by co-participants to see what action(s) may be being done through it. And all series of turns can be inspected or tracked (by the parties and by us) to see what course(s) of action may be being progressively enacted through them, what possible responses may be being made relevant, what outcomes are being pursued, what "sequences" are being constructed or enacted or projected. That is, sequences of turns are not haphazard but have a shape or structure, and can be tracked for where they came from, what is being done through them, and where they might be going. (Schegloff, 2007, p. 3)

The concept of *sequence organization* has thus been introduced by analysts to describe actions performed by conversationalists in interaction. The most common type of sequence in which turns at talk are organized is *adjacency pairs* (Liddicoat, 2011; Sacks et al., 1974; Schegloff, 2007). Question-answer, greeting-greeting, offer-acceptance, and/or offer-decline are examples of *adjacency pairs*. *Adjacency pairs* are turns at talk which occur in pairs and have certain characteristics. First, they are composed of two turns which are adjacently positioned; that is, they generally occur one after the other. Second, they are uttered by two different speakers. Third, *adjacency pairs* are ordered; that is, they are composed of *first* and *second pair parts*. In other words, one part of the pair has always to occur first and the other second, and these positions are not interchangeable. Finally, *adjacency pairs* are organized into pair types, such that not any *second pair part* can follow a specific *first pair part*. This is because the *first pair part* that initiates the sequence generally establishes the *second pair part* which has to complete it. For example, a question cannot be followed by a greeting, the course of action initiated by this *first pair part* in fact requires a particular response, an answer, to be completed (Liddicoat, 2011; Sacks, 1992; Schegloff, 2007; Schegloff and Sacks, 1973).

The idea behind *adjacency pairs* is that conversationalists perform actions while uttering turns at talk. Turns at talk are "tied" together because of the course of action implemented by speakers while interacting. Moreover, one action makes another action relevant, which in turn generates another action, and so on. Hence, turns at talk do not occur casually, but they are sequentially organized. Strong evidence that this is the case comes from *adjacency pairs* (Liddicoat, 2011; Sacks, 1992; Schegloff, 2007; Schegloff and Sacks, 1973).

One type of sequence which is very common in everyday conversation and FB comment threads is the telling sequence; this will be discussed in the following section.

Tellings

Previous studies have identified two types of tellings in spoken conversation: announcements and stories (Bamberg and Georgakopoulou, 2008; C. Goodwin, 1984; M. Goodwin, 1982, 1991, 1993; Jefferson, 1978; Labov and Waletzky, 1997; Liddicoat, 2011; Mandelbaum, 1989; Maynard, 2006; Norrick, 2000; Sacks, 1974, 1978, 1986, 1992; Terasaki, 2004). As Schegloff (2007) states, an announcement is "a telling packaged in a single, grammatically simple, turn-constructional unit" (p. 42). On the other hand, Liddicoat (2011) defines stories as "tellings which occur as multi-unit, extended turns at talk" (p. 320). Therefore, announcements and stories are both tellings, but they have different formats. The former are commonly short and simple, while the latter are long and complex. While announcements may occur casually in a conversation, stories generally do not, and in fact they are usually triggered by something which has been previously said in an interaction (Liddicoat, 2011; Sacks, 1992).

A very important moment in a conversation is when a teller wants to start a telling, as he or she must solve two interactional problems before uttering it. The first is to secure a recipient, and the second is to secure the interactional space for the telling. These problems are commonly dealt with in a pre-telling sequence, which is a sequence of two turns at talk that may precede an announcement or a story. In a pre-telling sequence, a teller asks a recipient if he or she is interested in listening to a telling, and the recipient accepts or refuses to listen to it (Liddicoat, 2011; Maynard, 2006; Sacks, 1992; Schegloff, 2007; Terasaki, 2004). The problem of securing a recipient for a telling is common to both announcements and stories. This is because it is impossible (at least in spoken conversation) to perform a telling without a recipient who listens to it. However, securing the space to perform a telling is a problem which affects stories only. Stories require multiple TCUs and turns at talk to be completed; hence, both the teller and the recipient have to stop the *turn-taking system* in order to provide the teller with enough space to perform his or her story. Once a teller has secured the space and a recipient for his or her story, the story may occur (Jefferson, 1978; Liddicoat, 2011; Maynard, 2006; Sacks, 1992; Terasaki, 2004).

When a telling is completed, a response is relevant. So, on completion of a telling, the teller expects the recipient to respond to it. This response shows how the recipient has understood the telling. A common way to respond to both stories and announcements is by using an assessment (Liddicoat, 2011; Sacks, 1992; Terasaki, 2004). A second telling is another possible type of response to a first telling (Jefferson, 1978; Liddicoat, 2011; Sacks, 1992; Terasaki, 2004). In this case, the first telling triggers the second telling. In other words, the recipient of the first telling shows his or her understanding of the previous telling by uttering a second telling which generally refers to the previous one.

Tellings seem also to be very frequent in FB (Georgakopoulou, 2013a, b; Page, 2010b), especially in status updates (Farina, 2015). These narratives appear to be similar to small stories (Georgakopoulou, 2013a, b; Page, 2010b), consisting of "tellings of ongoing events, future or hypothetical events, shared (known) events, but also allusions to tellings, defferal of tellings, and refusal to tell" (Georgakopoulou, 2007b). Moreover, they may consist of textual messages only, combinations of textual messages with photos or hyperlinks, photos only, or hyperlinks only (Farina, 2015).

After pointing out that CA is a methodological approach which is mainly concerned with the study of the orderliness of naturally occurring social interactions, the final sections of this chapter have focused on some features of everyday conversation which will also be relevant in discussing FB comment threads, like the *turn-taking system* and the *sequence organization* of everyday conversation. A particularly common sequence—telling—was then briefly discussed.

The structure of this book

This book is organized into nine chapters. Following this Introduction, Chapter 2 presents the terminology utilized and describes the data and participants who took part in this study. Chapter 3 describes the impact of some of the features of FB on the organization of comment threads. Chapter 4 discusses the basic sequence that characterizes FB comment threads. This chapter shows that comment threads are commonly opened by tellings, and it presents the classification into which FB comment threads have been organized in this book. Chapter 5 discusses the interactional problems that characterize FB comment threads which contain tellings in their initial comments and the actions performed by FB users to overcome these problems. Chapter 6 focuses on tellings which occur in comments that are not the first contributions posted by FB users in comment threads and how these tellings impact on the overall structure of FB comment threads. Chapter 7 investigates responses posted by FB users after tellings which occur in comment threads, and Chapter 8 focuses on later comments posted in FB comment threads. Finally, Chapter 9 presents the findings of this study.

2

Research Design, Data Collection, and the Corpus

Introduction

After describing the aim of this book, Chapter 1 presented the findings of some of the linguistic studies that have examined FB and the interactions that take place in this social networking site. Chapter 1 also demonstrated that CA is a suitable methodology to take for investigating the structure of FB comment threads. It then introduced some features of everyday conversation, which will also be relevant in discussing the structure of FB comment threads, like the *turn-taking system*, *sequence organization*, and the telling sequence. This chapter introduces the terminology utilized in this book and presents the data and participants involved in this research.

FB Home, Friends, comment threads, and comments: Definitions

This book explores the organization of FB comment threads. Comment threads are interactions that occur on the FB Home, the webpage accessed by an FB user after completing the logging-in process. The Home is similar to the homepage of a discussion forum, and it contains interactions started by the "owner" of the Home and his or her Friends. The term *Friends* refers to FB users who share a "friendship status." To become Friends, an FB user has to send a friendship request to another user, who has to accept it. Therefore, each FB user has his or her network of Friends, and this may partially overlap with the networks of other users.

Comment threads generally consist of written messages, typed by FB users using computers, tablets, and smart phones, and then posted on the Home.

They appear as a separate "block" on the Home, and consist of one or more comments, where a comment is the single contribution published by an FB user in a comment thread, as indicated by Figure 2.1.

Figure 2.1 is a screen capture of the FB Home utilized in this study with boxes replacing profile pictures and real names. This figure does not show any comment thread started by the owner of this Home page, only comment threads started by his Friends. The comment thread in the black circle has been initiated by Guido, a Friend of the owner of this Home, and continued by Giorgio, Silvio, and Ruggero.

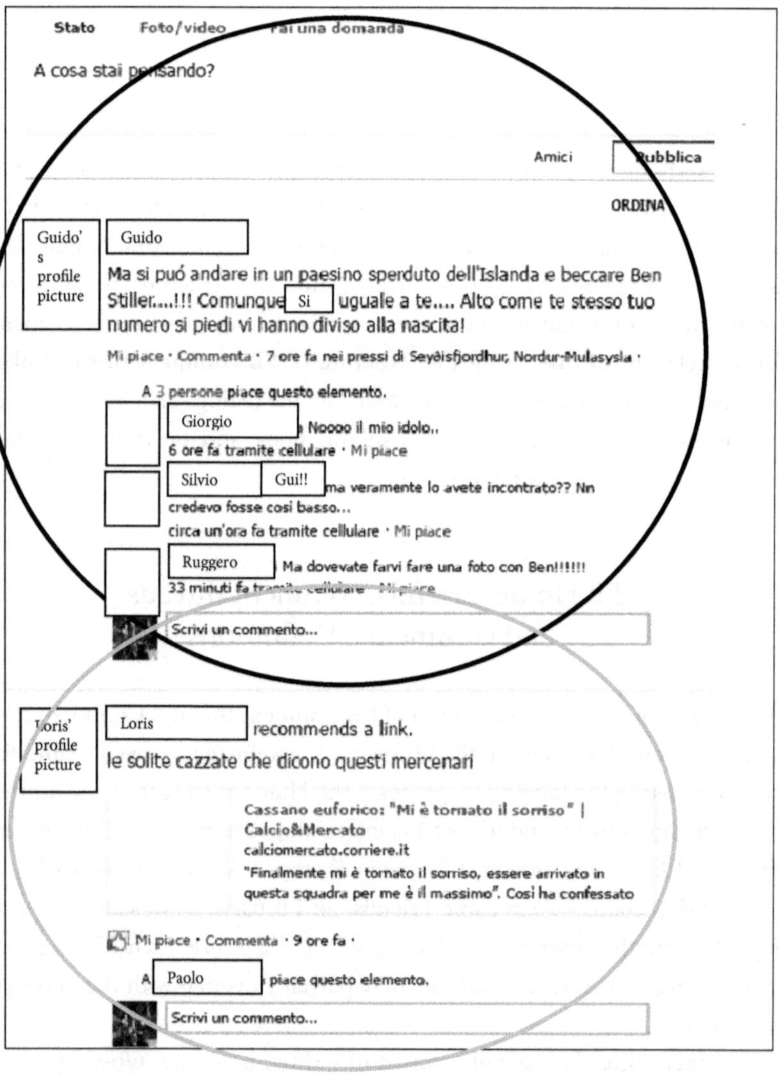

Figure 2.1 Comment threads on the FB Home.

While Silvio is a Friend of the owner of this Home, Giorgio and Ruggero are not. However, the owner of this Home can see the comments they have posted in this comment thread, because these comments have been posted in a comment thread started by Guido, one of the Friends of the owner of this Home.

Every FB user has his or her Home, which contains both the comment threads he or she has initiated and those started by his or her Friends. In other words, every FB Home is different. In fact, even in the hypothetical case in which two users, A and B, share exactly the same Friends, but they themselves are not Friends, their Homes will be different. This is because while A and B both could access the comment threads started by their Friends, A could not see the comment threads B has started and vice versa.[1]

As discussed in Chapter 1, interactions on FB are predominantly asynchronous. FB users do not need to be simultaneously online to post a comment in a comment thread, and this can be seen by the timestamps of the comments in the comment thread in the black circle in Figure 2.1. The time of publication of the first comment in this comment thread indicates that Guido launched this interaction seven hours before the screen capture that contains it was taken for the analysis (*7 hours ago*). Around one hour after the publication of the comment at Post 1, Giorgio published the comment at Post 2 (*6 hours ago via mobile*). Then, almost six hours after the publication of the first comment in this comment thread, Silvio published the comment at Post 3 (*about 1 hour ago via mobile*). Finally, after another half an hour, and therefore almost seven hours since the publication of Guido's initial comment, Ruggero posted the comment at Post 4 (*33 minutes ago via mobile*). We see here that "lags" between the publication of comments in comment threads are normal. Several hours have elapsed between the publication of the first and fourth comment in this comment thread.

On the FB Home, the first comment thread seen by an FB user when he or she accesses his or her Home is included between the dialogue boxes *A Cosa stai pensando?*[2] (What's on your mind?) and *Scrivi un commento* (Write a comment). On the other hand, all other comment threads are found between the two dialogue boxes *Write a comment* that precede and close them. This can be clearly seen in the two comment threads in Figure 2.1. While the comment thread in the black circle (the first presented on the Home) is preceded and closed by the dialogue boxes *What's on your mind?* and *Write a comment*, the comment thread in the gray circle (the second presented on the Home) is positioned between the two dialogue boxes *Write a comment*. Furthermore, a separation line, such as that which follows the comment thread in the black circle in Figure 2.1, is automatically generated by the system after every comment thread published on the Home.

Another important feature of FB comment threads is that there are several ways to publish a comment in a comment thread. If an FB user wants to start a new comment thread, that is, to post the first comment in a new interaction, he or she can either publish a comment using the dialogue box *What's on your mind?* within FB or he or she can simply use the *Condividi* (Share) button. Both these features allow FB users to launch a new comment thread on the Home. The first of these ways, the dialogue box *What's on your mind?*, has been designed as the *first pair part* of a question-answer sequence (Liddicoat, 2011; Sacks, 1992; Sacks et al., 1974; Schegloff, 2007). *First pair parts* require *second pair parts* to be completed, in other words, they project a relevant next action (Liddicoat, 2011; Sacks, 1992; Sacks et al., 1974; Schegloff, 2007). Thus, it appears that the designers of FB have specifically shaped the system prompt *What's on your mind?* as a question to stimulate users to launch new comment threads on the Home. The other way to begin a new comment thread is by using the *Share* button. This button is available on many websites, such as YouTube, and it allows FB users to publish contents from these websites directly onto the FB Home by simply clicking on it. The *Share* button also enables FB users, if desired, to comment on the content they want to post on the Home.

On the other hand, if an FB user wants to participate in an existing comment thread, he or she can use the dialogue box *Write a comment* or the button *Commenta* (Comment). These features (as clearly shown by Figure 2.1) are positioned directly after the first (*Comment*) and the most recent comment in a comment thread (*Write a comment*). Moreover, they have exactly the same function: to allow a Friend to participate in a comment thread by adding his or her new comment to the end of a comment thread. When an FB user publishes a new comment using the dialogue box *Write a comment* or the button *Comment*, this comment is automatically positioned after the last comment in the comment thread. For instance, if a Friend decides to publish a new comment using either the dialogue box *Write a comment* or the button *Comment* in the comment thread in the black circle shown in Figure 2.1, this comment will be positioned after Ruggero's comment (the fourth contribution in this comment thread).

In other words, FB users do not have control over the positioning of comments posted using the dialogue box *Write a comment* or the button *Comment*. This is because FB manages the publication of comments posted using these two features. In addition, contributions posted using these features are presented in order; this order reflects the times of publication of the comments in the comment thread. Moreover, while comment threads on the FB Home are presented in a reverse chronological order, where the first comment thread that appears on the Home is the most recent comment thread started by either the owner of the Home or one of his or her Friends, this is not the case for comments posted using the dialogue box *Write a comment* or the button *Comment*. Comments posted using these features are organized in a chronological order, where the last comment presented is the most recent contribution published in the comment thread, and the first is the oldest one.

Another way to participate in an existing comment thread is by using the *Rispondi* (Reply) button, which is positioned immediately under every comment posted in a comment thread[3] as clearly shown by Figure 2.2.

This button allows FB users to post a comment immediately after a contribution that has already been posted in a comment thread (with the exception of the first comment of a comment thread). If an FB user wants to post a comment

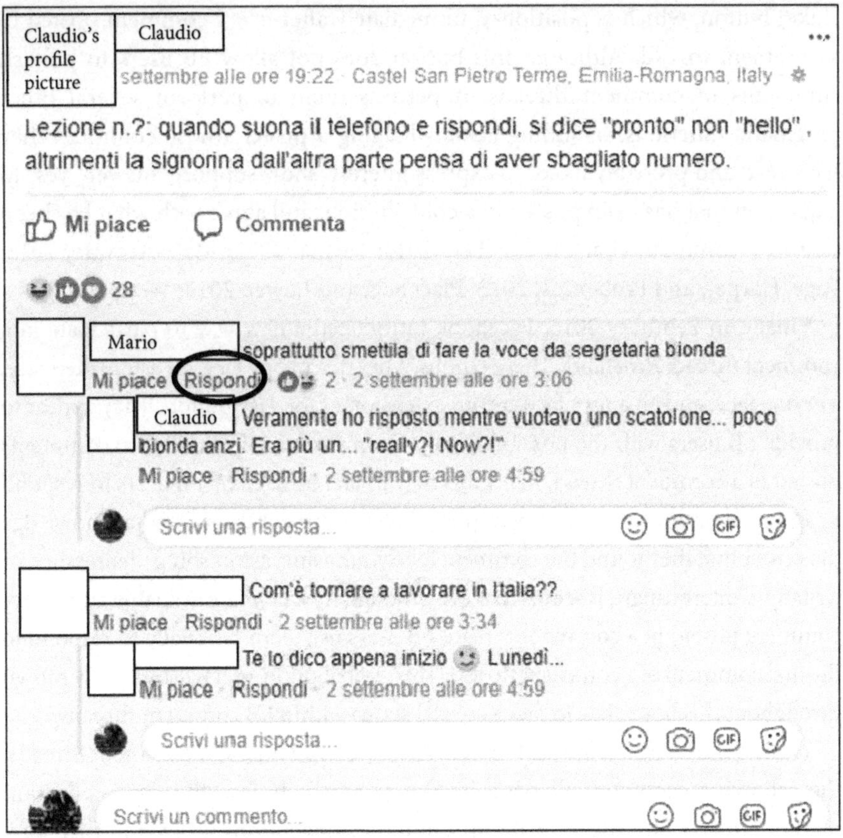

Figure 2.2 The *Rispondi* (Reply) button.

that responds to the first comment of a comment thread he or she can use the dialogue box *Write a comment* or the button *Comment* described above. It thus seems that the *Reply* button allows FB users to have control over the positioning of their comments in comment threads; however, this control does not apply to the contributions that respond to the first comments that open comment threads.

In summary, whether an FB user decides to start a new comment thread or join an existing one, he or she simply has to use the *Share* button or type a comment in the dialogue boxes *What's on your mind?*, *Write a comment*, *Comment*, or *Reply* and then click on either the *Pubblica* (Post) button on FB or the Enter button on his or her keyboard to publish it on the Home. Moreover, all of these features enable FB users to publish comments that can be made up of verbal and nonverbal elements, such as textual messages, photos, videos, and hyperlinks. These buttons in fact allow FB users to attach photos, videos, and hyperlinks to their comments, and if desired, to evaluate them.

Another way to participate in a comment thread is by clicking on the *Mi piace* (Like) button, which is positioned immediately after every comment posted in a comment thread. Although this button does not allow FB users to publish comments in comment threads, it permits them to perform several other pragmatic functions, including acknowledging a poster whose comment they have read and probably liked, to express interest, show support, answer "yes" to a question that has been posted in a contribution, and agree with what has been said in a comment (Barton and Lee, 2013; Farina, 2015; Maíz-Arévalo, 2013; Page, Harper, and Frobenius, 2013; Placencia and Lower, 2013; West, 2015).

Finally, in February 2016, Facebook introduced a new way to participate in a comment thread: *Reactions*. These emojis, a heart, a happy face, an astonished face, a crying face, and an angry face, are an extension of the *Like* button. They appear to provide FB users with the possibility to post an emotional response to comments posted in a comment thread. *Reactions* may in fact be used by FB users to respond to an initial or any other comment posted in a comment thread and acknowledge the poster that they found the comment lovely, amusing, astonishing, depressing, or irritating. Interestingly, it seems that even though *Reactions* are available after every comment posted in a comment thread, FB users use them especially to respond to the first comment of a comment thread. This contribution, as it will be clearly shown throughout this book, has in fact a special status within FB comment threads.

Having thus defined the FB Home, Friends, comments, and comment threads, the following sections will describe the research design, the data collection method, the corpus, the contributors, and the conventions utilized in this book to transcribe the comment threads examined in this study.

Research design

As mentioned in Chapter 1, one major concern in conversational analytic research is that the interactions being investigated should be natural. As Liddicoat (2011) has claimed, such interactions "should be interactions which would have happened anyway, not interactions which have been contrived by the researcher for the purposes of doing research" (p. 14). Thus, in order to explain how FB comment threads are organized, this book needed comment threads which took place naturally on the FB Home and that were not arranged specifically for the purpose of this book.

Data collection method and the corpus

I needed a method that would allow me to collect data without being intrusive and affecting the "naturalness" of comment threads. I thus chose to take screen captures of my FB Home. I followed a very simple procedure to take these screen captures; after completing the logging-in process and accessing my FB Home, I made sure that all the comments posted in the comment threads started by participants who agreed to take part in this study were visible on my Home.[4] I then selected the drop down menu "File" available on the top-left corner of the menu bar of my web browser, Mozilla Firefox. By clicking on the "File" menu, I could access several additional functions, including "Print." This function allowed me to select the device for printing my screen captures. One of the printing devices installed on my computer was Adobe Acrobat Professional 7.0. This software allowed me to save all the comment threads published on my FB Home in a single Adobe PDF file.

During the data collection period, which started in November 2011 and finished in August 2012, I took 132 screen captures of my FB Home, each screen capture containing between 56 and 135 comment threads. I chose to collect screen captures only every two or three days, so that the comment threads collected would not include any of the previously captured interactions. I wanted to have at least 200 analyzable comment threads; I chose to analyze only 10 of the 132 screen captures collected. Once I reached 200 comment threads, I continued until the end of the screen capture I was analyzing, and this produced a total of 213 comment threads. These 213 comment threads contained a total of 1,264 comments. The 213 comment threads included in the corpus of this study look broadly similar to the comment thread in Figure 2.3.

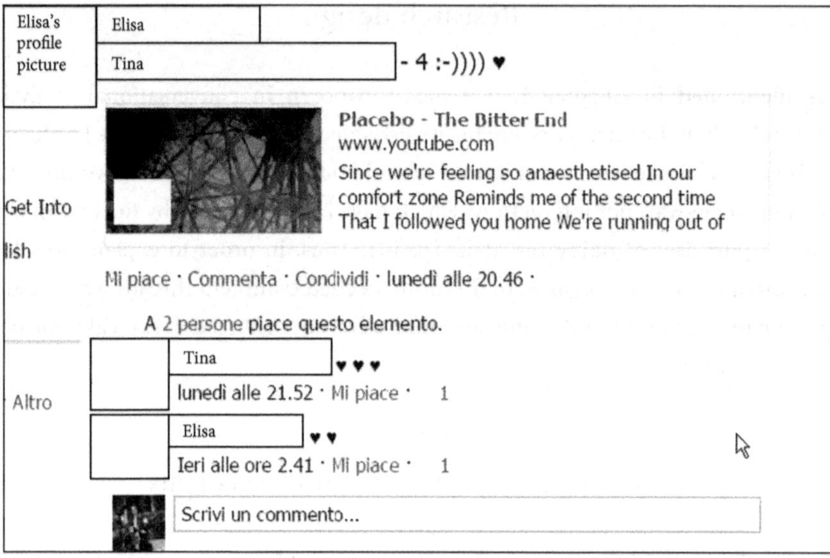

Figure 2.3 Screenshot of an FB comment thread.

In the comment at Post 1 Elisa launches the comment thread contained in Figure 2.3, in the comment at Post 2 Tina responds to it, and finally in the comment at Post 3 Elisa concludes this comment thread by responding to Tina's previous comment at Post 2.

As with the comment thread in Figure 2.1, most of the comment threads included in the corpus of this book are in Italian. However, it is not uncommon for other languages to be used as well, and so some of the comments in the corpus, such as the comments at Posts 1, 5, 6, 7, 8, 9, and 10 in Extract 2.1, are in languages other than Italian, especially English, as indicated by the arrows.

Extract 2.1: Tiramisù

→ 1 Claudio: Doesn't look very nice now??? :P
[Claudio publishes a photo which shows him and a bowl that contains half of a tiramisù cake]

A 2 persone piace questo
2 people like this

2 Raffaele: NO

3 Claudio: Cazzo! :P Ora ci manca che anche Yan se ne accorga:P
Claudio: Shit! :P I hope Yan [Claudio's personal trainer] *doesn't discover this:P*

4 Lucia: mi hanno detto che non scendi D:
Lucia: they told me you won't be back D:

→ 5 Alex: that's mineeeeeeeeeeeeeeeeeee[5]

→ 6 Claudio: run run ;)

→ 7 Jorge: poor tiramisù . . . didn't do anything to you . . . yet xD

→ 8 Claudio: it did! it was saying "you can't have meeeee . . . you're on a diet . . . ." So I showed you that for me the diet doesn't start on Monday :P

→ 9 Jorge: it's weird . . . some chocolate cookies said the same thing to me in the morning . . . is the word coming to an end? . . . Show that tiramisù who's the boss xD

→ 10 Claudio: 2012 is very close yep ;)

The majority of comments in this comment thread are in English. Even though there are almost no comment threads which are entirely in English, it is common to find a few comments written in this or other languages, especially Spanish. The presence of these languages is not surprising in the data. Previous studies have in fact found that foreign words (particularly English words) are commonly used by Italians of all ages in everyday interactions (Bistarelli, 2014; Gèorlach, 2003; Rando, 1970). In addition, it appears that the language used by FB users to post comments in comment threads depends on the audience they want to reach (Androutsopoulos, 2014a, 2014b, 2015; Seargeant, Tagg, and Ngampramuan, 2012). Participants in this study seem also to rely on code switching to resolve communicative problems that might arise in a comment thread, especially when an interaction occurs between speakers of different languages, as in Extract 2.1. The presence of English and Spanish words in comment threads may also depend on the countries in which the contributors lived at the time of the data collection. For example, Claudio, the initial poster of the comment thread in Extract 2.1, was living in England at the time of the publication of this comment thread, and it is therefore possible that he chose to make the comment at Post 1 in English because he wanted all of his Friends, or at least all of those who had some knowledge of the English language, to understand him.

On the other hand, some comments, like the one at Post 1 "*Tira un'aria che pela . . .*" (The wind is so cold that it chills you to the bone . . .) and the initial component of the comment at Post 8 "*Va a let e po cruvet!*" (Go to bed and stay warm!) in Extract 2.2 are in a regional variety of Italian, more specifically Emilian-Italian (*Tira un'aria che pela . . .*), and a dialect, Emilian dialect (*Va a let e po cruvet!*).

Extract 2.2: Weather discussion

→ 1 Claudio: Tira un'aria che pela . . .
Claudio: The wind is so strong that it chills you to the bone . . .

2 Maria: io sono stata a Parigi il febbraio scorso . . . che freddo porco che faceva . . . ti sono vicina ;)
Maria: last February I went to Paris . . . the cold was bloody freezing . . . I'm close to you ;)

3 Claudio: Stammi davvero vicino perchè qui ci rimango. Tra placche e febbriciattola, più st'aria . . . spero di rientrare nella nebbiosa Londra alive :)
Claudio: Stay really close to me because I'm going to die here. With a sore throat, the fever, and this wind . . . I hope to return alive to the foggy London:)

4 Maria: tra londra [*sic*] e parigi [*sic*] . . . meglio l'aria di bologna [*sic*]! :** (solo l'aria temo)
*Maria: between london and paris . . . better the air of bologna! :** (I'm afraid just the air)*

5 Claudio: Ve che a Bologna fa più freddo che a Londra. Però ci sono i ristoranti con ogni ben di dio!
Claudio: Bologna is colder than London. But there are restaurants full of delicacies!

6 Maria: caza vi! ;) e soprattutto . . . . ci sono le none [*sic*]!! ;) :)
Maria: caza vi! [probably an idiomatic expression in Emilian dialect which might work as an expletive] *;) and by the way . . . . there are the grandmothers!!;)*

7 Claudio: Merda l'hai detto!
Claudio: Shit well said!

→ 8 Nives: Va a let e po cruvet! Così ti scaldi
Nives: Go to bed and stay warm!

Regional varieties of Italian and dialects are commonly used by conversationalists in everyday interactions, especially in spoken conversation to create group identity (Cerruti, 2011), and their presence in the data is therefore not surprising.

Extracts 2.1 and 2.2 have shown that some of the comments posted in the comment threads included in the data of this book are written in other languages as well as in regional varieties of Italian and dialects. Even though these comments are not written in (standard) Italian, they have not been translated or deleted from the transcripts of this study, because the data would be distorted and not representative of naturally occurring interactions. Thus, all data is included for analysis, regardless of the language of the comments.

However, most comments are in standard Italian (allowing for abbreviations, emoticons, typos, etc.).

Contributors

I invited all of my Friends to participate in this study. At the time of the data collection I had 236 Friends, and I sent invitations to all of them using the e-mail feature embedded in FB. Twenty-nine of my Friends agreed to participate in this study, and they are referred to as the primary contributors to this research. Therefore, the primary contributors were my family members, friends, and acquaintances. I also contributed to some of the comment threads included in this study. My contributions have been examined as if they were posted by a contributor who participated in this research. Even though the relationship I shared with primary contributors did not affect the organization of FB comment threads, this preexisting relationship did provide me with background information for understanding some aspects of comments posted by these contributors on the comment threads. Primary contributors consisted of eighteen males and eleven females and they had at least thirteen years of formal instruction in Italian primary, junior high, and high school. Moreover, nineteen of them had an undergraduate qualification awarded by an Italian university; they were therefore considered to be speakers of Italian, and the primary use of this language in the data is not surprising. Furthermore, most or all the primary contributors had some knowledge of additional languages, especially English and Spanish; in addition, some of them spoke regional varieties of Italian, especially Lombard and Emilian dialects (the dialects spoken in the cities of Milano and Bologna).

Secondary contributors, such as Raffaele, Lucia, Alex and Jorge in Extract 2.1 and Maria and Nives in Extract 2.2, were also involved in this study. They were people who had not specifically agreed to participate in this study, but who contributed comments in comment threads which were begun by one of the primary contributors, and whose contributions were thus vital in examining the *sequence organization* of those comment threads. While there were 29 primary contributors, there were 237 secondary contributors. I did not necessarily know secondary contributors, nor share an FB "friendship status" with them. For this reason, I had no access to information regarding features such as their gender and linguistic or social background, although it appears from the data that many of them share broadly similar backgrounds with the primary contributors.

Conventions for transcribing FB comment threads

Even though comment threads such as those in Figures 2.1 and 2.3 do not need to be transcribed (in the sense that they are already in written form in the screen captures), for ethical reasons they are not presented as they appear in the original data. Comment threads contained in the PDF files gathered during the data collection period have been transcribed by using specific conventions, and these can be clearly seen in Extracts 2.1 and 2.2. First, names of both primary and secondary contributors have been replaced by pseudonyms. Pseudonyms have been carefully chosen in relation to both the gender and the language contributors utilized in their comments. For example, the pseudonym Jorge in Extract 2.1 was chosen because this secondary contributor appeared to be a male and a Spanish native speaker. Second, images of the profile pictures have been deleted from the transcripts, to protect the identities of primary and secondary contributors.

Third, information regarding the time of publication of comments, where not relevant to the analysis, has been removed from the data. In general, this information does not affect the sequential organization of comment threads, and moreover, information regarding time is not reliable in FB. This is because of the inconsistent way in which FB expresses the time of publication of comments in comment threads. In some cases, such as in the comment thread in Figure 2.3, the time of publication of comments is expressed by indicating the day and time at which comments have been posted in a comment thread, for example, *Monday at 9.52 p.m.* However, in other cases the time of publication of comments is expressed by indicating the number of hours that have elapsed between the publication of a comment in a comment thread and the time at which the screen capture was taken for the analysis, such as *8 hours ago*. Moreover, while I was in Australia when I collected the data, contributors were located in Italy, Spain, England, Australia, and Portugal. It is therefore possible that the different time zones might have affected information regarding the time of publication of comments in comment threads. Information regarding time may also be distracting for the reader, and has thus been removed from the presentation of the data. However, in those cases where the timing is potentially relevant, it has been explicitly included or discussed.

Fourth, the images, photos, videos as well as the textual and visual previews that generally follow hyperlinks published in comments contained in comment threads have been deleted from the transcripts and replaced by brief descriptions, in bracketed notes, of the contents of the items deleted (see comment 1 in the comment thread in Extract 2.1). This is for several reasons, including protecting the privacy of people portrayed in photos published on the FB Home, as well as readability. In fact, the reader cannot click on images, photos, videos, and hyperlinks, and indeed they are often no longer valid. At the time of analyzing the comment threads I was often able to access these contents, thus descriptions which enable the reader to understand the comment threads are given where relevant to understand the interactions and their analyses.

Fifth, any syntactic or other errors that appear in the original data have not been corrected in the transcripts. However, where relevant to clarify meaning, additional information has been added in brackets. Finally, as seen in the comment threads in Extracts 2.1 and 2.2, data are given in the original language, and a fairly literal translation into English, when required, is provided under comments posted in comment threads.

Summary

After introducing the terminology utilized in this book, this chapter has described the research design, the data collection method, the corpus, contributors, and the conventions utilized to transcribe data for the current study, which consists of 213 comment threads containing 1,264 comments mostly in Italian, with some contributions in regional varieties of Italian dialects and other languages. Comment threads included in this corpus have been written by 266 contributors, 29 primary and 237 secondary contributors, and they were collected between November 2011 and August 2012.

The next chapter will discuss some of the features of FB comment threads and describe the basic sequence that characterizes this type of interaction.

3

The Organization of FB Comment Threads

Introduction

In order to understand what happens in FB comment threads, we need to describe some of the characteristics of this type of interaction. After discussing some of the typical features of FB comment threads, this chapter shows that comments in comment threads do not follow one another incoherently, but are organized in an identifiable sequence. Strong evidence for this comes from the presence of *adjacency pairs* and comments that make sense only if interpreted in relation to the actions accomplished in previous comments posted in a comment thread.

Features of FB comment threads

As already noted in Chapter 2, one of the most noticeable characteristics of FB comment threads is that they consist of multiple comments.[1] This can be clearly seen in Extract 3.1, which is a comment thread about Guido and his encounter with the American comic actor Ben Stiller.

Extract 3.1 Ben Stiller

1 Guido: Ma si può andare in un paesino sperduto dell'Islanda e beccare Ben Stiller . . . !!! Comunque Si [Silvio's nickname] è uguale a te . . . alto come te stesso tuo numero si [*sic*] piede vi hanno diviso alla nascita!
Guido: Is it possible to go to a remote town in Iceland and come across Ben Stiller . . . !!! By the way Si he is like you . . . tall as you same shoe size you have been separated at birth!

A 3 persone piace questo[2]
3 people like this

2 Giorgio: Noooo il mio idolo . . .
Giorgio: Noooo my idol . . .

3 Silvio: Gui [Guido's nickname]! ma veramente lo avete incontrato?? Nn [*sic*] credevo fosse così basso . . .
Silvio: Gui! did you really meet him?? I didn't know he was so short . . .

4 Ruggero: Ma dovevate farvi fare una foto con Ben!!!!!!
Ruggero: Guys you should have had a photo taken with Ben!!!!!!

This comment thread consists of four related comments. After telling Friends about his unexpected encounter with the actor Ben Stiller (*Ma si può andare in un paesino sperduto dell'Islanda e beccare Ben Stiller . . . !!!*), in the comment at Post 1, Guido mocks Silvio (one of his Friends) by saying that he resembles Ben Stiller (*Comunque Si è uguale a te . . . alto come te stesso tuo numero si piede vi hanno diviso alla nascita!*). In the comment at Post 2 Giorgio picks up the humorous tone proposed by Guido in the comment at Post 1 and posts the second contribution in this comment thread when he says that Ben Stiller is his idol (*Noooo il mio idolo . . .*). In the contributions at Posts 3 and 4, Silvio and Ruggero publish the third and fourth comments in this comment thread. Specifically, in the comment at Post 3, after requesting that Guido confirm if he has really encountered the actor Ben Stiller (*Gui! ma veramente lo avete incontrato??*), Silvio, the addressee of Guido's facetious comment at Post 1, shows that he has understood the mocking insult (Jefferson, 1979) in the comment at Post 1. Silvio responds to it by mocking himself and saying that he did not know that Ben Stiller was so short (*Nn credevo fosse così basso . . .*). Then, in the final comment of this interaction, the contribution at Post 4, Ruggero responds to the comment at Post 1 by jokingly saying that Guido should have taken a photo with Ben Stiller (*Ma dovevate farvi fare una foto con Ben!!!!!!*).

The analysis of Extract 3.1 has shown that comment threads consist of multiple related comments. That is, an FB user types and then publishes a comment in a comment thread, then another user types and publishes a second comment in the same comment thread, and so on. In this sense, comments are similar to turns at talk in spoken conversations, where a speaker utters a turn, then another speaker utters another turn, and so on. Of course, while comment threads consist of comments, spoken conversations are made up of turns at talk.

Moreover, comment threads, like spoken conversations, contain points where one poster's comment stops and another poster contributes—hence, here it is the poster, rather than the speaker, who changes. This can be seen in Extract 3.2 about Loris's watch.

Extract 3.2 Loris's watch

1 Loris: genitori, mogli e suoceri cominciate la colletta Natalizia !! dev'essere [*sic*] mio !! [Loris publishes a hyperlink containing information on a technological watch]
Loris: parents, wives and in laws start saving money for Christmas !! I must have it !!

A 2 persone piace questo
2 people like this

2 Aleandro: Meglio un ipod nano . . . ;)
Aleandro: an ipod nano is better . . . ;)

Although the comment thread in Extract 3.2 contains two comments only, a poster change occurs between the comments at Posts 1 and 2. In the comment at Post 1, Loris, the initial poster, types and publishes a contribution where he tells his family members to start saving money because he wants the watch described in the following hyperlink as a Christmas present (*genitori, mogli e suoceri cominciate le colletta Natalizia !! dev'essere mio !!*). After the publication of the comment at Post 1, Aleandro presumably reads this contribution and posts a comment at Post 2, so that a poster change has occurred between the comments at Posts 1 and 2. In the comment at Post 2 Aleandro says, referring to the watch described in the hyperlink at Post 1, that an iPod nano is better; he then closes the comment at Post 2 with a smiling emoticon (*Meglio un ipod nano . . .;)*). The function of this emoticon is probably to mitigate the seriousness expressed in the previous statement about the watch. Aleandro in fact disagrees with Loris's statement in the comment at Post 1, where he says that he wants the watch described in the hyperlink at Post 1.

Comment threads are generally made up of several related comments and poster changes are common in this type of interactions. This is because, as already mentioned above, Friends type and publish comments in comment threads, then other Friends type and post other related comments in the same comment threads, and so on.

Another typical feature of comment threads is that when an FB user publishes a comment in a comment thread, he or she cannot predict who will respond to it. For example, in Extract 3.1, Guido receives a response from three different Friends, though he specifically names only one of them as the intended recipient of his initial comment. The unpredictability of responders can also be seen in Extract 3.3, which contains a comment thread about Loris's car.

Extract 3.3 Loris's car

1 Loris: Ho dovuto lavarla
Loris: I had to wash it

2 Luca: era ora
Luca: finally

3 Fausto: Bravo Loris . . .
Fausto: Well done Loris . . .

4 Franco: Era più bella sporca!!!!
Franco: It looked better when it was dirty!!!!

5 Loris: pulita o sporca che sia è una Jeep
Loris: dirty or clean it is a Jeep

6 Loris: minkia [*sic*] sono commosso
Loris: shit I'm so moved

7 Guido: ti ho visto lavarla al pinduino [*sic*] [name of a car wash]!!!
Guido: I saw you washing it at the car wash!!!

8 Fausto: Anch'io . . . L'unico che piangeva mentre lavava la macchina! Ehehehe . . .
Fausto: me too . . . he was the only one crying when washing his car! Ehehehe . . .

In the comment at Post 1, Loris (the same user who has begun the comment thread in Extract 3.2) opens the interaction with a comment about his car (*Ho dovuto lavarla*). Loris tells his Friends that he has washed "it," referring to his car—the image of which he has set as his profile picture. When Loris published the comment at Post 1, he could not know that Luca, Fausto, Franco, and Guido would respond to it. In contrast to a spoken conversation, where speakers normally know the recipients of their turns at talk, this is not the case in FB comment threads. When an FB user publishes a comment in a comment thread, he or she does not know who will read it, especially if he or she is typing the first comment in a new comment thread. Given this, an FB user must design his or her comment knowing that all of his or her Friends can potentially read it.

In addition to the issue of an unknown number of readers, the number of potential participants in a comment thread is also unknown to FB users at the time of the publication of a comment in a comment thread. That is, when an FB user posts a comment in a comment thread, he or she does not know how many Friends will respond to it. For example, when in Extract 3.3 Loris posted the comment at Post 1, he did not know that four Friends would respond to it. Therefore, another typical feature of FB comment threads is that the number of potential participants is unknown to Friends at the time of publication of a comment in a comment thread. This is different from what normally happens in a spoken conversation, where speakers generally know the number of participants in an interaction.

A further feature which characterizes FB comment threads is that these interactions are generally asynchronous, that is, several hours might elapse between the publication of comments in comment threads. This means that "gaps" in the sense of time are common in FB comment threads. This can be seen in Extract 3.4, about Claudio and the spaghetti.

Extract 3.4 Spaghetti

1 Claudio: have a single portion of spaghetti and some ragu [*sic*] . . . attempted for a sec to use them instead of opening a new box of penne: I need a doctor!!! (But I've opened the box :)) 13 hours ago

2 David: CARBOIDRATI?!? 8 ore fa
David: CARBOHYDRATES?!? 8 hours ago

3 David: e cmq [*sic*], gli spaghetti al ragù non esistono . . . si inizia la scatola delle penne . . . x forza . . . [Italian people normally eat spaghetti with tomato sauce and penne with Bolognese sauce and not vice versa] 8 ore fa
David: and by the way, spaghetti with Bolognese sauce do not exist . . . it's better if you open the box of penne . . . you have to . . . 8 hours ago

4 Claudio: Yes! Finally!!! :) Winter is coming ;) 8 hours ago

5 Claudio: Infatti ;) Ma x un attimo stavo prendendo quelli x finirli ma una voce dall'alto mi ha fermato :p 8 ore fa
Claudio: Exactly ;) For a second I was tempted to use them [the spaghetti] *but then a voice stopped me :p 8 hours ago*

6 David: EMMENOMALE! Dio serve anche per questo. . . ! 8 ore fa
David: LUCKILY! God is useful even for this . . . ! 8 hours ago

7 Ray: Oh dear, looks like Claudio is using Facebook to wrtite a food diary . . .! 6 hours ago

8 Claudio: this time no pics Ray . . . aren't you happy? ,D 6 hours ago

9 Ray: Yes, last night's photographs were traumatic (and quite scarry!) 4 hours ago

10 Claudio: scary for my belly . . . ;P 4 hours ago

11 Ray: Well and your hair . . . what's going on with it? 4 hours ago

12 Claudio: ahahah . . . need an hair cut ;) I'll do as soon as I can ;) 4 hours ago

13 Ray: Yes please do! 4 hours ago

This comment thread, as indicated by the approximate times of publication of its comments (on the right side of this extract), is asynchronous. It was opened by Claudio thirteen hours before I took a screen shot of the page (*13 hours ago*). In the comment at Post 1, Claudio tells Friends about his intention of cooking some spaghetti rather than penne with ragù (*have a single portion of spaghetti and some ragu . . . attempted for a sec to use them instead of opening a new box of penne: I need a doctor!!! (But I've opened the box :)*). Five hours after the publication of the comment at Post 1 (*8 hours ago*), David (one of Claudio's Friends) publishes the comment at Post 2 where he asks Claudio why he is eating carbohydrates (*CARBOIDRATI?!?*).

This comment is followed by a series of contributions: the comments at Posts 3, 4, 5, and 6 which were all published around the same time as the comment at Post 2 (*8 hours ago*). FB does not give us any detailed timing,[3] just that these comments were all published within the same hour, and were posted in the order in which they appear here. Furthermore, approximately two hours after the publication of the comment at Post 6 (*6 hours ago*), that is, seven hours after the publication of the comment at Post 1, Ray publishes his first contribution in this interaction, the comment at Post 7 (*6 hours ago*). At around the same time, but after the comment at Post 7, Claudio publishes the comment at Post 8 (*6 hours ago*). In the comment at Post 7 Ray teases Claudio by ironically saying that he is using FB as a cooking diary (*Oh dear, looks like Claudio is using Facebook to wrtite a food diary . . . .!*), then in the comment at Post 8 Claudio responds to Ray by saying that he should not complain, because this time he (Claudio) did not publish any photo of his food (*this time no pics Ray . . . aren't you happy? ,D*). Another two hours go by, and then Ray publishes the comment at Post 9 (*4 hours ago*). In this contribution he responds to Claudio's comment at Post 8, and humorously says that the photos Claudio posted the night before were traumatic (*Yes, last night's photographs were traumatic (and quite scarry!)*). The comment at Post 9 stimulates another series of contributions: the comments at Posts 10, 11, 12, and 13, which have once again been posted within a short span of time (*4 hours ago*).

The analysis of Extract 3.4 supports what was found by previous studies on FB, which is that comment threads are generally asynchronous (Baron, 2013; Maíz-Arévalo, 2013; Tagg and Seargeant, 2012; West, 2013); several hours can in fact elapse between the publication of one comment and the response that follows it. On the other hand, my data show that sometimes comment threads can also be quasi-synchronous. The term quasi-synchronous has been introduced to describe the *turn-taking system* in real-time text chats (Garcia and Jacobs, 1999), where only a few seconds may elapse between the time in which a message is typed and made available to its recipients for inspection; however, in a sense, this term may also be used to describe comments in some comment threads, especially those where only a few minutes or possibly seconds elapse between the publication of comments. This can be seen in Extract 3.5, which is about Metroman, an amateur singer who performs on the underground in Milan and uploads the videos of his performances on the website YouTube.com.

Extract 3.5 Metroman[4]

1 Mauro: Cmq [*sic*] ormai siamo arrivati ad un Livello Superiore. L'anno prossimo partecipa agli EMA's [Mauro publishes a hyperlink about Metroman] Lunedì alle 9:27

Mauro: by the way it's clear that he has reached a higher Level. Next year he will participate in the European Music Awards *Monday at 9:27am*

A 5 persone piace questo
5 people like this

2 Mauro: Parola d'ordine: SUBBBLIMARE [quote taken from the video contained in the hyperlink at Post 1] Metroman . . . mannagia a te . . . Lunedì alle 9:27

Mauro: password: SUBBBLIMARE [term probably created by Metroman which is impossible to translate] *damn you Metroman . . .* *Monday at 9:27 a.m.*

3 Mauro: Gianni Zaira Valeria Amelia Claudia Sara Aldo Monday at 9:28 a.m.

→ 4 Vanessa: hahahahhahahhahahaahahhahaahhaahhahhahaahhaah sto piangendo Lunedì alle 9:29

Vanessa: hahahahhahahhahahaahahhahaahhaahhahhahaahhaah I'm crying *Monday at 9:29am*

→ 5 Mauro: Alessio Chiara Auron Monday at 9:29 a.m.

→ 6 Vanessa: io sono un artista perchè mio padre da giovane era un'artista [*sic*] [quote taken from the video contained in the hyperlink at Post 1]. Lunedì alle 9:30

Vanessa: I'm an artist because my father was an artist when he was young *Monday at 9:30 a.m.*

→ 7 Alessio: quella mattina a cascina gobba [*sic*] [metro station] mi ha cambiato la vita . . . lo ammetto . . . Lunedì alle 9:30

Alessio: that morning at Cascina Gobba he changed my life . . . I have to admit *Monday at 9:30 a.m.*

→ 8 Mauro: [Mauro publishes a hyperlink containing another video about Metroman] Monday at 9:30 a.m.

9 Vanessa: ma . . . milano777 su utube [*sic*] è lui che si fa i video da solo sul suo canale suppongo ahahhah :D Lunedì alle 9:31
Vanessa: but . . . milano777 on utube I suppose that he shoots his own videos and then uploads them on his channel ahahhah :D Monday at 9:31 a.m.

→ 10 Mauro: Parole Grosse che faranno tremate [*sic*] La Critica Musicale Internazionale: "IO SO [*sic*] MEGLIO DI BAGLIONI, IO Sò [*sic*] MEGLIO DI RENATO ZERO . . . IO sò [*sic*] MEGLIO DE GIORG MAIKOL [*sic*]" [quote probably taken from the video contained in the hyperlink at Post 1] Applausi. Lunedì alle 9:32
Mauro: Important words that will shake the International music critics: "I'M BETTER THAN BAGLIONI, I'M BETTER THAN RENATO ZERO [Italian singers] . . . *I'M BETTER THAN GIORG MAIKOL* [English musician]" *Applause. Monday at 9:32 a.m.*

→ 11 Vanessa: AHHAHAHHAAH mio padre e [*sic*] di torino [*sic*] mia madre e [*sic*] siciliana e io ho origini romane [quote probably taken from the video contained in the hyperlink at Post 1] ODDDIOOOOOO Lunedì alle 9:32
Vanessa: AHHAHAHHAAH my father was from Turin and my mother was Sicilian and I have roman origins OH MY GODDDDDDDD Monday at 9:32 a.m.

[. . .]

As it can be seen from the times of publication of the comments in Extract 3.5, this comment thread is quasi-synchronous. One minute after the publication of the first three comments of this interaction (the contributions at Posts 1, 2, and 3), where Mauro has introduced, published, and selected the intended recipients for his hyperlink-telling, Vanessa publishes the comment at Post 4 (*Lunedì alle 9:29 a.m.*). In this comment Vanessa evaluates Mauro's hyperlink-telling at Post 1 with a representation of laughter (*hahahahhahahhahahaahahhahaahhaahhahhahaahhaah sto piangendo*). "At the same time" that Vanessa publishes the comment at Post 4, Mauro posts the comment at Post 5 (*Lunedì alle 9:29 a.m.*).

The relative positioning indicates that Vanessa's comment entered the system before Mauro's, although the times of publication of the comments at Posts 4 and 5 state that these contributions were published "at the same time," at 9:29 a.m. In the comment at Post 5, Mauro names other potential recipients for his initial hyperlink-telling (*Alessio Chiara Auron*). In other words, in the comment at Post 5 Mauro does not respond to Vanessa's previous comment at Post 4, but apparently continues on with the action he has initiated in the comment at Post 3, where he has selected the possible recipients for his hyperlink-telling. It seems that while Mauro was typing the comment at Post 5, Vanessa posted the comment at Post 4. Therefore, in the comments at Posts 4 and 5, we could say that we have an apparently quasi-synchronous interaction.

This also happens in the comments at Posts 6, 7, and 8, where Vanessa, Alessio, and Mauro seem to post three other comments around the same time. One minute after the publication of the comment at Post 5, Vanessa publishes the comment at Post 6 (*Monday at 9:30 a.m.*). The comment at Post 6 appears to be oriented to the comment at Post 1; in this contribution Vanessa seems to post a quote taken from the hyperlink-telling at Post 1 (*io sono un artista perchè mio padre da giovane era un'artista*). At around the same time that Vanessa publishes the comment at Post 6, Alessio posts the comment at Post 7 (*Monday at 9:30 a.m.*). Similar to what Vanessa has done in the comment at Post 6, in the comment at Post 7 Alessio responds to the comment at Post 1, jokingly saying that encountering Metroman has completely changed his life (*quella mattina a cascina gobba mi ha cambiato la vita . . . lo ammetto . . .*). At the "same time" that Vanessa and Alessio publish the comments at Posts 6 and 7, Mauro apparently posts the comment at Post 8 (*Monday at 9:30 a.m.*). In this contribution Mauro seems to respond to Vanessa's comment at Post 6, by publishing another hyperlink-telling about Metroman.

Thus, even though the system reports that the comments at Posts 6, 7, and 8 are simultaneous, this is probably not the case. While the comments at Posts 6 and 7 could potentially have been posted at the "same time," with the poster of the comment at Post 7 not having seen the comment at Post 6, the comment at Post 8 seems to have been published a few seconds after the comment at Post 6, at least long enough for Mauro to receive Vanessa's comment, read it, and type and publish his response. Here, we can see the apparent quasi-synchronous interaction continuing.

Around one minute (or less) after the publication of the comment at Post 8, Vanessa publishes the comment at Post 9 (*Monday at 9:31 a.m.*). In this contribution she evaluates Mauro's hyperlink-telling at Post 8 by saying that Metroman has a channel on the website YouTube.com where he uploads his own videos (*ma . . . milano777 su utube è lui che si fa i video da solo sul suo canale suppongo ahahhah :D*). Around one minute after the publication of the comment at Post 9, Mauro makes a comment at Post 10 (*Monday at 9:32 a.m.*). In this contribution Mauro picks up the idea introduced by Vanessa in the comment at Post 6 and publishes another quote probably taken from one of the videos about

Metroman; then he comments on it. Mauro ironically says that what Metroman has said in his video will shake the critics (*Parole Grosse che faranno tremate La Critica Musicale Internazionale: " IO SO MEGLIO DI BAGLIONI, IO Sò MEGLIO DI RENATO ZERO . . . IO sò MEGLIO DE GIORG MAIKOL" Applausi*). Once again, at what appears to be the same time that Mauro publishes the comment at Post 10, Vanessa posts the comment at Post 11 (*Monday at 9:32 a.m.*).

Therefore, based on the system timing, the comments at Posts 10 and 11, like the comments at Posts 4 and 5, and those at Posts 6, 7, and 8, appear to occur at around the same time, probably because those who posted the comments were simultaneously online at the time of the publication of these comments in this comment thread. In the comment at Post 11 Vanessa ironically posts laughs to introduce another quote taken from Metroman (*AHHAHAHHAAH mio padre e di torino mia madre e siciliana e io ho origini romane ODDDIOOOOOO*). This contribution thus appears to respond to the comment at Post 10, where Mauro has quoted and mocked Metroman (*Parole Grosse che faranno tremate La Critica Musicale Internazionale: " IO SO MEGLIO DI BAGLIONI, IO Sò MEGLIO DI RENATO ZERO . . . IO sò MEGLIO DE GIORG MAIKOL" Applausi*). Although the system once again reports that the comments at Posts 10 and 11 are simultaneous, this is probably not the case. In the comment at Post 11 Vanessa has apparently received and read the comment at Post 10, and then typed and published her contribution. Therefore, like the comments at Posts 4, 5, 6, 7, and 8, here, given the timing and the available pragmatic evidence, we most likely have a quasi-synchronous interaction.

Comment threads can thus be quasi-synchronous as well as asynchronous; this means that FB users may be simultaneously online at the time of an interaction. However, comments are not interactionally co-constructed in comment threads in the way that turns at talk are co-constructed in spoken conversation. FB users do not have access to each other's comments in progress. That is, when an FB user is typing a comment in a comment thread, his or her Friends cannot know what is being typed or even that something is being typed.[5] Therefore, even though Friends can simultaneously be online at the time of a comment thread, they cannot monitor each other's comments in progress. In the comment at Post 5 Mauro did not know that Vanessa was constructing the comment at Post 4, and similarly it seems that in the comment at Post 7 he did not know that Vanessa was posting the comment at Post 6.

After publishing the comment at Post 6 Vanessa did not know that Mauro was reading her contribution, and constructing a response, at least until after Mauro finished his comment and pushed the *Post* button; similarly after publishing the comment at Post 8 Mauro did not know that Vanessa was reading it and responding, until she published the comment at Post 9. This means that although poster change occurs in comment threads, it is not interactionally achieved by FB users in the course of these interactions. This is in contrast with what normally happens in spoken conversations, where speaker changes are interactionally achieved by participants in these interactions. In other words, unlike spoken conversations, where conversationalists can monitor each other's turns at talk and predict when a TCU could be complete and a speaker change could occur, in comment threads FB users can only access comments which have already been posted on a comment thread and not those that are in progress.

This also means that although comments are presented on screen, when an FB user is typing a comment in a comment thread, he or she cannot know if another comment will appear in the comment thread before he or she has posted his or her own contribution in the comment thread. Therefore, the longer a comment takes to type, the more likely it is that another comment will appear in the comment thread before one's own contribution. It is probably for this reason that, as it will be discussed in Chapter 7, the first comment posted by an FB user in a comment thread commonly orients to the action performed in the initial comment of a comment thread, rather than to the action performed in the most recent comment (which may no longer be the most recent by the time the user publishes his or her comment in the comment thread). We see here the importance of the fact that FB users do not have control over the positioning of comments in comment threads. In other words, the system presents comments in comment threads in relation to when they have been posted on the Home. That is, if two FB users type two contributions and then press on the *Post* button at around the same time, these comments will not overlap. The system will post these comments in relation to the times at which the server has received them, and if they are more or less simultaneous, it will present them one after the other with the same time of publication. FB users do not have control over the positioning of their first comments in comment threads, and this affects the way they design their comments, as we will see.

While poster changes are not cooperatively achieved by FB users in comment threads, making them different from spoken conversation, FB users construct comments by using pragmatically complete units, in the same way that speakers construct contributions to spoken conversation. Pragmatically complete units are units that count as actions in comment threads, such as a question, a telling, and so on. This can be seen in Extract 3.6.

Extract 3.6 Soundgarden

1 Mauro: finitela di postare i Soundgarden . . . bastardi.
Mauro: stop posting Soundgarden . . . you bastards.

2 Elvira: ahahahahah

3 Elvira: e tu vai a vedere gli off al magnolia, no?
Elvira: but're you going to see the off [possibly the name of a band] *at magnolia* [possibly the name of a club], *aren't you?*

4 Alfredo: . . .

5 Denise: prrrrrrrrrrrr :)

This comment thread consists of five comments which are made up of several complete units. In the comment at Post 1 Mauro opens this interaction with a contribution that contains a unit which is pragmatically complete (*finitela di postare i Soundgarden . . . bastardi*). He in fact performs an action in this comment, humorously requesting his Friends to stop posting messages about Soundgarden, a band that has probably recently performed live in Milan. In the comment at Post 2, Elvira publishes her first contribution in this comment thread (*ahahahahah*). Although this comment only contains a representation of laughter, it counts as another action (the second) in this comment thread as it acts as a response to Mauro's request in the comment at Post 1.

After the comment at Post 2, Elvira goes on to publish another comment, the contribution at Post 3 (*e tu vai a vedere gli off al magnolia, no?*). Although its intention is somewhat unclear, this comment is once again pragmatically complete. It seems to be declining the suggestion of the comment at Post 1—Elvira says to Mauro that he should not complain about missing the concert by Soundgarden since he will be attending another concert, that of *off*, which is probably the name of another band. In the comment at Post 4 Alfredo posts his first comment in this comment thread (. . .). Although this contribution consists of a series of suspension points only, it constitutes a complete action (the fourth) in this comment thread; presumably another rejection of Mauro's request in the comment at Post 1. Then, in the comment at Post 5 Denise posts her first comment in this comment thread, which consists of only a raspberry, but once again it constitutes an action in this comment thread like the others in previous contributions. Denise rejects Mauro's request, in her case with a raspberry (*prrrrrrrrrrrr*) followed by a smiling emoticon (:)).

So, comments in comment threads consist of pragmatically complete units. Furthermore, even though this is not always the case, the units that compose comments may also be grammatically complete. That is, the units which compose a comment may be pragmatically and grammatically complete; where a grammatically complete unit is an item which consists of a sentence or a phrase, such as a full grammatically complete sentence. This can be seen in the comments at Posts 1 and 3 in Extract 3.6, where Mauro and Elvira publish two comments which are made up of pragmatically and grammatically complete units; these contributions in fact constitute actions in this comment thread (a facetious request and its decline) and are also grammatically complete utterances (Comment at Post 1: *finitela di postare i Soundgarden . . . bastardi.* Comment at Post 3: *e tu vai a vedere gli off al magnolia, no?*).

Other comments may not be grammatically complete—indeed may not consist of "words" at all; however, they are still pragmatically complete. Thus, like in spoken conversation, where, as already noted in Chapter 1, for speaker changes it is important that TCUs are pragmatically complete (even though they may also be grammatically and intonationally complete), this is also the case of the units that compose comments in comment threads. Although poster changes are not interactionally achieved by FB users in comment threads, for the organization of comment threads it is important that the units that compose comments are pragmatically complete. This is because comments are designed by FB users in relation to the actions accomplished by other users in previous comments.

On the other hand, another feature of comments in comment threads is that a single comment can consist of multiple pragmatically complete units, rather than a single complete unit. This can be seen in the comment at Post 8 in Extract 3.7, where Linda publishes a contribution which is made up of two elements that accomplish two actions in this comment thread, and are addressed to two different Friends.

Extract 3.7 iPhone[6]

1 Renzo: non ce l'ho fatta . . . alla fine l'ho preso!!! il [*sic*] mio primo iphone!!!!
Renzo: I couldn't resist . . . at the end I bought it!!! my first iphone!!!!

A Loris, Mauro e altre 4 persone piace questo elemento
Loris, Mauro, and other 4 people like this

[. . .]

7 Alberto: renz [*sic*] non darlo in mano alla linda [*sic*] . . .;) e nemmeno a ferrò che se no lo usa come sasso da far rimbalzare sull'acqua . . .
Alberto: renz don't give it to linda . . . ;) or to ferrò [probably the nickname of one of Renzo's Friends], *otherwise he'll use it as a stone to bounce on the water . . .*

→ 8 Linda: ooohhh . . . Albe problemi!?!? Renz [*sic*] t [*sic*] capisco . . . avevi la scimmietta . . .
Linda: ooohhh . . . Albe do you have a problem!?!? Renz I understand you . . . you had to have it ["*scimmietta*" is a slang term which means to strongly desire something] . . .

9 Alberto: io no . . . l'iphone di renzo [*sic*] si se lo da in mano a te . . .!
Alberto: I don't . . . but renzo's iphone does, if he gives it to you . . .!

[. . .]

After a series of comments in the contributions at Posts 1, 2, 3, 4, 5, 6, and 7 where Friends evaluate Renzo's initial telling about his new iPhone (*non ce l'ho fatta . . . alla fine l'ho preso!!! il mio primo iphone!!!!*), in the comment at Post 8 Linda publishes her third contribution to this comment thread (*ooohhh . . . Albe problemi!?!? Renz t capisco . . . avevi la scimmietta . . .*). This comment consists of two complete units: one directed to Alberto, a Friend who participates in this comment thread, and the other directed to Renzo, the initial poster. The first unit of the comment at Post 8 (*ooohhh . . . Albe problemi!?!?*) is Linda's response to Alberto's ironic comment at Post 7, where he suggested to Renzo that he should not give his new phone to Linda (*renz non darlo in mano alla linda . . . ;)*). The second unit of this comment, on the other hand, (*Renz t capisco . . . avevi la scimmietta . . .*) orients to the comment at Post 1, and is a positive evaluation of Renzo's telling in this contribution, where he says that he bought an iPhone.

What Extract 3.7 has shown is that comments in comment threads can be made up of multiple complete units. In a sense, comments can be thought as consisting of one or more TCUs. However, as already mentioned above, there is a big difference between the items that compose comments in comment threads and TCUs in spoken conversation. While participants in spoken conversations can access TCUs when in progress, and predict when a single TCU will be complete, this is not the case in comment threads, where FB users can only access complete comments that have already been posted in a comment thread, and not those that are in progress.

In addition, Extract 3.7 suggests another interesting feature of comment threads—that FB users can use turn allocation components to select the recipients of their comments[7]. This is once again clear in the comment at Post 8, where in the first unit of this contribution Linda explicitly selects Alberto as the addressee of her comment, and humorously asks him if he has got problems (*ooohhh . . . Albe problemi!?!?*). The action in the comment at Post 8, formulated as a question, projects the next relevant action in this comment thread: an answer from Alberto. In the comment at Post 9 Alberto in fact responds to Linda; continuing with the ironic tone of the contributions in previous comments, he states that though he does not have any problem if Linda gets the phone, Renzo's phone may have an issue if Renzo gives it to her (*io no . . . l'iphone di renzo si se lo da in mano a te . . .!*).

As in spoken conversation, FB users may use turn allocation components to select the next poster and project the next action in a comment thread. However, Extract 3.8 shows that in cases where a poster appears to explicitly select recipients, this does not necessarily mean that only those Friends will respond.

Extract 3.8 Music discussion-Bancale[8]

1 [Mauro publishes a hyperlink which contains a video of one of the songs of Bancale, an unknown Italian band]

A 3 persone piace questo
3 people like this

→ 2 Mauro: eccolo, questo è il nuovo Guru—Il Neubauten Italiano [*sic*] che sembra TufKad (e molti altri—meno che un cantante diciamo . . .) Alessia, Zaira, Claudia, Chiara, Bono, Cinzia
Mauro: here it is, the new Guru—The Italian Neubauten who looks like TufKad [names of two singers] *(and many others—apart from let's say a singer . . .) Alessia, Zaira, Claudia, Chiara, Bono, Cinzia*

3 Dario: sopra tutto [*sic*] . . . la cariola [*sic*]!
Dario: especially . . . the wheelbarrow!

4 Gianni: E MI CHIEDI CHE COS'E' IL MIO VUOTO!?!?!?
Gianni: AND YOU ASK ME WHAT IS MY EMPTINESS!?!?!?

5 Alessia:—oddio, ma è il numero uno O_ò
Alessia:—oh my god, but he is the number one O_ò

6 Claudia: Mi piace!
Vorrei che mi parlasse di notte, seduto per terra accanto al mio letto.
Io lo so da che libro vengo.
Claudia: I like it/him!
I wish he would talk to me at night, sitting on the floor close to my bed.
I know from which book I come from.

7 Mauro: io porto Torce.
Mauro: I bring Torce [the term *Torce* could refer to the Human Torch, one of the characters of the comic book Fantastic Four]

[. . .]

In the comment at Post 1 Mauro launches this comment thread by publishing a hyperlink only; then in the contribution at Post 2, after commenting on this hyperlink-telling, Mauro selects the intended recipients of this comment by explicitly naming them (*eccolo, questo è il nuovo Guru—Il Neubauten Italiano che sembra TufKad (e molti altri—meno che un cantante diciamo . . .) Alessia, Zaira, Claudia, Chiara, Bono, Cinzia*). Although in the comment at Post 2 Mauro has in a sense selected the possible next posters in this comment thread, in the comments at Posts 3 and 4, Dario and Gianni, two Friends who have not been selected by Mauro as the explicit intended recipients of his contribution, ignore his selection and respond to the comment at Post 1.

In the comment at Post 3 Dario posts a textual message which refers to the wheelbarrow that appears on the video in the comment at Post 1 (*sopra tutto . . . la cariola!*). Then, in the comment at Post 4 Gianni, another Friend who has not been selected by Mauro as a recipient of this comment thread, posts a contribution which appears to orient to the comment at Post 1. Although this contribution is unclear, Gianni seems to respond to Mauro's hyperlink-telling at Post 1 by using an exclamation (*E MI CHIEDI CHE COS'E' IL MIO VUOTO!?!?!?*).

Two other comments are then published by Alessia and Claudia, two of the addressees who were selected by Mauro in the comment at Post 2. Alessia and Claudia use two positive evaluations to tell Mauro that they like the hyperlink-telling in the comment at Post 1 (Comment at Post 5:—*oddio, ma è il numero uno O_ò*. Comment at Post 6: *Mi piace! Vorrei che mi parlasse di notte, seduto per terra accanto al mio letto. Io lo so da che libro vengo*). Although unclear, the comment at Post 7 seems to respond to the comment at Post 6. In this contribution Mauro apparently says that he will bring the Human Torch (*io porto Torce*) to interrupt the scene described by Claudia in the comment at Post 6, where she says that she would like the singer of Bancale to sit by her bed at night time and talk to her (*Vorrei che mi parlasse di notte, seduto per terra accanto al mio letto. Io lo so da che libro vengo*).

The action accomplished by Mauro in the comment at Post 7, responding to Claudia's previous comment at Post 6, shows that although Dario and Gianni, two Friends who have not been explicitly selected as the intended recipients of the comment at Post 1, have responded to it, this is unproblematic for this interaction. So, even though turn allocation components are present in comment threads, they do not necessarily function in the way one might expect. In fact, even though FB users may have apparently selected the Friends whose comments they want next, for example, by explicitly naming them, this does not stop Friends who have not been selected as recipients from participating in a comment thread.

In summary, therefore, it seems that comment threads are generally made up of several related comments, and that poster changes are common in these interactions. In addition, when an FB user publishes a comment in a comment thread, he or she does not know the identity and the number of Friends who will respond to it, and when people posting comments attempt to restrict the set of recipients by naming them, as in Extract 3.8, this does not stop other Friends from participating. Comment threads appear also to be generally asynchronous, which means that "lags" in the sense of time are common between comments. On the other hand, some comment threads seem quasi-synchronous, with FB users being simultaneously online at the time of contributing to a comment thread.

However, even though FB users can be simultaneously online when posting comments in comment threads, they do not have access to each other's comments in progress. This has an impact on comment threads; the system, rather than FB users, controls the positioning of comments in comment threads, and poster changes are not interactionally achieved by FB users in these interactions. So, although poster change is not interactionally achieved in comment threads, comments are normally designed using single or multiple pragmatically complete units, which may also be grammatically complete (even though they do not necessarily have to be).

Finally, even though Friends may use turn allocation components in comments within comment threads, these do not necessarily function in the way expected. In fact, Friends who were not selected as intended recipients of a comment sometimes respond to it. Nevertheless, these responses are not treated as problematic by the other Friends who contribute to the comment thread.

Sequence organization in FB comment threads

Comment threads are made up of several related comments. These comments do not follow one after the other incoherently, but are organized in a meaningful way. This organization is called *sequence organization* and it is based on the idea that FB users perform actions when they post a comment in a comment thread. In other words, the action performed by an FB user in a comment within a comment thread generates another action which makes another action the relevant next and so on.

The *sequence organization* of FB comment threads is identifiable in all the interactions analyzed in this chapter. For example, it characterizes the structure of the comment thread in Extract 3.1 where the action accomplished by Guido in the opening comment of this interaction has generated the actions performed by Giorgio, Silvio, and Ruggero in the comments at Posts 2, 3, and 4. These are in addition to the actions performed by the other three Friends who have read Guido's comment and used the *Like* button to respond to it. *Sequence organization* can also be found in Extract 3.4 where the action performed by Claudio in the comment at Post 1 has generated the actions performed by David and Ray in the comments at Posts 2, 3, and 7 which have then generated the actions performed by Claudio in the comments at Posts 4, 5, and 8 and so on.

Strong evidence of the presence of *sequence organization* in FB comment threads comes from comments that contain obvious *adjacency pairs*. *Adjacency pairs* have been analyzed by researchers to show the *sequence organization* of spoken conversations. As noted in Chapter 1, *adjacency pairs* are composed of two turns at talk that are adjacently positioned, ordered, and organized into pair types according to the actions performed in these contributions. Moreover, *adjacency pairs* are uttered by different speakers and they may consist of sequences such as question-answer, greeting-greeting, request-acceptance or decline, and so on (C. Goodwin, 1989; Liddicoat, 2011; Sacks, 1992, 2004; Sacks et al., 1974; Schegloff, 2007). *Adjacency pairs* can be seen in the comments at Posts 2, 3, 4, 5, and 6 in Extract 3.9, which is a comment thread about Valeria and Chiara's own activities.

Extract 3.9 The mosaic course

1 [Valeria publishes a hyperlink with information about a mosaic course]

A 3 persone piace questo
3 people like this

→ 2 Chiara: ciao . . . si la tua bomboniera è sopra il mobil [*sic*] del bagno, [*sic*] vedessi come st [*sic*] bene
Chiara: hi . . . yes your bomboniera is on the vanity in my bathroom, if you could see how beautiful it looks

→ 3 Valeria: Ciao Chiara!!! Che bello sentirti!!! La puoi usare tranquillamente come porta sapone se vuoi, è super resistente!!!
Valeria: Hi Chiara!!! Nice to hear from you!!! If you want, you can definitely use it as soap container, it's super resistant!!!

→ 4 Chiara: Ciao Valeria . . . non soo [*sic*] ma anche bella . . . complimenti sei proprio brava . . . come state??
Chiara: Hi Valeria . . . I don't know it's also wonderful . . . congrats you've done well . . . how are you??

→ 5 Valeria: Grazie . . . ehehehhe . . . A parte un pò di raffreddore tutto ok!! Sto preparando la fiera dell'artigianato di Milano . . . è vicinissima!!! E voi??
Valeria: Thanks . . . ehehehhe . . . Apart from a cold everything is fine!!! I'm working for fiera dell'artigianato [name of a fair] *in Milan . . . it's really close!!! And you??*

→ 6 Chiara: noi per ora parliamo piano m [*sic*] niente malanni . . . e coma [*sic*] al solito si lavora nel grigiore dell'ufficio . . . ma tanta manna che si lavora . . . con lla [*sic*] pessima ari ache [*sic*] tira!!!
Chiara: touching wood we're [probably referring to Chiara's family] *fine . . . we work in the sadness of our offices . . . but considering the current economic crisis, we can't complain . . .!!!*

[. . .]

After an initial telling, this comment thread consists of comments that contain *adjacency pairs*. In the comment at Post 1, Valeria, a mosaic artist, performs the first action in this comment thread: she accomplishes a telling when she posts a hyperlink about a mosaic course. This telling generates a second action which is performed in the comment at Post 2. Chiara opens this contribution with the *first pair part* of a greeting sequence (*ciao*). Then, she continues by performing another action which also includes a compliment; she posts a second telling about the "*bomboniera*," an object that Valeria has probably crafted for Chiara, and says that it looks amazing. Chiara tells Valeria that the "*bomboniera*" looks beautiful in her bathroom (*si la tua bomboniera è sopra il mobil del bagno , vedessi come st bene*).

In the comment at Post 3, Valeria completes the greeting sequence started by Chiara in the comment at Post 2. More precisely, she responds to Chiara with another greeting (*Ciao Chiara!!! Che bello sentirti!!!*). Then, in the final component of the contribution at Post 3 Valeria performs another action (the second) in this comment; she posts a response to Chiara's compliment about the "*bomboniera*" in the contribution at Post 2. Valeria says to Chiara that she can even use the "*bomboniera*" as a soap dispenser (*La puoi usare tranquillamente come porta sapone se vuoi, è super resistente!!!*).

Other *adjacency pairs* can be seen in the comments at Posts 4, 5, and 6, where Chiara and Valeria perform other actions in this comment threads; specifically, two how-are-you sequences. In the comment at Post 4, after complimenting Valeria for her "*bomboniera*" (*Ciao Valeria . . . non soo ma anche bella . . . complimenti sei proprio brava . . .*), Chiara publishes the *first pair part* of a how-are-you sequence (*come state??*). This *adjacency pair* is completed by the action performed by Valeria in the comment at Post 5. In this contribution after thanking Chiara for her compliment, Valeria tells Chiara that she has a cold, and goes on to say that she is preparing some items for an imminent exhibition in Milan (*Grazie . . . ehehehhe . . . A parte un pò di raffreddore tutto ok!! Sto preparando la fiera dell'artigianato di Milano . . . è vicinissima!!!*).

Then, Valeria closes the comment at Post 5 by performing another action in this interaction; she starts another how-are-you sequence (*E voi??*). This action is responded to by Chiara with an action in the comment at Post 6 where she reports on the well-being of her family and her work situation (*noi per ora parliamo piano m niente malanni . . . e coma al solito si lavora nel grigiore dell'ufficio . . . ma tanta manna che si lavora . . . con lla pessima ari ache tira!!!*). It therefore appears that the action performed by Valeria in the opening comment of this comment thread has generated the actions performed by Chiara in the comment at Post 2, which have then generated the actions performed by Valeria in the comment at Post 3, and so on.

Comments in comment threads seem to contain *adjacency pairs*. This can be seen again in the comments that make up Extract 3.10, where in the contributions at Posts 3 and 4 there is another how-are-you sequence.

Extract 3.10 Elisa's farewell

1 Elisa: Time to pack. Again.

A 2 persone piace questo
2 people like this

2 Vanda: buon viaggio Eli [Elisa's nickname], e boa sorte!
Vanda: have a good trip Eli, and good luck!

→ 3 Elisa: grazie Va [Vanda's nickname]. stavolta [*sic*] non ne ho per niente voglia . . . poi torno in Italy e in febbraio vado in portogallo. [*sic*] tu [*sic*] come stai?
Elisa: thanks Va. this time I don't feel like leaving at all . . . but after a while I'll be back in Italy and in February I'll go to portugal. how are you?

→ 4 Vanda: qui a Roma tutto discretamente bene, studio con una bella tazza de [*sic*] camomilla per aiutare la concentrazione :) mi mancano le cene a casa insieme! intanto [*sic*] un bacio grande
Vanda: here in Roma everything is going well, I'm studying while having a cup of chamomile tea to help my concentration:) I miss our dinners at home together! a big kiss

In the comment at Post 1 Elisa performs the first action in this interaction; she opens this comment thread with a comment that contains a telling, saying to Friends that she is leaving (*Time to pack. Again*). After the comment at Post 2 where Vanda accomplishes the second action in this comment thread, she responds to Elisa's initial telling (*buon viaggio Eli, e boa sorte!*). In the comment at Post 3, Elisa performs the third action in this interaction—she reports on her future activities (*grazie Va. stavolta non ne ho per niente voglia . . . poi torno in Italy e in febbraio vado in portogallo*). More precisely, Elisa says to Vanda that she does not want to leave and that in the following months she will be in Italy and Portugal. Then, she closes the comment at Post 3 by performing another action in this comment thread; she posts the *first pair part* of a how-are-you sequence (*tu come stai?*).

This sequence is completed by the action performed by Vanda in the comment at Post 4, where she publishes the *second pair part* of the how-are-you sequence launched by Elisa in the comment at Post 3. Vanda does this by reporting to Elisa that she is fine, that she is having a cup of chamomile tea while studying, and that she misses dinners with Elisa (*qui a Roma tutto discretamente bene, studio con una bella tazza de camomilla per aiutare la concentrazione :) mi mancano le cene a casa insieme! intanto un bacio grande*).

The analysis of Extract 3.10 supports the hypothesis that FB users perform actions in comment threads. Moreover, these actions can be organized in *adjacency pairs*. This comment thread also indicates that comments within comment threads generally make sense only when considered as part of a sequence and not when analyzed separately. This can be seen even more clearly in the comments at Posts 2, 3, and 4 in Extract 3.11, about Giorgio's brain.

Extract 3.11 Giorgio's brain

1 Alberta: E' ufficiale mio marito si è "bruciato" il cervello!!!!
Alberta: It's official my husband has lost his mind!!!!

A 2 persone piace questo
2 people like this

→ 2 Serena: capita . . . pure io il mio da anni . . . :)))))))))))
Serena: it happens . . . I lost mine years ago . . . :)))))))))))

→ 3 Giorgio: è da parecchi anni che lavoro su qst [*sic*]
Giorgio: I've been working at this for years

→ 4 Alberta: su cosa??? Sul riuscire a bruciartelo per bene??? Amorsigno ce l'hai fattaaaaaaaa!!!
Alberta: at what??? on losing it definitely??? My love you succeeded!!!

In the comment at Post 1 Alberta performs the first action in this comment thread; she posts an exclamation about Giorgio, her husband. Alberta tells Friends that Giorgio has lost his mind (*E' ufficiale mio marito si è "bruciato" il cervello!!!!*). In the comment at Post 2, Serena accomplishes the second action in this interaction: she publishes a comment which makes sense only if interpreted as a response to the comment at Post 1. Serena humorously tells Alberta that "it" happens and that "she lost hers years ago" (*capita . . . pure io il mio da anni . . . :))))))))))))))*. The action performed by Serena in the comment at Post 2 cannot be established except with reference to the action in the comment at Post 1.

Similarly, Giorgio's action in the comment at Post 3 makes no sense if considered separately; however, if interpreted in relation to the action in the comment at Post 1, it gains meaning: "I've been working at it for years" (*è da parecchi anni che lavoro su qst*). This comment stimulates another action, the comment at Post 4, which once again makes sense only if interpreted as a response to the action performed in the comment at Post 3. Here Alberta responds to Giorgio's comment at Post 3 by teasing him and saying that he should be proud of his actions, because he has definitely succeeded in losing "it" (*su cosa??? Sul riuscire a bruciartelo per bene??? Amorsigno ce l'hai fattaaaaaaaa!!!*).

So, in general, comments in comment threads make sense only if interpreted as part of a sequence, and not if analyzed as separate items. In addition, it appears that comments generate other comments, which make successive comments relevant and so on. This is because, as already mentioned in this section, FB users perform actions when they post comments in comment threads. These actions generate other actions which make other actions the relevant next. This can be seen again in Extract 3.12, which contains a segment taken from a Woody Allen movie.

Extract 3.12 Woody Allen

1 Aldo: corro ad accenderla [Aldo publishes a hyperlink that contains a segment of the movie *Deconstructing Harry*, including a joke about the Pope and air-conditioning]
Aldo: I must turn it on

A 2 persone piace questo
2 people like this

2 Vera: mi ricordi tanto peppone [one of the characters of the book *Don Camillo*], ma dov'è il tuo don camillo [main character of this book]??!!
Vera: you remind me so much of peppone, but where is your don camillo??!!

3 Aldo: il ruolo è libero
Aldo: the role is available to anyone

Although the comment thread in Extract 3.12 is made up of three comments only, these contributions are tied together; the comment at Post 1 launches the comment at Post 2, which then projects the comment at Post 3. In the comment at Post 1, Aldo opens this interaction by performing the first action in this comment thread. He introduces and posts a hyperlink-telling. He tells Friends that he intends to turn "it" on (*corro ad accenderla*), where "it" refers to the air-conditioning which is the focus of the movie segment in the hyperlink in the comment at Post 1.

This action generates the second action in this comment thread: the response in the comment at Post 2. Here Vera tells Aldo, based on what he has posted in the comment at Post 1, that he reminds her of Peppone, one of the characters of the book *Don Camillo* (*mi ricordi tanto peppone*). Vera continues the comment at Post 2 by mocking Aldo and ironically asking him who is his Don Camillo, another character from the same book (*ma dov'è il tuo don camillo??!!*). Vera's mocking tone in the comment at Post 2 projects another action in this interaction: the response at Post 3. In this contribution Aldo responds to Vera by saying that "the role" is still available (*il ruolo è libero*).

The analysis of Extract 3.12 has thus confirmed the hypothesis introduced earlier in this section, that comments in comment threads make sense only if considered in a sequence and not if analyzed separately. This is because of the actions performed by FB users in comments within comment threads.

In general, therefore, comments in comment threads do not incoherently follow one after the other, but they are organized in an identifiable structure. This is because FB users perform actions when they post comments within comment threads. Strong evidence that this is the case comes from the presence of comments that make sense only when interpreted in relation to earlier comments, forming part of an *adjacency pair* or a more complex sequence. These issues will be taken up in following chapters, where the organization of sequences beginning with tellings will be explored in more detail.

Conclusions

In analyzing FB comment threads, this chapter found that there are specific features that characterize these interactions. For instance, comment threads consist of several related comments, and poster changes regularly occur in these interactions.

In addition, comment threads can be asynchronous or quasi-synchronous. However, in neither case do FB users have access to comments in progress. This means that although simultaneously online at the time of an interaction, FB users cannot negotiate poster change. In fact, as will be seen later on in this book, the system, and not FB users, has control over the positioning of almost all the comments posted in comment threads. This chapter has also demonstrated that FB users construct comments by using pragmatically complete units, which may also be grammatically complete sentences. Moreover, these elements may also consist of multimodal elements, such as the hyperlink posted by Aldo in the opening comment of Extract 3.12. These multimodal elements seem to complement the verbal material published in comments within comment threads.

Turn allocation components also appear to be present in FB comment threads, although they do not necessarily function in the way one might expect. In fact, while these elements may select next posters in a comment thread, they do not stop Friends who have not been selected as the intended recipients of a comment from participating in a comment thread.

Finally, comments in comment threads are generally organized in an identifiable structure. This is because FB users perform actions when they post comments in comment threads. Strong evidence for this comes from the presence of *adjacency pairs* and comments that make sense only if interpreted in relation to previous comments in a thread. Having now established that there is *sequence organization* in FB comment threads, the following chapters will look at how FB users open these interactions and how Friends respond to them.

4

The Basic Sequence of FB Comment Threads: Tellings

Introduction

After showing in Chapter 3 that comments in FB comment threads are organized in an identifiable structure, this chapter focuses on the contributions that open these interactions, and demonstrates that the basic sequence which opens FB comment threads is the telling sequence. Chapter 5 will then go on to analyze the interactional problems that may arise when an FB user begins a comment thread by using a telling, and the resources he or she may use to overcome them. Chapter 6 will contrast tellings that occur in the opening comments of comment threads with tellings that take place in comments that are not the first contributions in comment threads, and Chapter 7 will focus on responses to initial and non-initial tellings.

After demonstrating that FB comment threads are commonly opened by comments that contain tellings, this chapter discusses the format of these tellings. Then, it introduces the classification utilized in this book to describe tellings occurring in the first comments of FB comment threads.

First-post tellings

This section shows that FB comment threads are almost always opened by comments containing tellings; indeed only 8 out of the 213 comment threads included in the corpus of this study were opened by comments which do not contain a telling. In this book, a telling is understood as a narrative that occurs in a comment thread. A typical example of a first-post telling[1] can be seen in Extract 4.1, where in the comment at Post 1 Alberta, the first-post teller, launches this interaction by posting a textual message that functions as a telling.

Extract 4.1 The purse snatching

→ 1 Alberta: Ma che bella giornata di merda . . . iniziata bene ma finita stramalissimo con tanto di scippo in diretta!
Alberta: What a crappy day . . . . It has started well but it ended terribly and included a live purse snatching

2 Alessia: e delle mie 700 euro per riparare la macchina . . . ne vogliamo parlare!!!! ufff
Alessia: tell me about it!!! what about me and the 700 euros I had to pay to fix my car . . .!ufff

3 Alberta: Fidati! noi [*sic*] ci andiamo vicino . . .
Alberta: Trust me! I know what you mean . . .

4 Chiara: bhe finita stramalissimo . . . e della telefonata con me che mi dici?!? ho [*sic*] pure seguito lo scippo in diretta! =)
Chiara: ok so it ended terribly . . . and what about our phone conversation? I also witnessed the purse snatching live!=)

5 Alberta: No comment!!!!!!! Arrivo al corso e racconto lo scippo, e poi mi chiedono ma poi com'è finite [*sic*]? Niente mi hanno suonato e me ne sono andata, ma non ho detto che tu mi ha suggerito: SCAPPAAAAAA!
Alberta: No comment!!!!!!! I arrived at the class and I told people about the snatching and people asked me how it all ended? Nothing I said, someone beeped me and I had to drive on, but I didn't mention what you suggested to me: RUUUUN!

6 Lucia: ma Alberta che cavolo e [*sic*] successo?
Lucia: but Alberta what the hell happened?

In the comment at Post 1 Alberta launches this comment thread by publishing a contribution which consists of two pragmatically complete units: an evaluation of her day (*Ma che bella giornata di merda . . .*) and a telling (*iniziata bene ma finita stramalissimo con tanto di scippo in diretta!*). In the first unit of the comment at Post 1, Alberta gives a "summary" comment, alerting Friends as to how they should interpret the following telling; she says to Friends that she had a "crappy" day (*Ma che bella giornata di merda . . .*). The second unit of the comment at Post 1, on the other hand, is the telling; Alberta tells Friends about how she witnessed a purse snatching (*iniziata bene ma finita stramalissimo con tanto di scippo in diretta!*).

As can be seen from the comment at Post 1, the first actions accomplished by FB users in comment threads appear to be tellings. Moreover, these tellings may consist of multiple units which overall function as single tellings. In fact, even though the first unit of the comment at Post 1 seems to be an evaluative summary, while the second appears to be the telling itself, together they constitute the telling.

Although the telling in the comment at Post 1 occurs within a contribution only, thus seeming to correspond to what conversation analysts refer to as a spoken announcement (Liddicoat, 2011; Maynard, 2006; Sacks, 1992; Schegloff, 2007; Terasaki, 2004), it is also made up of multiple units, like a story told in a spoken conversation. Thus, tellings occurring in FB comment threads seem to share features of both spoken announcements and stories (C. Goodwin, 1984; M. Goodwin, 1982, 1991, 1993; Jefferson, 1978; Liddicoat, 2011b; Mandelbaum, 1989; Norrick, 2000; Sacks, 1986, 1992). In addition, it seems that the telling occurring in Extract 4.1 is similar to a small story (Georgakopoulou, 2007a; Page, 2012) or to what Bolander and Locher (2010) refer to as an expressive speech act.

The actions performed by Alessia, Chiara, and Lucia in the comment that follow the contribution at Post 1 demonstrate that these Friends have interpreted the entire comment as a single telling. In the comment at Post 2, Alessia responds to Alberta by performing another telling. She says that she had to pay seven hundred euros to fix her own car (*e delle mie 700 euro per riparare la macchina . . . ne vogliamo parlare!!!! ufff*). Thus, here we have Alessia using a second story (Georgakopoulou, 2007a; C. Goodwin, 1984, 1986; C. Goodwin & Goodwin, 1992; Liddicoat, 2011; Page, 2012; Sacks, 1992; Schegloff, 2007; Vàsquez, 2015) to show affiliation with Alberta about what a crappy day it is. In the comment at Post 3, when she says that these two tellings are similar, Alberta explicitly accepts the affiliation (*Fidati! noi ci andiamo vicino . . .*).

Similar to what Alessia has done in the comment at Post 2, in the comment at Post 4 Chiara performs another action which shows that she has interpreted the comment at Post 1 as a telling. In this contribution Chiara is supportive, responding with a negative evaluation of the day, telling Alberta that her day did indeed end terribly (*bhe finita stramalissimo*). Then, after a series of suspension points, Chiara performs another action in this comment thread. She continues with the comment at Post 4 by talking about how they were on the phone when Alberta was witnessing the purse snatching (*. . . e della telefonata con me che mi dici?!? ho pure seguito lo scippo in diretta! =)*). In the comment at Post 6, Lucia accomplishes another action which indicates that she has interpreted all the units that compose the comment at Post 1 as a single telling. Lucia shows that she needs to know more about the events of the telling in the comment at Post 1 by explicitly requesting that Alberta explain what happened to her (*ma Alberta che cavolo e successo?*).

The actions performed by Alessia, Chiara, and Lucia in the comments at Posts 2, 4, and 6 clearly show that these Friends have interpreted the first comment in this comment thread as a telling. Moreover, these responses suggest that, similar to spoken conversation, second tellings, evaluations, and requests for clarification might be typical responses that follow first-post tellings. This issue will be taken up in more detail in Chapter 7.

A somewhat different example of a telling is also evident in Extract 4.2, where Alberta opens a comment thread with another first-post telling.

Extract 4.2 *Le Petite Prince*

1 Alberta: Il piccolo prince
→ [Alberta publishes a photo which contains the necklace she has created. This necklace has a pendant, which is reminiscent of the image of the Little Prince, the main character of Antoine de Saint Exupéry's book *Le Petite Prince*.]
Alberta: The little prince

con Eleonora[2]
with Eleonora

2 Eleonora: Alberta è meraviglioso!!! Grazieeeeeee! Non vedo l'ora di metterlo!
Eleonora: Alberta it's marvellous!!! Thanks! I can't wait to wear it!

Like the first contribution in Extract 4.1, the comment at Post 1 in Extract 4.2 consists of two pragmatically complete units which function as a single action, a telling. The first unit is the textual message which introduces the telling (*Il piccolo prince*), while the second is the photo-telling. In other words, Alberta, who crafts jewellery in her free time, is letting Friends know that she has finished the necklace she was working on.

Once again, strong evidence that this is the case comes from the action Eleonora, the only other contributor to this comment thread, has performed in the comment at Post 2. In the comment at Post 2 Eleonora publishes a positive evaluation of the content of the telling in the comment at Post 1; after explicitly telling Alberta that her necklace is marvellous, she thanks her for the necklace by saying that she cannot wait to wear it (*meraviglioso!!! Grazieeeeeee! Non vedo l'ora di metterlo!*).

The action performed by Eleonora in the comment at Post 2 supports the hypothesis introduced earlier in this section, which is that the first action normally accomplished by an FB user in a comment thread is a telling. Therefore, comment threads are normally opened by first-post tellings. Moreover, these tellings may consist of multiple units which function as single actions, and evaluations are a possible type of response to first-post tellings.

The same interpretation of a comment made up of multiple units which function as a single telling can be seen again in Extract 4.3, where in the comment at Post 1 Mauro talks about the band Crippled Black Phoenix.

Extract 4.3 Music discussion

→ 1 Mauro: Sono Tornati. Hanno deciso. Dall' intellettualismo [*sic*] alla ribellione. [Mauro publishes a hyperlink that contains a video of the band Crippled Black Phoenix] Valeria Giorgio Alice Zara Alberto
Mauro: They're back. They've decided. From philosophers to rebels Valeria Giorgio Alice Zara Alberto

A Valeria piace questo
Valeria likes this

2 Mauro: forse ora si faranno conoscere ma la loro storia è lunga.
Mauro: maybe they'll become popular, but they've a long history.

3 Alice:—eccellente; tra un pò parto e vengo in Danelleria. Mi riservo l'ascolto lì.
Alice:—excellent; I'll be leaving in a while and come to Danelleria [name used by Friends to refer to Mauro's bar]. *I'll listen to them once I'm there.*

4 Antonio: buono, buon. Han davvero tre batteristi? O_O
Antonio: good, good. Do they really have three percussionists? O_O

The first comment in this extract once again consists of four potentially pragmatically complete units that function as a single action in this interaction; more precisely a telling. The first unit consists of the textual message where Mauro, the first-post teller, introduces his telling; the second unit is the hyperlink that contains the video of the band Crippled Black Phoenix; the third is a list of intended recipients for the telling; and the final unit consists of some extra information provided by Mauro about the band.

In the textual message at Post 1 Mauro provides Friends with a framework to interpret his telling, by saying that Crippled Black Phoenix have finally returned, changing from an intellectual to a rebellious style (*Sono Tornati. Hanno deciso. Dall' intellettualismo alla ribellione*). Then, after publishing a hyperlink-telling, Mauro closes the comment at Post 1 by naming the intended recipients of his telling (*Valeria Giorgio Alice Zara Alberto*). In the comment at Post 2, Mauro continues on with the telling, providing Friends with more information about Crippled Black Phoenix; he says that although this band will probably become popular, it already has a long history (*forse ora si faranno conoscere ma la loro storia è lunga*).

The actions performed by Alice and Antonio in the comments at Posts 3 and 4 show that these Friends have interpreted all the actions contained in the comments at Posts 1 and 2 as a single telling. Although in the final component of Post 3 Alice says that she did not listen to the song in the comment at Post 1, because she wants to do it in "*Danelleria*," which is the name used by Friends to refer to Mauro's bar (*tra un pò parto e vengo in Danelleria. Mi riservo l'ascolto lì*), she opens the comment at Post 3 with "*eccellente*," which can be interpreted as a recipient token (Maynard, 2006). In other words, in the initial unit of the comment at Post 3 Alice acknowledges to Mauro that she has read the comments at Posts 1 and 2. In the comment at Post 4 after publishing a positive evaluation of the video at Post 1 (*buono, buon*), Antonio asks Mauro to confirm if Crippled Black Phoenix have three percussionists (*buono, buon. Han davvero tre batteristi? O_O*). Thus, in this extract we have Alice and Antonio using a recipient token and an evaluation to respond to the comments at Posts 1 and 2, suggesting that these Friends have interpreted these contributions as a single telling.

It seems that the first action accomplished by an FB user in a comment thread is a telling. Therefore, comment threads are normally opened by first-post tellings. The interactions so far analyzed in this chapter have also indicated that tellings occurring in the opening comments of FB comment threads may consist of multiple units. In a sense, first-post tellings can be thought of as corresponding to stories in spoken conversation, as these may consist of multiple units that together operate as a single narrative; however, first-post tellings are also like spoken announcements, in that they occur in single comments only with no interaction from addressees within the telling (Liddicoat, 2011b; Maynard, 2006; Sacks, 1986, 1992; Schegloff, 2007; Terasaki, 2004).

In addition, as will be discussed in more detail in Chapter 7, this section has shown that the actions performed by Friends in the comments that follow the tellings appear to be similar to the actions performed by conversationalists after tellings occurring in spoken conversation (Jefferson, 1979; Liddicoat, 2011b; Maynard, 2006; Sacks, 1992; Schegloff, 2007; Terasaki, 2004). That is, Friends, as conversationalists, use second tellings, assessments, requests for clarification, and recipient tokens to respond to first-post tellings occurring in FB comment threads, as clearly demonstrated by the comments that follow the initial tellings in Extracts 4.1 to 4.3.

Overall, FB comment threads are generally opened by first-post tellings, and therefore tellings constitute the basic sequence that characterizes FB comment threads.

Formats of first-post tellings

In arguing that FB comment threads are normally opened by first-post tellings, the previous section has also suggested that tellings can have different formats. In fact, while the telling in the comment at Post 1 in Extract 4.1 consists of a textual message only, the tellings in the comments at Post 1 in Extracts 4.2 and 4.3 are made up of a textual message followed by a photo and a hyperlink-telling respectively.

Therefore, this section will demonstrate that first-post tellings may have five different formats: textual messages only, photos only, hyperlinks only, or combinations of textual messages with either photos or hyperlink-tellings (see also Farina, 2015), as can be seen in Extracts 4.4 to 4.8.[3]

Extract 4.4 Claudio's early dinner

→ 1 Claudio: Cazzo! Sono le 18:40e [*sic*] sto cenando! Peggio di mio nonno O_o
Claudio: Fuck! It's 6:40 p.m. and I'm having dinner! I'm worse than my grandfather O_o

A 2 persone piace questo
2 people like this

2 Aleandro: sei un vecchio!
Aleandro: you're an old man!

3 Claudio: fossero tutti così i vecchi . . . (tiè:P)
Claudio: If only all the old people were like me . . . (tiè:P) [exclamation which normally accompanies hand gesture used to ward off evil]

4 Esteban: i guess you're talking about Berlusconi [the former Italian prime minister], everyone does!

5 Claudio: I'm different ☺ Didn't you recognize this yet???? ; P I'm just saying . . . . "[*sic*] Fuck, It's 6:40 p.m. and I'm having dinner. Worst than what my grandfather does O_o"

6 Aleandro: Berlusconi is dead. Forever.

In the comment at Post 1 Claudio performs a telling. He publishes a textual message that contains three pragmatically complete units: an initial expletive (*Cazzo*); an intended humorous telling, where he says that he is having an early dinner (*Sono le 18:40e sto cenando!*); and an ironic negative evaluation oriented to his own telling, where Claudio tells Friends that even his grandfather generally eats later (*Peggio di mio nonno O_o*). The action performed by Aleandro in the comment at Post 2 shows that he has interpreted all the units that make the contribution at Post 1 as an overall telling. Specifically, in the comment at Post 2, Aleandro shows that he has understood the facetious tone embedded in Claudio's initial telling. Aleandro mocks Claudio by ironically agreeing with him when he says that Claudio is old (*sei un vecchio!*).

The other contributor to this comment thread is Esteban, and as indicated by his pseudonym he is apparently not a native speaker of Italian. The action accomplished by Esteban in the comment at Post 4 shows that he has a problem in understanding the telling in the comment at Post 1. Esteban guesses that this comment refers to Silvio Berlusconi, the former Italian prime minister (*i guess you're talking about Berlusconi, everyone does!*). The comment at Post 4 is in English. In the comment at Post 5 Claudio responds to Esteban and posts the English translation of the comment at Post 1. Claudio switches to English to resolve the communicative problem that Esteban raised in the comment at Post 4. In other words, here we have Claudio seeming to use code switching as a strategy to explain his contribution in the comment at Post 1 (Androutsopoulos, 2014a, b, 2015; Seargeant et al., 2012).

In the comment at Post 6, Aleandro, who has already posted the comment at Post 2, performs another action in this comment thread. He switches to English to post another response to Esteban's comment at Post 4. Aleandro makes an ironic comment on the political career of Berlusconi. He says that Berlusconi is dead (*Berlusconi is dead. Forever.*). Thus, it seems that Aleandro has used English to avoid any other potential communicative problem in this comment thread; he wants to make sure that his ironic comment is understood by Esteban. Therefore, it appears that, similar to what happens in spoken conversation, FB users use code switching as a strategy to resolve communicative problems that may occur in a comment thread.

In contrast to Extract 4.4, the initial telling that launches the comment thread in Extract 4.5 has a photo format; moreover, this comment is not accompanied by any textual message that introduces it or evaluates it.

Extract 4.5 Lying in the sun

→ 1 [Vanessa publishes the photo-telling which portrays herself and her colleagues lying in the sun during working hours.]

A Roberto piace questo
Roberto likes this

2 Elia: AH MA BRAVI è COSì CHE SI PRODUCE !!!
Elia: AH WELL DONE THIS is THE WAY YOU PRODUCE!!!

3 Vanessa: erano le 15.30 e approfittavamo del sole!!!
Vanessa: it was 3:30 P.M. and we were making the most of the sun!!!

4 Alessia: ke [*sic*] belli ke [*sic*] siete!!!!
Alessia: what a spectacle you are!!!!

5 Vanessa: Eravamo tanti [*sic*] stanchi è stata una settimana dura!!!!
Vanessa: We were really tired, it's been a busy week!!!!

6 Piera: ah però! devo [*sic*] cambiare ufficio . . . ho deciso
Piera: wow! I've got to move to your office . . . I've made up my mind

In the comment at Post 1 Vanessa launches this comment thread by performing the first action in this interaction. She posts a contribution that contains a photo-telling. The photo in the comment at Post 1, in contrast to that seen earlier in Extract 4.2, is not preceded by any textual message that introduces it. This photo shows Vanessa and her colleagues lying in the sun during working hours.

The actions performed by Elia, Alessia, and Piera in the comments at Posts 2, 4, and 6 demonstrate that even though the comment at Post 1 is a photo, they have interpreted it as a telling. Specifically, in the comment at Post 2 Elia publishes an ironic positive evaluation of the productivity of both Vanessa and her colleagues (*AH MA BRAVI è COSì CHE SI PRODUCE !!!*). Another positive evaluation, which once again responds to the photo-telling in the comment at Post 1, is published by Alessia in the comment at Post 4, with Alessia telling Vanessa that she and her colleagues look wonderful (*ke belli ke siete!!!!*).

In the comment at Post 6 Piera publishes another comment which explicitly responds to the photo-telling at Post 1. Piera ironically says that after seeing Vanessa's photo, she is considering moving office (*ah però! devo cambiare ufficio . . . ho deciso*). In other words, as a way of evaluating Vanessa's telling, Piera ironically tells Vanessa that she is envious because Vanessa is lying in the sun, while she is working.

Thus, although the comment in the contribution at Post 1 is a photo, and therefore potentially more open to interpretations than a textual telling, the actions performed by Elia, Alessia, and Piera in the comments that follow it indicate that this is not the case. In fact, the actions performed in these contributions are similar to the actions accomplished in the responses posted in Extract 4.4. All the actions performed in the responses in these two comment threads orient to the initial tellings, even though the telling in Extract 4.5 is a photo and the telling in Extract 4.4 is a textual message.

The following extract, Extract 4.6, shows that a first-post telling may also consist of only a hyperlink. Mauro in fact launches this comment thread by simply publishing the hyperlink-telling in the comment at Post 1, which shows up on the screen as a frame from a video that refers to a segment of the TV show *Il più grande spettacolo dopo il weekend* (The biggest show after the weekend).

Extract 4.6 TV show

→ 1 [Mauro publishes a hyperlink which links to a segment of the TV show *Il più grande spettacolo dopo il weekend*]

A Valeria piace questo
Valeria like this

2 Valeria: Belle le coriste ultra :D
Valeria: the hooligan chorister are wonderful :D

3 Arturo: skazz le minl
Arturo: skazz le minl [title of one of the songs performed in the video at Post 1]

The hyperlink which opens this comment thread refers to a video of a segment of one of the episodes of the TV show *Il più grande spettacolo dopo il weekend.* In contrast to the comment at Post 1 in Extract 4.3, where Mauro has performed an additional action to introduce his telling—more specifically, he has posted a textual message to introduce his hyperlink-telling—Mauro here does not perform any additional action to introduce his telling. However, the actions performed by Friends in the comments that follow this contribution show that although it is a hyperlink, they have interpreted it as a telling.

In the comment at Post 2 Valeria publishes a positive evaluation of the choristers that appear in the video at Post 1 (*Belle le coriste ultra :D*); commenting positively on an aspect of a telling is a common type of response utilized by Friends to respond to first-post tellings. In the comment at Post 3 Arturo publishes the title of one of the songs performed in this video (*skazz le minl*), presumably indicating that he particularly likes it or finds it amusing, once again showing that he is treating the hyperlink at Post 1 as a telling.

First-post tellings may therefore consist of textual messages only, photos only, and hyperlinks only. However, Extracts 4.7 and 4.8 demonstrate that this is not always the case. In fact, the tellings that open these interactions consist of multiple units which overall function as tellings, more specifically a textual message followed by a photo and a hyperlink-telling respectively.

Extract 4.7 Andrea Pirlo

→ 1 Mauro: Comunque mi manchi . . .
[Mauro publishes a photo of Andrea Pirlo, an Italian soccer player]
Mauro: By the way I miss you . . .

A 4 persone piace questo
4 people like this

2 Serena: A me no :-P
Serena: I don't :-P

3 Carlo: A chi lo dici . . .
Carlo: tell me about . . .

4 Chiara: io l'ho sempre detto
Chiara: I've always said this

5 Mauro: Era uno dei motive [*sic*] per cui ancora guardavo le partite del Milan. Ora devo ammettere di avere perso un'altra buona parte di affezionamento.
Mauro: He was one of the reasons I used to watch Milan matches. To be honest, now I've lost a big part of my attachment to the team.

In the comment at Post 1 Mauro opens this comment thread by posting a contribution which consists of two units that overall function as a complete telling. The first unit is the textual message where Mauro says that he misses Andrea Pirlo (*Comunque mi manchi . . .*), and the second unit is the photo of this soccer player. The actions performed by Serena, Carlo, and Chiara in the responses to the comment at Post 1 indicate that these Friends have interpreted this contribution as a telling. In the comment at Post 2, in disagreeing with Mauro, Serena shows that she has treated the comment at Post 1 as a telling. Serena in fact says that she did not miss Pirlo (*A me no :-P*). Similar to what Serena has done in the comment at Post 2, in the comments at Posts 3 and 4 Carlo and Chiara show that they have interpreted the comment at Post 1 as a telling.

In the comment at Post 3, Carlo agrees with Mauro when he says that he misses Pirlo too (*A chi lo dici . . .*), and in the comment at Post 4 Chiara is once again supportive when she says that she has always said to people that she misses Pirlo (*io l'ho sempre detto*). So, in expressing their agreement and disagreement with Mauro Serena, Carlo, and Chiara have shown that they interpreted the comment at Post 1 as a telling.

On the other hand, Extract 4.8 demonstrates that a first-post telling may also consist of the combination of a textual message with a hyperlink-telling.

Extract 4.8 The affair[4]

→ 1 Elisa: oh signur!!!
[Elisa publishes a hyperlink which contains the news about the affair between Barbara D'Urso and Massimiliano Allegri, two celebrities]
Elisa: oh my god!!!

2 Franco: Nooooo . . . quella ce lo demotiva!!!! Salvatelo!!!
Franco: Nooooo . . . that [woman] *will have a negative impact on his motivation!!!! Save him!!!*

[. . .]

8 Sandro: gran MILF bravo max
Sandro: great MILF well done max [Allegri's name]

Elisa, like Mauro has previously done in Extract 4.7, launches this comment thread by performing a telling. More precisely, she posts a contribution that consists of two pragmatically complete units that function as a single telling: the textual message "*oh signur!!!*" and the hyperlink at Post 1. In the comment at Post 1 Elisa uses an expletive in Lombard dialect, specifically the *Milanese* dialect spoken in the city of Milano, to provide an evaluation of the telling contained in the hyperlink at Post 1 (*oh signur!!!*). Interestingly, this textual message shares some features of a *first pair part* of a pre-telling sequence (Liddicoat, 2011b; Maynard, 2006; Sacks, 1992; Schegloff, 2007; Terasaki, 2004); this issue will be taken up in more detail in Chapter 5.

The actions accomplished by Franco and Sandro in the comments that follow the comment at Post 1 indicate that these Friends have interpreted this contribution as a telling. In the comment at Post 2 Franco picks up the facetious tone embedded in Elisa's comment at Post 1; he publishes a negative evaluation which supports the interpretation of the affair between Barbara D'Urso, an Italian TV personality, and Massimiliano Allegri, former coach of the soccer team A. C. Milan, proposed by Elisa in the comment at Post 1. Franco says that Barbara D'Urso will have a negative effect on the motivation of the coach (*Nooooo . . . quella ce lo demotiva!!!! Salvatelo!!!*).

After a series of contributions where Elisa and Franco post several humorous comments on the affair between the two celebrities, in the comment at Post 8 Sandro demonstrates that he has interpreted the comment at Post 1 as a telling. He uses an expletive to describe Barbabra D'Urso (*gran MILF*), then he congratulates the coach for his romantic conquest (*bravo max*). In this extract Franco and Sandro perform two actions: they use two evaluations to show that they have interpreted the textual message and the hyperlink in the comment at Post 1 as a single telling.

First-post tellings may therefore consist of contributions that are made up of several units, such as textual messages, photos, and hyperlinks which overall function as single tellings. In summary, this section enriches what was noted by a previous linguistic study on FB (Farina, 2015), which is that tellings occurring in the first comments of FB comment threads may have five different formats: textual messages only, photos only, hyperlinks only as well as combinations of textual messages with photos or hyperlink-tellings. So, in general, tellings in FB comment threads may consist of explicit text, written representations of non-verbal elements (emoticons, laughter, etc.), photos, hyperlinks, and combinations of textual messages with photos or hyperlinks. In other words, they appear to be similar to other contents published on the web, they are multimodal. Comments in comment threads may in fact consist of combinations of photos, images, spoken and written language, music, and sounds (Androutsopoulos, 2010; Georgalou, 2015a, b; Lee, 2011; Page, 2010a; Page, Harper, and Frobenius, 2013).

In addition, first-post tellings also seem intertextual (Kristeva, 1980); they reshape already existing texts, such as photos, images, and videos found online to create new texts (Androutsopoulos, 2010; West and Trester, 2013). First-post tellings integrate written and visual elements. This is probably because of the resources available on FB which may affect the format of first-post tellings. In other words, the presence of photos and hyperlinks in the opening comments of FB comment threads probably depends on FB users taking advantage of the tools available on the FB Home, such as the *Add Photo/Video* and *Share* buttons. These buttons allow FB users to publish photos, videos, and hyperlinks in comment threads, and if desired, to post written messages that refer to them.

On the other hand, although first-post tellings may consist of textual messages only, photos only, hyperlinks only, or combinations of textual messages with photos or hyperlinks, these formats do not seem to affect the ways in which Friends respond to tellings. In fact, as clearly demonstrated by the actions accomplished by Friends in the responses in Extracts 4.4 to 4.8, they respond in the same way regardless of the format of the telling. In other words, the format of a telling occurring in the first comment of an FB comment thread does not appear to impact on the *sequence organization* of a comment thread. This has been clearly seen in Extracts 4.5 and 4.6, where the actions performed by Friends in the comments that follow the visual tellings that have opened these interactions (the former is a photo while the latter is a hyperlink-telling) are similar to the actions performed by Friends in comments that come after the textual telling in Extract 4.4. The issue of responses to first-post tellings will be taken up again in Chapter 7.

Autobiographical and third-person event tellings

Turning briefly to consider the content of first-post tellings, it is possible to see that a narrative occurring in the first comment of a comment thread may be autobiographical or about a third-person event and may refer to a past, current, or future activity or event.

This was clearly shown by the analysis of Extracts 4.1 to 4.8 presented above. For example, the telling published by Claudio in Extract 4.4 is autobiographical because it refers to his own activities; Claudio says that he is having an early dinner (*Cazzo! Sono le 18:40e sto cenando! Peggio di mio nonno O_o*). On the other hand, the telling in Extract 4.6 is about a third-person event; it refers to an event in which Mauro has no involvement. This telling is in fact a hyperlink containing a fragment of the TV show *Il più grande spettacolo dopo il weekend.* Although it is usually clear when a first-post telling is autobiographical, sometimes establishing whether a telling is about a third-person event can be complicated; because even when a telling seems to explicitly refer to a third-person event, it may in some way relate to the person posting the comment.

This can be seen in Extract 4.9, where Elena in the comment at Post 1 publishes an invitation prior to introducing the following hyperlink-telling.

Extract 4.9 The drama course

→ 1 Elena: iscrivetevi numerosi
[Elena publishes a hyperlink with information about a drama course]
Elena: please enrol

Although the hyperlink-telling in the comment at Post 1 apparently refers to a third-person event (the drama course described in the hyperlink at Post 1), the textual message that introduces it suggests that this telling may be autobiographical. In the textual message in the comment at Post 1, Elena invites Friends to participate in the drama course described in the following hyperlink-telling (*iscrivetevi numerosi*); therefore, she shows a possible personal involvement in this course. So, even though the hyperlink-telling in the comment at Post 1 refers to a third-person event, the textual message that introduces it suggests that this telling may also refer to the initial poster, making it difficult to establish whether the telling is autobiographical or about a third-person event. This is the case of the majority of the third-person event tellings included in the corpus of this book where, even when the telling clearly refers to a third-person event, the person posting the comment must feel some sort of connection with it—if only that the telling depresses or entertains him or her—since otherwise he or she would not have posted it.

Another interesting feature that characterizes first-post tellings is that whether referring to the poster's own activities or third-person events, these tellings can refer to a past, current, or future activity or event. This can be seen in

Extracts 4.10 to 4.15. Extract 4.10 is an autobiographical telling. In the comment at Post 1 Elisa, the first-post teller, posts a textual message followed by a photo-telling, more precisely, a selfie—a photograph of oneself typically taken with a smartphone (*Oxford English Dictionary Online*, 2017)—which shows her and her Friend Serena during a concert. The photo in the comment at Post 1 refers to Elisa herself, therefore it is autobiographical; moreover, it refers to a past activity.

Extract 4.10 Ligabue's concert

→ 1 Elisa: LIGA 16/07/10 [Elisa publishes a photo which shows herself and Serena during a concert by Luciano Ligabue, a famous Italian rock star]
Elisa: LIGA 16/07/10

2 Elisa: Serena [Elisa's Friend] amoooo ti ricordi?:-)
Elisa: Serena daaaaaarling do you remember it?:-)

3 Serena: Certo che si!!!!!!!!!!!!!! Bellissimo concerto!!!!! Uscire dal centro estivo per andare da liga non ga [*sic*] prezzo!!
Serena: Of course!!!!!!!!!!!!!! Great concert!!!!! To leave the summer school to go and see liga is priceless!!

4 Elisa: ♥♥♥♥♥♥

The selfie in the comment at Post 1 shows Elisa and Serena during a concert by the Italian rock singer Luciano Ligabue. This contribution seems to promote "knowing participation," a specific type of participation triggered by some previous knowledge shared by a restricted group of Friends and normally based on offline interactions or experiences (Georgakopoulou, 2016). In other words, as will be discussed in more detail in Chapter 5, it appears that Elisa is using the selfie at Post 1 to secure Serena's response at Post 3. In addition, in the textual message that precedes the photo-telling in the comment at Post 1, Elisa, before producing the telling, performs an additional action which is aimed to help Friends interpreting her telling. She provides them with information regarding the telling; she says that the concert was held in 2010 (*LIGA 16/07/10*). The comment at Post 1 was posted in 2011, and therefore it refers to a past activity (Georgalou, 2016). In other words, the telling in the comment at Post 1 is about Elisa's own activities, which happened in the past. On the other hand, the opening comment of Extract 4.11, although autobiographical, is about an ongoing activity.

Extract 4.11 Daily plan

→ 1 Claudio: to reduce the guiltiness about this Mascarpone's day, the plan is to finish my breakfast now (still without Mascarpone) and go to the gym ASAP :P

A 2 persone piace questo
2 people like this

2 Marta: se fai il mascarpone montato con un pò di panna diventa più leggero e si risolve il tuo problema☺
Marta: if you mix the mascarpone with a little bit of cream it becomes lighter and you fix your problem☺

3 Claudio: AHHAHAHA :D Vedo che la Chiara ha insegnato bene :P Purtroppo no, solo uova, mascarpone e zucchero a velo (e un pò di caffè, irish cream e cioccolato in polvere):D
Claudio: AHHAHAHA :D Chiara taught you well :P Unfortunately no, I only use eggs, mascarpone and icing sugar (and a little bit of coffee, irish cream and powdered chocolate):D

4 Christian: E se, poi ci aggiungi della crema pasticcera diventa ancora più leggera [*sic*] ☺
Christian: and if, you add some custard it becomes even lighter☺

5 Marta: dai che fa lo stesso. Oggi possiamo tutto.
Marta: come on it doesn't matter. These days everything is possible.

6 Claudio: non so perchè ma mi piace la tua filosofia Marta☺
Claudio: I don't know why but Marta I like your philosophy☺

Claudio opens this comment thread with a contribution on his ongoing activities; he tells Friends what he is doing, having breakfast, and that he plans to immediately go to the gym in order to burn some of the calories he has accumulated after eating a huge amount of mascarpone (*to reduce the guiltiness about this Mascarpone's day, the plan is to finish my breakfast now (still without Mascarpone) and go to the gym ASAP :P*). The telling in the comment at Post 1 is about Claudio, the initial poster, and refers to his activities at the time of publication of this contribution on the FB Home; thus, it is a current autobiographical telling.

In contrast to the initial telling in Extract 4.11, the first-post telling in Extract 4.12 is about Mauro's future activities.

Extract 4.12 Metroman-Carnevale[5]

→ 1 Mauro: ho Deciso . . . A CARNEVALE MI VESTO DA METROMAN [the busker mentioned in Extract 3.5]
Mauro: I have decided . . . AT THE NEXT CARNEVALE PARTY I'LL DRESS UP AS METROMAN

A Elisa ed altre 12 persone piace questo
Elisa and other 12 people like this

2 Auro: non dormo più!
Auro: I can't sleep anymore

3 Filippo: io da banana
Filippo: and I will dress up like a banana

[. . .]

In the comment at Post 1 Mauro performs a telling about his future activities, referring to his own plan for the upcoming Carnevale party. Carnevale is an Italian celebration where people go to parties wearing masks and dressing up as fantasy characters, such as Pinocchio, Mickey Mouse, and so on. Mauro states that for the next Carnevale party he wants to dress up as Metroman (*ho Deciso . . . A CARNEVALE MI VESTO DA METROMAN*). The telling in the comment at Post 1 is autobiographical, referring to Mauro's own activities; furthermore, Mauro is explicitly referring to a future plan. Therefore, the comment thread in Extract 4.12 is an autobiographical telling about a future activity (Georgakopoulou, 2002). In this case, of course, the future plan is probably intended only humorously.

First comments that open FB comment threads may contain autobiographical tellings that refer to past, current, or future activities. Similarly, first-post tellings may also refer to past, current, and future third-person events as clearly indicated by the analysis of Extracts 4.13 to 4.15.

The first comment in Extract 4.13, like that in Extract 4.6, refers to a segment of the TV show *Il più grande spettacolo dopo il weekend.*

Extract 4.13 *Il più grande spettacolo dopo il weekend*

→ 1 Mauro: Elisa [Italian singer] in presobenismo [non-standard expression utilized to describe people who are always positive] [Mauro publishes a hyperlink which contains a segment of the TV show *Il più grande spettacolo dopo il weekend.* This episode was broadcast on November 28, 2011]
Mauro: Elisa in presobenismo

A 3 persone piace questo
3 people like this

2 Aldo: ride come la maionchi [*sic*] [Italian music producer] tra l'altro ahahah!
Aldo: by the way she [Elisa] *laughs like mara maionchi ahahah!*

3 Fabio: Spassosa!. . . :-D
(p.s.: avete notato che Mr Saxobeat [probably one of the musicians in the video in the comment at Post 1] la interpreta con una metrica diversa dall'originale?. . .).

Fabio: Funny!. . . :-D (p.s.: did you notice that Mr Saxobeat interprets this song using a different lyric? . . .).

4 Laura: Ho scoperto di ridere come Elisa!!! O_O
Laura: I've discovered that I laugh like Elisa!!! O_O

Mauro launches this comment thread by publishing the textual message which introduces the hyperlink-telling in the comment at Post 1 (*Elisa in presobenismo*). This hyperlink is about a third-person event, a segment of the TV show *Il più grande spettacolo dopo il weekend*. As indicated by the information published in the preview of the hyperlink-telling in the comment at Post 1, this video refers to an episode which was broadcast on November 28, 2011. However, Mauro has posted this comment thread on December 1, 2011. Three days have elapsed since this show was broadcast on TV; therefore, because the first-post telling in Extract 4.13 refers to a past event, it is a past third-person event telling.

Unlike the telling in Extract 4.13, the first-post telling in Extract 4.14 is about a current third-person event. In fact, Auro, the original poster, begins this comment thread by commenting on the current weather conditions in Milan.

Extract 4.14 It can't rain forever[6]

→ 1 Auro: "Non può piovere per sempre" [quote taken from the Italian version of the movie *The Crow*]
Auro: "It cannot rain forever"

A Claudio piace questo
Claudio likes this

2 Alex: ma può smettere per un pò . . . .
Alex: but it can stop for a while . . . .

3 Matteo: però può continuare per un bel pò . . .
Matteo: or it can keep raining for a long time . . .

[. . .]

In the comment at Post 1, Auro performs a telling by publishing a quote taken from the movie *The Crow* ("*Non può piovere per sempre*") to comment on the weather in Milan. Because Auro's initial telling is about a third-person event—the weather, this contribution is a third-person event telling. Moreover, because this narrative refers to an unfolding event, it is a current third-person event telling.

On the other hand, the telling in the comment at Post 1 in Extract 4.15 is about a future event, a soccer match between A. C. Milan and F. C. Barcelona.

Extract 4.15 The soccer match

→ 1 Elisa: stasera spettacolo a S.Siro [a stadium in Milano] . . . non vedo l'oraaa ☺
Elisa: tonight there's a show at S.Siro . . . I can't waaait ☺

A 3 persone piace questo
3 people like this

2 Jay: speriamo dell'orrore ahahahaha!!;-)
Jay: I hope it's going to be a horror show ahahahaha!!;-)

3 Elisa: noooo . . . solo vedere giocare il Barcellona dal vivo è un onore!!!☺
Elisa: noooo . . . just watching Barcelona playing live is a honor!!!☺

[. . .]

Elisa launches this comment thread by reminding Friends of the upcoming soccer match between A. C. Milan and F. C. Barcelona (*stasera spettacolo a S.Siro . . . non vedo l'oraaa* ☺). This telling is about a third-person event, the soccer match; Elisa explicitly says in the comment at post 1 that a match will take place later on the same day (*stasera*). Therefore, the first-post telling in Extract 4.15 is a third-person future event telling.

This section has confirmed what was indicated by previous linguistic studies on FB, which is that the comments that open FB comment threads (the so-called status updates) normally consist of autobiographical tellings or tellings about national and international events, such as TV shows, political and other public events (Androutsopoulos, 2015; Bolander and Locher, 2010; Georgakopoulou, 2007a, 2013b, 2014; Georgalou, 2015a, b; Lee, 2011; Page, 2010b, 2012; Page, Harper, and Frobenius, 2013; Stæhr, 2015; West, 2013; West and Trester, 2013). Moreover, it has also demonstrated that autobiographical and third-person event tellings may refer to past (Georgalou, 2016), current, future (Georgakopoulou, 2002) activities or events in relation to the contents of the tellings.

Conclusions

Looking at the first comments of FB comment threads is important because it shows that the first action accomplished by an FB user in a comment thread is a telling. Therefore, the telling sequence is the basic sequence that opens FB comment threads.

This chapter has analyzed how FB users perform first-post tellings in comment threads and what the content of these tellings can be. After showing that FB comment threads are generally opened by first-post tellings, this chapter has found that these tellings may consist of single as well as multiple units. This chapter has also demonstrated that first-post tellings may have five different formats: textual messages only, photos only, hyperlinks only and combinations of textual messages with either photos or hyperlinks.

It has then found that first-post tellings may refer to activities in which the poster was involved (autobiographical), or events in which the poster had no involvement (third-person events). Finally, this chapter has also indicated that autobiographical and third-person event tellings may refer to past, current, or future activities or events.

The frequent occurrence of tellings in the opening comments of FB comment threads presumably relates to the way the system is framed. Three distinct factors encourage tellings. First, as mentioned in Chapter 2, the system prompt in the dialogue box *What's on your mind?* is designed as what might be called a telling elicitor. In other words, it projects a telling as the first relevant action in a comment thread. Second, the type of contents that Friends can share using the *Share* button are predominantly tellings, consisting of post news, photos, and videos. Finally, of the various actions an FB user may perform in a comment thread, tellings are somehow the easiest to perform asynchronously. They do not require Friends to be simultaneously online to interact. So, the occurrence of a telling in the first comment of an FB comment thread seems to be occasioned by the system itself. Having now established that FB comment threads are almost always opened by tellings, at least in the data collected for this study, the following chapters will look at the interactional problems that may be associated with first-post tellings, and the actions Friends perform in the comments that follow tellings.

5

The Nature of First-Post Tellings

Introduction

Having shown in Chapter 4 that comment threads are commonly opened by tellings, this chapter discusses the interactional problems that may arise when an FB user performs a telling in the opening comment of a comment thread, and the techniques he or she can use to overcome these problems.

While securing space to perform a telling is a concern in spoken conversation, this chapter demonstrates that it is unproblematic in comment threads. However, securing recipients for a telling is an interactional problem for FB users. This chapter discusses the actions performed by FB users to secure recipients to first-post tellings, and it focuses especially on the most common of these actions—the use of humor.

Securing the space for a first-post telling

In spoken conversation, speakers often need to secure the conversational space for a telling, at least if it consists of more than a single TCU (i.e., a story rather than an announcement). This is commonly done using a pre-telling sequence (Liddicoat, 2011; Maynard, 2006; Sacks, 1986, 1992; Schegloff, 2007; Terasaki, 2004). Pre-tellings normally precede tellings and consist of two turns at talk; a *first pair part* in which a potential teller projects a telling as the next relevant action in the interaction, and a *second pair part* in which another speaker aligns or refuses to align him or herself as the recipient of the telling.

The interactional job of the *first pair part* of a pre-telling sequence is to project a *second pair part* that encourages the telling. For this reason in the *first pair part* of a pre-telling a potential teller may perform one or more of the following actions: inform a recipient that what follows is a telling; characterize, assess, or mention the topic of the telling; provide a recipient with information about the newsworthiness of the telling; and project the telling as the next relevant activity in the interaction. On the other hand, in the *second pair part* of a pre-telling sequence, a recipient may produce a go-ahead or a blocking response oriented to the telling (Liddicoat, 2011; Maynard, 2006; Schegloff, 2007; Terasaki, 2004). If the recipient produces a go-ahead, the speaker has a warrant to tell his or her narrative, having secured the space (and recipient) to do so.

While it may be necessary to secure the space for a telling in a spoken conversation, this is not a part of FB interactions. This can be clearly seen in Extract 5.1 about Alberta and the purse snatching. This example has already been discussed in Chapter 4; however, it is reproduced here for convenience.

Extract 5.1 The purse snatching

→ 1 Alberta: Ma che bella giornata di merda . . . iniziata bene ma finita stramalissimo con tanto di scippo in diretta!
Alberta: What a crappy day . . . It has started well but it ended terribly and included a live purse snatching

2 Alessia: e delle mie 700 euro per riparare la macchina . . . ne vogliamo parlare!!!! ufff
Alessia: tell me about it!!! what about me and the 700 euros I had to pay to fix my car . . .! ufff

3 Alberta: Fidati! noi [*sic*] ci andiamo vicino . . .
Alberta: Trust me! I know what you mean . . .

4 Chiara: bhe finita stramalissimo . . . e della telefonata con me che mi dici?!? ho [*sic*] pure seguito lo scippo in diretta! =)
Chiara: ok so it ended terribly . . . and what about our phone conversation? I also witnessed the purse snatching live!=)

5 Alberta: No comment!!!!!!! Arrivo al corso e racconto lo scippo, e poi mi chiedono ma poi com'è finite [*sic*]? Niente mi hanno suonato e me ne sono andata, ma non ho detto che tu mi ha suggerito: SCAPPAAAAAA!
Alberta: No comment!!!!!!! I arrived at the class and I told people about the snatching and people asked me how it all ended? Nothing I said, someone beeped me and I had to drive on, but I didn't mention what you suggested to me: RUUUUN!

6 Lucia: ma Alberta che cavolo e [*sic*] successo?
Lucia: but Alberta what the hell happened?

As already noted in Chapter 4, in the comment at Post 1 Alberta opens this comment thread by performing two actions. She makes an assessment, where she says that she had a "crappy" day (*Ma che bella giornata di merda . . .*), and then she performs a telling: she tells Friends that she witnessed a purse snatching (*iniziata bene ma finita stramalissimo con tanto di scippo in diretta!*). In some ways the first action in the initial unit of the comment at Post 1 is similar to the action normally performed in the *first pair part* of a pre-telling sequence, as it characterizes the telling. However, Alberta does not use this element to secure the space for her telling, but rather to introduce it. Even though in the first unit of the comment at Post 1 Alberta gives an assessment relating to the following telling, thus seeming to launch a pre-telling sequence, she does not stop this comment after this unit, but continues straight on with the telling itself.

In other words, although the first action performed in the comment at Post 1 looks like the action accomplished in the *first pair part* of a pre-telling sequence, this is not aimed at securing the space to perform the telling immediately following it, nor to provide Friends with the opportunity to produce a go-ahead or a blocking response. In contrast to spoken conversation, where tellings are interactionally achieved by participants in these interactions (M. Goodwin, 1982; Jefferson, 1978; Liddicoat, 2011; Mandelbaum, 1989; Maynard, 2006; Sacks, 1986, 1992; Schegloff, 2007), first-post tellings are not interactionally achieved by FB users in comment threads.

This reflects the realities of the medium. First, as already noted in Chapter 3, comment threads are generally asynchronous, which means that FB users are not simultaneously online at the time of an interaction, and therefore, they cannot negotiate the occurrence of a telling in a comment thread. Having launched a pre-telling, requesting space for a telling, the poster would have to return to the comment thread later to see if there was a response, before beginning the telling. Second, FB users do not negotiate poster changes in comment threads; therefore, even though they could be simultaneously online at the time of a telling, they do not need to deal with the problem of securing the space to perform it. Unlike in a spoken conversation, where only one participant speaks at a time, and each participant is present in a single conversation, FB users can simply begin their own comment threads, thus "securing space" with no negotiation.

Returning to Extract 5.1, this is all reflected in the actions performed by Alberta and the Friends involved in this comment thread. Although in the initial unit of the comment at Post 1 Alberta produces an assessment to introduce her telling, similar in some ways to the action normally performed by a conversationalist in the *first pair part* of a spoken pre-telling sequence, she does not wait for Friends to respond to it, but rather in the second unit of the same comment she performs another action; she produces the basic telling, making potential responses to the "pre-telling" irrelevant. The actions performed by Friends in the comments at Posts 2, 4, and 6 confirm this hypothesis. These comments do not contain *second pair parts* oriented to the pre-telling, but contain responses to the first-post telling.

In the comment at Post 2 Alessia accomplishes her first action in this interaction; she responds to the comment at Post 1 with a second telling that shows affiliation with Alberta. Alessia tells Alberta that she had to pay seven hundred euros to fix her own car (*e delle mie 700 euro per riparare la macchina . . . ne vogliamo parlare!!!! ufff*). Similar to what Alessia has done in the comment at Post 2, the action performed by Chiara in the first unit of the comment at Post 4 orients to the telling at Post 1. Chiara shows her support for Alberta in saying that Alberta's day indeed ended terribly (*bhe finita stramalissimo . . . e della telefonata con me che mi dici?!? ho pure seguito lo scippo in diretta! =)*). Another action which orients to the comment at Post 1 is performed by Lucia in the comment at Post 6. In this contribution Lucia uses what seems to be a topicalization (Liddicoat, 2011) to project further "talk" from Alberta, explicitly asking Alberta to expand the telling and provide her with more information about the snatching (*ma Alberta che cavolo e successo?*).

So, although the action performed by Alberta in the initial unit of the comment at Post 1 is similar to the action normally accomplished by a conversationalist in the *first pair part* of a pre-telling sequence, this is not intended by Alberta to secure the space to perform her telling, as this occurs immediately after it, and makes responses to the "pre-telling" irrelevant.

This can be seen again in Extract 5.2, another example that has already been presented in this book (see Chapter 4) and reproduced here. In the comment at Post 1 Claudio packages what seems to be the *first pair part* of a pre-telling sequence and a telling in the same contribution, making responses to the pre-telling irrelevant, and once again showing that the problem of securing the space for a first-post telling does not affect FB comment threads.

Extract 5.2 Claudio's early dinner

→ 1 Claudio: Cazzo! Sono le 18:40e [*sic*] sto cenando! Peggio di mio nonno O_o
Claudio: Fuck! It's 6:40 p.m. and I'm having dinner! I'm worse than my grandfather O_o

A 2 persone piace questo
2 people like this

2 Aleandro: sei un vecchio!
Aleandro: you're an old man!

3 Claudio: fossero tutti così i vecchi . . . (tiè:P)
Claudio: If only all the old people were like me . . . (tiè:P) [exclamation which normally accompanies hand gesture used to ward off evil]

4 Esteban: i guess you're talking about Berlusconi [the former Italian prime minister], everyone does!

[. . .]

As already noted in the analysis of Extract 4.4, in the comment at Post 1 Claudio opens this interaction with a contribution that consists of three complete units: an initial exclamation (*Cazzo!*); the basic telling, where he says that he is having an early dinner (*Sono le 18:40e sto cenando!*); and a humorous self-critical comment on his own telling, where Claudio tells Friends that even his grandfather generally eats later (*Peggio di mio nonno O_o*).

Similar to Extract 5.1, with the expletive in the initial unit of the comment at Post 1 (*Cazzo!*) Claudio performs the first action in this comment thread; he assesses the telling that is to come. However, Claudio does not accomplish this action to secure the space for his telling, which is published immediately after it. In other words, like Alberta in Extract 5.1, in the comment at Post 1, Claudio does not provide Friends with the opportunity to post a go-ahead or a blocking response following the expletive, which would negotiate the space to perform the telling, but he simply posts the basic telling immediately, making responses to the expletive irrelevant. The actions performed by Friends in the comments that follow the contribution at Post 1 support this interpretation. In the comments at Posts 2 and 4, Aleandro and Esteban do not publish the *second pair parts* of a pre-telling sequence, but respond to the basic telling in the comment at Post 1. At Post 2 Aleandro mocks Claudio by saying that he is old (*sei un vecchio!*), and in the comment at Post 4 Esteban asks Claudio if the contribution at Post 1 refers to Silvio Berlusconi, the former Italian prime minister (*i guess you're talking about Berlusconi,everyone does!*).

The irrelevance of the problem of securing the space for a first-post telling is also evident in Extract 5.3, where Elisa publishes a multiunit comment, without providing Friends with the opportunity to issue a go-ahead or blocking response to the telling.

Extract 5.3 Elisa and the three Welsh workers

→ 1 Elisa: three mighty Welsh workers at my door! If I overcome and understand their working-class slang, it could be love.

A Marta piace questo
Marta likes this

2 Eluana: It sounds like you are too upper class to understand their "working class slang." Classy diva, please come down we humans are here ☺

3 Elisa: ahahaa, no! all [*sic*] the contrary! that [*sic*] means I'm ignorant! my [*sic*] English is not a real one! I miss a big part! Anyway, they left and that's the end of my story ☹

4 Eluana: you surprise me, love does not need words . . .

In the comment at Post 1 Elisa begins this interaction with a contribution that, like the previous examples, consists of two complete units: an initial unit which seems to foreshadow the topic of the telling, saying that there were three Welsh workers at her door (*three mighty Welsh workers at my door!*); and the basic telling, where Elisa humorously says that if she could understand the slang spoken by these workers, she would probably fall in love with them (*If I overcome and understand their working-class slang, it could be love*). The contribution at Post 1 is once again opened by a comment that looks like the *first pair part* of a pre-telling sequence, because it anticipates the topic of what is likely to be the telling. However, the action performed by Elisa in this comment is not aimed at securing the space for her telling. In fact, in the comment at Post 1 Elisa does not provide Friends with the interactional space to provide a response to her "pre-telling," but rather she immediately publishes the telling. This is reinforced by the action performed by Eluana in the comment at Post 2. This contribution, like those in Extracts 5.1 and 5.2, does not contain a go-ahead or a blocking response oriented to the "pre-telling," but a response to the telling at Post 1. The action accomplished by Eluana explicitly refers to the comment at Post 1 when she says that Elisa did not understand the slang spoken by the Welsh workers because she is an "upper class diva" (*It sounds like you are too upper class to understand their "working class slang." Classy diva, please come down we humans are here* ☺).

So, although the actions performed by FB users in certain units of the opening comments of FB comment threads appear to correspond to those accomplished by conversationalists in the *first pair parts* of pre-telling sequences, they are not used by FB users in the way that might be expected. FB users in fact package "pre-tellings" and the basic tellings within single comments. The problem of securing the space for tellings does not affect participants in FB comment threads, and thus they do not need to negotiate this space using pre-tellings.

On the other hand, as will be discussed in the following section, securing recipients for a telling does appear to be problematic for FB users who perform tellings in the opening comments of comment threads.

Securing recipients for a first-post telling

As discussed in Chapter 1, FB is about social interaction. As in a conversation, posters are aiming for interaction—wanting someone to respond to their comments. Evidence for this comes from comment threads where posters have received no responses, and then have had to perform additional actions in order to receive responses from Friends, as Mauro has done in Extracts 5.4 and 5.5 on an upcoming event in Milan.

Extract 5.4 Mauro's problematic invitation

→ 1 Mauro: Domani, Via Candiani, Milano, Bovisa [Mauro publishes a hyperlink that contains some information about an upcoming event] 15 ore fa
Mauro: Tomorrow, Candiani Street, Milan, Bovisa *15 hours ago*

A Valeria piace questo
Valeria likes this

2 Mauro: e loro si stanno scaldando :-D! [Mauro publishes a hyperlink which contains a video of the band that will play live during the event described in the comment at Post 1] 14 ore fa
Mauro: and they are warming up :-D! *14 hours ago*

Extract 5.5 Mauro's successful invitation

→ 1 Mauro: Domani sera vi aspetto in via Candiani 127, ed ora andate a dormire . . . dopo questa dormite sicuro . . . qualche incubo magari. By Babylon Alessia, Valeria, Claudia, Gianluca, Chiara, Zaira [nicknames of Mauro's Friends] [Mauro publishes a hyperlink that contains the video of the song Rivers of Babylon by Josh T. Pearson] 3 ore fa
Mauro: Tomorrow night I'll be waiting for you in Candiani street 127, and now you can go to sleep . . . after this [song] *you'll sleep for sure . . . maybe with some nightmares. By Babylon Alessia, Valeria, Claudia, Gianluca, Chiara, Zaira* *3 hours ago*

A Zaira piace questo
Zaira likes this

2 Elena: anna dai capelli rossi, la sigla era uguale, lo giuro 3 ore fa
Elena: anna dai capelli rossi [name of a cartoon character], *the theme song was the same, I swear it* *3 hours ago*

3 Alessia: sembra l'uomo più triste del mondo 2 ore fa
Alessia: he seems to be the saddest man in the world *2 hours ago*

4 Zaira: è lui quello di ieri sera Polpets [probably Alessia's nickname]!! ho [*sic*] già ascoltato abbastanza ieri Mauro, magari stasera passo dai ;) 2 ore fa

Zaira: Polpets, he is the singer we watched last night!! I had enough of him yesterday, tonight I reckon I'll pass;) *2 hours ago*

5 Claudia: dio come lo dice bene il tuo nome, quanta meridionalità. Ad un certo punto sembra che quelle dita non si fermeranno mai più 2 ore fa
Claudia: god he pronounces your name so well, so southern [probably referring to the accent of the singer in the video]. *At a certain point it seems that his fingers will never ever stop* *2 hours ago*

Before analyzing Extracts 5.4 and 5.5 it is important to notice that those comment threads have been collected on the same day, November 16, 2011; moreover, as shown by the timing, Mauro posted Extract 5.4 several hours before Extract 5.5. Those comment threads have the same topic, an event that will be held in Milan. It seems that Mauro published Extract 5.5 because none of his Friends had responded to Extract 5.4.

Mauro opens Extract 5.4 by seeming to invite Friends to participate in an event. In the comment at Post 1 he in fact provides Friends with the address of the club and the hyperlink that describes the event he wants them to attend (*Domani, Via Candiani, Milano, Bovisa*). Then, in the comment at Post 2 Mauro provides Friends with a hyperlink about the band who will perform live during this event (*e loro si stanno scaldando :-D!*). The comment at Post 2 was published approximately an hour after the comment at Post 1, suggesting that it was posted because none of Mauro's Friends had responded to this contribution.

Strong evidence that this is the case comes from the publication of Extract 5.5, where Mauro redoes the comment at Post 1 of Extract 5.4, but with additional actions. In this extract Mauro redesigns his invitation, provides Friends with a new hyperlink that contains a telling (a video of a song by Josh T. Pearson), publishes a framework to interpret the telling, and selects the recipients for his telling.

While the comment at Post 1 in Extract 5.4 contains only the address of the club in which the event will be held (*Domani, Via Candiani, Milano, Bovisa*), the first unit in the comment at Post 1 in Extract 5.5 is more clearly designed to be an invitation; hence, Friends know how to respond to this comment (*Domani sera vi aspetto in via Candiani 127*). Moreover, this invitation is followed by a hyperlink introduced by a comment where Mauro tells Friends that after listening to this song they can go to sleep (*ed ora andate a dormire . . . dopo questa dormite sicuro . . . qualche incubo magari. By Babylon*). Then, in the final unit of the comment at Post 1, Mauro performs another action; he explicitly selects the recipients for his comment by naming them (*Alessia, Valeria, Claudia, Gianluca, Chiara, Zaira*).

The additional actions performed by Mauro in Extract 5.5 strongly support the idea that FB users post comments in comment threads because they want Friends to respond to them. When Mauro received no responses to his first comment in Extract 5.4, he added a second comment, and then in Extract 5.5 Mauro began a new comment thread, not having received any response to the previous one. Like participants in spoken conversation, FB users need to secure recipients for a telling. This problem is perhaps more acute for FB users. While in a spoken conversation, there is a set of participants who are copresent, for FB users, there is always the possibility that no one will respond at all to a telling, thus defeating the aim of engaging in social interaction.

There are examples in the corpus of first comments that do not receive any comments in response. As well as the first example above (Mauro's invitation), this can be seen in Extract 5.6 about Fausto's arrival.

Extract 5.6 Fausto's arrival

1 Donatella: e finalmente arriva Fausto :-) 8 ore fa
Donatella: and Fausto is finally arriving :-) 8 hours ago

A Maria piace questo
Maria likes this

Although the comment thread in Extract 5.6 was published eight hours before its screen shot was taken, none of Donatella's Friends responded to it. In the comment at Post 1 Donatella opens this interaction with a comment that is unclear—a textual message where she says that Fausto is finally arriving (*e finalmente arriva Fausto :-)*). Even though the action performed by Donatella in this comment appears to be a telling which refers to the birth of a new baby (Fausto); Friends did not respond to it with explicit comments.[1]

A similar lack of response can be seen in Extract 5.7, where the photo-telling in the comment at Post 1 fails to secure any response from Friends.

Extract 5.7 Women in the Monti and Berlusconi governments

1 [Michele publishes a photo that shows the women in the Monti and Berlusconi governments] Saturday at 9:53 a.m.

In the comment at Post 1 Michele launches this comment thread by publishing a photo that shows the women who worked in the Monti and Berlusconi governments (two former Italian prime ministers). Even though this interaction was published two days before its screen shot was taken, none of Michele's Friends had responded to it.

Extracts 5.6 and 5.7 are examples of first comments which have not generated responses, and have thus "failed," in the sense that they have not allowed the poster to participate in social interaction. While the reason these comments may have failed will be discussed in the following section, what matters here is that these contributions show that there is an issue of FB users having to secure recipients for a telling in a comment thread.

Techniques to secure responses to first comments

As noted in the previous section securing recipients can be problematic in FB comment threads. It is possible that a first comment may receive no responses from Friends. One feature which is common to Extracts 5.6 and 5.7 is that they consisted of bare tellings, with no other elements. In other words, the actions performed in these comments did not project a clear relevant next action from Friends. This is not common in the data. It is much more common for FB users to perform other actions in an initial first comment beyond the basic bare telling itself. These additional actions seem to be designed to increase the chance that a first-post telling will receive responses. There are three typical actions which are used to secure responses from Friends: naming the intended recipients of a telling; providing recipients with enough information to interpret a telling; and the use of humor. The first two of these are discussed here; the most complex, the use of humor, is discussed separately in the following section.

From the analysis of Extracts 5.8 to 5.10 we can see how first-post tellers select recipients for a telling, and make it more likely to secure responses from them. In Extract 5.8, Claudio, the first-post teller, selects Alex as recipient of his comment, and secures his response to the telling.

Extract 5.8 Claudio and the tiramisù cake

→ 1 Claudio: Alex se non ti muovi, lo finisco . . . oggi è ancora meglio di ieri!!!!!!!!
Claudio: Alex hurry up or I'll finish it . . . today it's even better than yesterday!!!!!!!!

A Alex piace questo
Alex likes this

2 Alex: già . . . purtroppo il teletrasporto oggi non và cmq [*sic*] mi appunto per la prossima volta . . . Thanks Claudio :D
Alex: I know . . . but unfortunately today the teletransportation system is out of order, but I'll come next time . . . Thanks Claudio :D

3 Claudio: no problem ☺ ☺

4 Claudio: ma no, non penso potrei . . . mi sentirei non in grado di competere con te in cucina
Claudio: I don't think . . . I can compete against you in the kitchen

5 Alex: ah ah ah ma sono sicuro che lo fai buonissimo :D
Alex: ah ah ah I'm pretty sure you make an excellent [tiramisù] *:D*

[. . .]

This comment thread is one of a series of eight interactions about Claudio and the tiramisù cake, which are discussed throughout this book. In the comment at Post 1 Claudio performs the first action in this comment thread; he says to Alex that he has to hurry up if he wants to taste the tiramisù before he (Claudio) finishes it (*Alex se non ti muovi, lo finisco . . . oggi è ancora meglio di ieri!!!!!!!!*). In the comment at Post 1 Claudio specifies the recipient of his telling, Alex, by naming him. It is therefore likely that Claudio has specifically selected Alex, because he wants him, rather than other Friends, to respond to his telling. And indeed, in the comment at Post 2 Alex responds to Claudio by declining his invitation, humorously saying that the "teletransportation" system is currently out of order and that he will taste the tiramisù another time (*già . . . purtroppo il teletrasporto oggi non và cmq mi appunto per la prossima volta . . . Thanks Claudio :D*).

The action of naming a Friend to secure his or her response to the telling can be seen again in Extract 5.9, a comment thread that has already been discussed in Chapter 4, where Elisa refers to a concert of Luciano Ligabue, a famous Italian singer.

Extract 5.9 Ligabue's concert

1 Elisa: LIGA 16/07/10 [Elisa publishes a photo which shows herself and Serena during Luciano Ligabue's concert, a famous Italian singer]
Elisa: LIGA 16/07/10

→ 2 Elisa: Serena [Elisa's Friend] amoooo ti ricordi?:-)
Elisa: Serena daaaaaarling do you remember it?:-)

3 Serena: Certo che si!!!!!!!!!!!!! Bellissimo concerto!!!!! Uscire dal centro estivo per andare da liga non ga [*sic*] prezzo!!
Serena: Of course!!!!!!!!!!!!! Great concert!!!!! To leave the summer school to go and see liga is priceless!!

4 Elisa: ♥♥♥♥♥♥

As noted in Chapter 4, the first action performed by Elisa in the comment at Post 1 is to provide Friends with some information to interpret her telling. She posts the nickname of the artist and the date of the concert to which the photo-telling in the comment at Post 1 refers (*LIGA 16/07/10*). Then, in the comment at Post 2, Elisa performs another action in this comment thread; she explicitly asks Serena if she remembers the concert (*Serena amoooo ti ricordi?:-)*). It therefore seems that Elisa is referring to an experience she shared with Serena (Georgakopoulou, 2016) to secure her response to this initial telling. In the comment at Post 3 Serena responds to Elisa by saying that she remembers the concert (*Certo che si!!!!!!!!!!!!!! Bellissimo concerto!!!!!*); then she positively evaluates the concert and says that finishing work to go to see Ligabue was priceless (*Uscire dal centro estivo per andare da liga non ga prezzo!!*).

The analysis of Extract 5.9 supports the hypothesis that the action of selecting the recipients of a telling ensures responses from Friends. It seems that in this way these tellers are more likely to receive at least a response from the named Friends. Extract 5.10 provides further evidence that the action of naming is specifically used in an attempt to gain recipients for a telling.

Extract 5.10 Amarcord video

1 Mauro: Momento Amarcord [Mauro publishes a hyperlink which contains a cartoon on "*metallari*," which is the Italian term used to refer to people who love heavy metal music] Lunedì alle 18:19
Mauro: Amarcord moment *Monday at 6:19 p.m.*

→ 2 Mauro: Antonio, Anita, Giorgio, Valeria, Zaira, Arturo [Mauro's Friends] Monday at 6:35 p.m.

3 Valeria: 0.46 posa alla Vasco. Lunedì alle 19:50
Valeria: 0.46 Vasco [a famous Italian singer] *style pose.* *Monday at 7:50 p.m.*

In the comment at Post 1 Mauro performs two actions: he posts a textual message and a hyperlink-telling. The textual message "*Momento Amarcord*" characterizes the following hyperlink-telling. *Amarcord* is the title of one of the movies of the director Federico Fellini. This word comes from the *Emiliano* dialect spoken in the city of Bologna and used by Fellini and means "I remember." It therefore seems that Mauro publishes the comment "*Momento Amarcord*" to tell Friends that the cartoon in the hyperlink-telling in the comment at Post 1 reminds him of "*metallari*," people who love heavy metal music. Then, in the comment at Post 2 Mauro performs another action: he selects the intended recipients of his comment by explicitly naming them (*Antonio, Anita, Giorgio, Valeria, Zaira, Arturo*).

The action performed by Valeria in the comment at Post 3 shows that she has understood the intention of Mauro's textual message in the comment at Post 1. Valeria, one of the addressees selected by Mauro in the textual message at Post 2, says that at minute 0.46 the character of the video performs a movement that reminds her of one of the moves performed by the singer Vasco Rossi (*0.46 posa alla Vasco*). The timing of the comments in Extract 5.10 is highly revealing. Mauro's original comment at Post 1 is published at 6:19 p.m. He receives no responses for the next fifteen minutes; then he posts a list of names, as potential recipients, in the comment at Post 2 and Valeria responds to this comment. It seems that Mauro posted this list of names as a result of not having received any responses. That is, this example indicates explicitly that the action of naming is used by FB users in an attempt to trigger responses.

In selecting the intended recipients of their tellings, FB users are aiming to secure responses from Friends.[2] This action seems to work, with named participants often responding, although as has been seen in Chapter 3, Friends other than those named may also respond.

Another important technique that appears to secure responses to first-post tellings is to provide Friends with an interactional framework to interpret the telling. This technique can be seen in Extracts 5.11 to 5.13. Extract 5.11 is on the upcoming visit of the Pope to Milan.

Extract 5.11 The Pope

→ 1 Aleandro: mi sa che domenica vado ai giardini . . . [Aleandro publishes a hyperlink which contains the news about the Sunday visit of the Pope to Milan]
Aleandro: I'm thinking of going to the public gardens on Sunday . . .

A Marco piace questo
Marco likes this

2 Marco: vieni a teatro !!!! ☺
Marco: come to the theater!!!! ☺

3 Aleandro: hai ragione! ci [*sic*] sei fino a domenica?
Aleandro: you're right! are you on stage on Sunday?

4 Marco: replichiamo stasera e domani!
Marco: we rerun the show tonight and tomorrow!

[. . .]

The first action performed by Aleandro in the comment at Post 1 is to introduce a hyperlink-telling which indicates that the Pope is coming to Milan. In his textual message Aleandro says that on Sunday he is considering going to the public gardens (*mi sa che domenica vado ai giardini . . .*). Here Aleandro provides Friends with an interactional framework to interpret the hyperlink-telling: he is not interested in the visit of the Pope to Milan and wishes to avoid it. The action performed by Marco in the comment at Post 2 shows that he has understood the intention of the textual message in the comment at Post 1. Marco uses the framework introduced by Aleandro to respond to him; he invites Aleandro to go to the theater (*vieni a teatro !!!! ☺*).

Another example of providing Friends with a framework to interpret a telling is seen in Extract 5.12. This extract has already been discussed in Chapter 4, and a full version is presented in Appendix A.

Extract 5.12 The affair

→ 1 Elisa: oh signur!!! [Elisa publishes a hyperlink which contains the news about the affair between Barbara D'Urso and Massimiliano Allegri, two Italian celebrities]
Elisa: oh my god!!!

2 Franco: Nooooo . . . quella ce lo demotiva!!!! Salvatelo!!!
Franco: Nooooo . . . that [woman] *will have a negative impact on his motivation!!!! Save him!!!*

[. . .]

8 Sandro: gran MILF bravo max
Sandro: great MILF well done max [Allegri's name]

[. . .]

In the comment at Post 1, Elisa performs the first action in this interaction. She publishes a hyperlink about an affair between Barbara D'Urso, a TV personality, and Massimiliano Allegri, who was, at the time of Extract 5.12, the coach of the soccer team A. C. Milan. In addition, though, in the textual message at Post 1 (*oh signur!!!*) Elisa performs another action: she suggests to Friends how she wants them to interpret her hyperlink-telling, which is to humorously comment on the news about the affair between the two celebrities making clear that she does not think it is good news.

The actions performed by Franco and Sandro in the comments at Posts 2 and 8 show that they have used the comment at Post 1 to respond to Elisa's telling. In line with the general tone of Elisa's comment at Post 1, in the comment at Post 2 Franco humorously tells Elisa that Barbara D'Urso will have a negative effect on the motivation of the coach (*Nooooo . . . quella ce lo demotiva!!!! Salvatelo!!!*); in the comment at Post 8, Sandro, after an expletive which works as a positive evaluation directed to Barbara D'Urso (*gran MILF*), ironically congratulates Allegri for his romantic conquest (*bravo max*).

From the analysis of Extracts 5.11 and 5.12 we can see that an action which is commonly used by FB users to secure responses to first-post tellings is to provide Friends with interactional frameworks to interpret the tellings.

In some cases, the interactional framework provided for interpreting a telling is designed in a way which resembles an explicit question (thereby projecting an answer as the next relevant action). This is particularly true with photo-tellings and hyperlink-tellings, as exemplified in Extracts 5.13 and 5.14.

Extract 5.13 Alberta's necklace

→ 1 Alberta: E di questa che ne pensate???
[Alberta publishes a photo of the necklace that she has recently created]
Alberta: What do you think of it???

A 4 persone piace questo
4 people like this

2 Yana: Hai superato te stessa . . . grande
Yana: You outdid yourself . . . great

3 Eluisa: Mi piace anche di più!!!
Eluisa: I like it a lot!!!

4 Vanessa: Alberta complimenti sei proprio brava!!!
Vanessa: Alberta well done, you're really good!!!

5 Sabina: bravissima . . . è proprio bella
Sabina: bravo . . . it's really nice

6 Joanna: sempre meglio
Joanna: you're getting better every day

Alberta opens this comment thread by performing two actions: she posts a photo of a necklace, and she makes the comment "*E di questa che ne pensate*???" (And what do you think of this one???). While similar in form to a question, it is clear from the repeated question marks that the action accomplished in the textual component of the comment at Post 1 is not a simple question. Rather it is a request for an opinion, thus providing the context within which Friends can respond. Since her Friends are aware that Alberta designs and creates necklaces, this textual comment gives them sufficient information to know that it is a necklace she created herself, and it is clear from the actions they perform in the comments that follow the initial telling that all have understood this.

The action performed in the textual message at Post 1 gives Friends an easy way to respond, essentially answering the "question" by explicitly evaluating the necklace. Several Friends respond to this, at least in part: Yana says the necklace is "great" (*grande*); Eluisa says that she likes it more than ever (*Mi piace anche di più!!!*); Vanessa congratulates Alberta (*Alberta complimenti sei proprio brava!!!*); Sabina comments that it is beautiful (*è proprio bella*); and Joanna says that Alberta's talent for making necklaces is constantly improving (*sempre meglio*). However, Friends also show their understanding that, rather than an explicit question they should answer, the action accomplished by Alberta in the comment at Post 1 is to provide them with an interpretive framework. Rather than "answering the question" they congratulate Alberta on her skills—Yana says that Alberta has outdone herself (*Hai superato te stessa . . .*); Vanessa and Joanna praise her skills (comment at Post 4: *Alberta complimenti sei proprio brava!!!* and comment at Post 6: *sempre meglio*); and Sabina congratulates her (*bravissima*).

Another example of a textual comment phrased as an apparent question providing an interpretive framework for a telling can be seen in Extract 5.14. This interaction has already been mentioned in Chapter 2; therefore, only a short version is presented below.

Extract 5.14 The tiramisù cake

→ 1 Claudio: Doesn't look very nice now??? :P
[Claudio publishes a photo which shows him and a bowl that contains half of a tiramisù cake]

2 Raffaele: NO

3 Claudio: Cazzo! :P Ora ci manca che anche Yan se ne accorga:P
Claudio: Shit! :P I hope Yan [Claudio's personal trainer] *doesn't discover this:P*

4 Lucia: mi hanno detto che non scendi D:
Lucia: they told me you won't be back D:

5 Alex: that's mineeeeeeeeeeeeeeeeeee

6 Claudio: run run ;)

7 Jorge: poor tiramisù . . . didn't do anything to you . . . yet xD

[. . .]

In the comment at Post 1 Claudio publishes a selfie of himself and a tiramisù cake. This cake has been the topic of several comment threads prior to this one. In this photo, only half of the tiramisù is still in the bowl. Claudio contextualizes the photo with a textual message (*Doesn't look very nice now??? :P*). This message bears some resemblance to a question, but it is clearly not a real question, with three question marks and an emoticon that close it. Rather the action performed by Claudio in this comment is to provide Friends with an evaluation which they can use as a framework to interpret his photo-telling (*Look I've eaten lots of the tiramisù since last time I wrote about it*).

The actions accomplished by Friends show that they have clearly understood the photo in the way that Claudio intends. Their comments are humorous, and relate to the situation as a whole, not to the "question" in Claudio's comment. The action performed by Alex in the comment at Post 5 where he responds with "that's mineeeeeeeeeeeeeeeeeee" shows that he has understood Claudio's action in the contribution at Post 1 as relating to Claudio having eaten much of the tiramisù. Similarly the action accomplished by Jorge in the comment at Post 7 (*poor tiramisù . . . didn't do anything to you . . . yet xD*) relates to Claudio's eating the tiramisù, rather than being an answer to how it looks. The action performed by Raffaele in the contribution at Post 2 is in capitals (*NO*) and it seems to be a humorous comment that indicates Raffaele's shock that Claudio has eaten so much, rather than being a simple "No" answer to Claudio's question. This interpretation gains force from Claudio's action in the response in the comment at Post 3, where he (humorously) worries suddenly that Yan (his personal trainer) will now realize that he has eaten tiramisù (thus ruining his diet)[3] (*Cazzo! :P Ora ci manca che anche Yan se ne accorga:P*).

Extract 5.14, then, contains another example of an FB user providing an interpretive framework which Friends can use in understanding a telling in a comment thread. The importance of the action of providing Friends with some indication of how to interpret a telling can be seen in those cases where no context is given for a response. The previous section contained two examples (Extracts 5.6 and 5.7) which consisted of bare tellings with no contextual information—a textual message and a photo-telling respectively. These tellings received no responses, and it is possible to hypothesize that the lack of a textual message that provides a framework within which Friends could interpret the comments and thus project the next relevant action in these interactions has led to a lack of responses. Friends in fact are given no help in interpreting why they are being told these tellings, and they do not respond.

FB users, therefore, post first-post tellings because they want Friends to respond to them. This is similar to what happens in spoken conversation, where on completion of a telling, a teller expects a recipient to respond (Liddicoat, 2011; Sacks, 1992; Terasaki, 2004). Moreover, in their aim to secure responses to first-post tellings, there are certain actions which FB users can perform. So far, two of these actions or techniques have been presented—the explicit naming of Friends as (potential) recipients, and the use of additional elements in a telling to allow Friends to understand how to interpret the telling. However, the most noticeable technique used by FB users to secure responses to first-post tellings is the use of humor.

Humor in first-post tellings

After showing that in order to encourage responses from Friends FB users often select the recipients for their tellings and provide interactional frameworks to interpret these tellings, this section presents what appears to be a very frequent action performed by FB users to secure responses to first-post tellings—the use of humor.

Previous research has pointed out that in spoken conversation humorous tellings may be classified in a variety of ways, as jokes, puns, riddles, allusions, wordplays, personal anecdotes, mockeries, and sarcasm (Adetunji, 2013; Norrick, 1993, 1994; Sacks, 1978, 1986, 1992; Schegloff, 1987b). In addition, these studies have found that although there are different types of humorous tellings, these narratives are generally responded to in similar ways, including laughter, assessments, and other humorous tellings (Jefferson, 1979; Kristeva, 1980; Norrick, 1993, 1994).

This section argues that overt and covert forms of humor are common in first-post tellings, and first-post tellings containing humor seem to secure responses from Friends. Overt forms of humor as defined here are those where FB users use emoticons, representations of laughter, exaggerations, jokes, puns, riddles, wordplays, entertainment, personal anecdotes, mimicries, mockeries, or sarcasm in their textual, photographic, and hypertextual tellings. On the other hand, covert forms of humor are those where nothing in what FB users write is clearly "funny," but responses published by Friends indicate that they have interpreted the tellings in a humorous way. The comment thread in Extract 5.15 is opened by a first-post telling that is overtly humorous.

Extract 5.15 The pilates class

→ 1 Elisa: stasera prima lezione di pilates . . . sono già stanca prima di iniziare . . . ahaha 6 ore fa
Elisa: tonight I've got the first pilates class . . . I'm already tired even before starting it . . . ahaha 6 hours ago

A 6 persone piace questo
6 people like this

→ 2 Elisa: :-(sono a pezzi e mi gira la testa . . . lo sport non fa per me :-) preferisco fare i km per negozi . . . uahuahuahauhuhauah 4 ore fa
Elisa: :-(I'm exhausted and I feel dizzy . . . sport is not for me :-) I prefer to walk kilometers shopping . . . uahuahuahauhuhauah 4 hours ago

3 Giorgia: ma . . . ma . . . teso! . . . hahahaha . . . 4 ore fa
Giorgia: but . . . but . . . honey! . . . hahahaha . . . 4 hours ago

The actions performed by Elisa in the comment at Post 1 already suggest the facetious intention of this contribution. The final laughter token (. . . *ahaha*) as well as the unlikely statement in the middle of this comment about Elisa's tiredness even before attending a class (*sono già stanca prima di iniziare*) both indicate the intended humorous approach of this telling, which is about Elisa's intention to attend a pilates class (*stasera prima lezione di pilates . . .*).

In the comment at Post 2, which as indicated by the timing was probably posted two hours after the comment at Post 1 (*4 ore fa*), Elisa performs other two actions in this interaction. She posts an emoticon which could represent disappointment (*:-(*); then she continues on with the telling, ironically describing her tiredness after the class, saying that she is physically exhausted and dizzy (*sono a pezzi e mi gira la testa*); Elisa closes this contribution by performing an ironic comment followed by a representation of laughter, where she says that she prefers going shopping rather than playing sport (*lo sport non fa per me :-) preferisco fare i km per negozi . . . uahuahuahauhuhauah*).

The response at Post 3 is probably secured by the humorous approach of the comments at Posts 1 and 2: the actions performed by Giorgia in this contribution show that she has understood Elisa's humorous intention. Giorgia opens the comment at Post 3 with an apparent initial reprimand (*ma . . . ma . . . teso!*) followed by a representation of laughter (*. . . hahahaha . . .*).

Humor seems also to characterize Extract 5.16, which is about Mauro's announcement of dressing up as Metroman during the next Carnevale party. Although the textual message at Post 1 is not overtly humorous, the responses published by Friends (and Mauro himself) indicate that they have interpreted it in an ironic way.

Extract 5.16 Metroman-Carnevale[4]

→ 1 Mauro: ho Deciso . . . A CARNEVALE MI VESTO DA METROMAN
Mauro: I have decided . . . AT THE NEXT CARNEVALE PARTY I'LL DRESS UP AS METROMAN

A Elisa ed altre 12 persone piace questo
Elisa and other 12 people like this

2 Auro: non dormo più!
Auro: I can't sleep anymore

3 Filippo: io da banana
Filippo: and I will dress up like a banana

4 Aria:—ti prego fallo davvero, non illudermi/ci.
Aria:—please do it, don't let us down.

5 Mina: Oltre a vestirti come lui, però dovrai cantare tutta la sera sennò non vale!! ;D
Mina: If you dress up like him [Metroman], *you will have to sing all night long or otherwise it won't count!! ;D*

6 Mauro: sai bene quanto io sia serio in queste occasioni.
Mauro: you know how serious I am in these circumstances,

7 Mauro: Mina: OVVIO.
Mauro: Mina: OF COURSE.

[. . .]

10 Richard: sexy
Richard: sexy

11 Daniele: @Mina: purtroppo ti conosco è un insulto gravissimo. . . io non ti parlerei + a vita ;) @Mauro: io mi vesto da palo della metro, così puoi attaccarti al palo e girare!!!
Daniele: @Mina: unfortunately "I know you" is a terrible offence . . . I feel like not talking to you anymore;) @Mauro: I will dress up as an underground pole, so you can attach yourself to the pole and swing around me!!!

12 Mauro: e li salto! sicuro [*sic*]?
Mauro: and then I'll jump! Are you sure?

[. . .]

In this extract, which has been discussed in Chapter 4, Mauro performs the first action by posting a comment at Post 1, where he announces his plan to dress up as Metroman at the next Carnevale party. The use of capital letters suggests "shouting," a convention of electronic communication utilized to emphasize a point (Crystal, 2006). It is likely that the nickname Metroman comes from the term *Metropolitana*, which is the name of the underground metropolitan system in Milan.

While there is nothing explicit indicating humor in the action performed by Mauro in the textual message in the comment at Post 1, it is clear from the content and form, as well as the actions performed by Friends in the comments that follow this comment, that this contribution is not serious. In the textual message at Post 1 Mauro tells Friends about his plan to dress up like Metroman (*ho Deciso . . . A CARNEVALE MI VESTO DA METROMAN*). In the comment at Post 2, Auro accomplishes an action in this interaction when he responds to Mauro with a textual message that seems ironic. Auro tells Mauro that after reading his comment, he will not be able to sleep, presumably because he is anticipating the supposed excitement of watching Mauro dressed up as Metroman (*non dormo più!*). The action performed by Filippo in the comment at Post 3 is another response to the comment at Post 1; he mocks Mauro by saying that he will dress up as a banana, if Mauro dresses up like Metroman (*io da banana*). Similarly, in the comment at Post 4 Aria responds to the comment at Post 1; she apparently plays along with Mauro and challenges him to pursue his plan of dressing up as Metroman. Aria tells Mauro that after publishing the comment at Post 1, he must dress up like Metroman, if he does not want to disappoint her and his Friends (*ti prego fallo davvero, non illudermi/ci*). The action performed by Mauro in the comment at Post 6 shows that he accepts the playful challenge Aria has proposed in her comment at Post 4. Mauro ironically tells Aria that he is "serious" about his plan of dressing up as Metroman (*sai bene quanto io sia serio in queste occasioni*).

In the comment at Post 5 Mina performs her first action in this interaction: she publishes another response to the comment at Post 1. The emoticon and the content of this contribution suggest Mina's intention to join the playful framework proposed by Auro, Filippo, and Aria in the comments at Posts 2 to 4. In the comment at Post 5 Mina tells Mauro that if he dresses up as Metroman, he will also have to sing as Metroman does on the underground for the entire duration of the Carnevale party (*Oltre a vestirti come lui, però dovrai cantare tutta la sera sennò non vale!! ;D*). In the comment at Post 7 Mauro seems to accept this "funny" challenge; indeed, he shouts to Mina that he will sing as Metroman does during the party (*Mina: OVVIO*). In the comment at Post 10 Richard performs another action in this comment thread; he says that if Mauro dresses up as Metroman, he will be sexy (*sexy*).

In the comment at Post 11 Daniele accomplishes two other actions in this interaction; he comments on Mina's previous response in the contribution at Post 5, where she has told Mauro that he will have to sing as Metroman does on the underground, and then he tells Friends that if Mauro dresses up as Metroman, he will dress up as an underground pole, so Mauro can swing around him (*io mi vesto da palo della metro, così puoi attaccarti al palo e girare!!!*). It is likely that the comment at Post 11 refers to a video of Metroman, where he swings around a pole while performing on the underground.

The humorous approach used by Mauro in the comment at Post 1 seems to have helped secure several responses from Friends. In addition, none of these responses is serious. In other words, the actions performed by Friends in the comments that follow Mauro's initial telling show that they have interpreted it as facetious. Furthermore, in the comments at Posts 6, 7, and 12 Mauro responds to some of these comments without repairing them and clearly participating in the playful framework of those responses.

A clearer example where an initial comment sparks humor, regardless of the intention of the person posting the comment, can be seen in Extract 5.17, where Friends respond to an apparently serious telling in a humorous way.

Extract 5.17 It can't rain forever

→ 1 Auro: "Non può piovere per sempre" [quote taken from the movie *The Crow*]
Auro: "It cannot rain forever"

A Claudio piace questo
Claudio likes this

2 Alex: ma può smettere per un pò . . .
Alex: but it can stop for a while . . .

3 Matteo: però può continuare per un bel pò . . .
Matteo: or it can keep raining for a long time . . .

4 Alex: non ci sono più le mezze stagioni . . . eggià!!! [Italian proverb]
Alex: there is no Spring or Autumn anymore . . . that's for sure!!!

5 Auro: pioev pioev pioev là gallina là fà il oef [Italian proverb]
Auro: it rains rains rains and the hen lays an egg

6 Mauro: Don't say the cat is in the sac [quote taken from Giovanni Trapattoni, former coach of the Italian national soccer team]

7 Auro: io adoro Giovanni trapattoni
Auro: I love Giovanni trapattoni

8 Mauro: Idem [Mauro publishes a YouTube video about Giovanni Trapattoni]
Mauro: me too

As discussed in Chapter 4, the first action performed by Auro in this comment thread is publishing a quote taken from the film *The Crow* to comment on the weather conditions in Milan, where it had apparently been raining for several days ("*Non può piovere per sempre*"). The comment at Post 1 is not blatantly humorous; indeed, nothing in what Auro writes clearly suggests that it is "funny." However, the actions accomplished by Friends in the contributions that follow the comment at Post 1 suggest that they have interpreted it in a playfully humorous way.

In the comment at Post 2 Alex performs an action that orients to the comment at Post 1; he responds to Auro with a linguistic play based on his initial quote, when he says that it can stop raining for a while (*ma può smettere per un pò . . .*). On the other hand, the action accomplished by Matteo in the comment at Post 3 orients to Alex's comment. Matteo continues with the play on words in the comment at Post 2 to tell Alex that it can continue raining for a while (*però può continuare per un bel pò . . .*). Moreover, the action in the comment at Post 3 seems to launch a joking competition (Norrick, 1993, 1994) which plays on the topic of weather. In the comment at Post 4 Alex joins this competition; he performs another action when he publishes an Italian cliché about seasons (*non ci sono più le mezze stagioni . . . eggià!!!*), which is followed by a proverb about the weather posted by Auro in the comment at Post 5 (*pioev pioev pioev là gallina là fà il oef*), and a quote taken from Trapattoni, the former coach of the Italian national soccer team, published by Mauro in the comment at Post 6 (*Don't say the cat is in the sac*). Even though the contribution at Post 6 is not about the weather, it seems to go on with the linguistic play started by the cliché and continued by the proverb in the comments at Posts 4 and 5.

The actions performed by Alex and other Friends in the joking competition in the comments at Posts 2 to 6 show that they have interpreted Auro's telling as a playful comment on the weather. Moreover, in the comment at Post 5 Auro joins this competition. The action he performs in this contribution suggests that Auro enjoys the way in which Friends have responded to his initial quote. Therefore, the analysis of Extract 5.17 has indicated that even when not overt, humor can be present in first-post tellings, and it seems to secure responses from Friends.

In addition to overtly and covertly humorous first comments, it is worth noting that even comment threads which begin with an initial non-humorous comment often receive at least some humorous responses.

Extract 5.18 Fabio Volo's quote[5]

1 Elisa: Forse c'è qualcosa di peggio dei sogni svaniti: la non voglia di sognare ancora. Fabio Volo [quote taken from a book of Fabio Volo, an Italian radio presenter] 10 ore fa

Elisa: Maybe there is something worst than vanished dreams: the desire to no longer dream. Fabio Volo 10 hours ago

A 11 persone piace questo

11 people like this

→ 2 Franco: Già . . . poveri interisti. 10 ore fa
Franco: yeah . . . poor interisti [nickname for F. C. Inter supporters]. *10 hours ago*

3 Elisa: :-) 10 ore fa
Elisa: :-) 10 hours ago

4 Franco: Però anche tu infierisci . . . sei cattiva! 10 ore fa
Franco: but you like to rub salt into a wound . . . you're mean! 10 hours ago

5 Elisa: ahhaha . . . si si cattivissima . . . ! 10 ore fa
Elisa: ahhaha. . . yeah yeah really mean . . .! 10 hours ago

6 Franco: Come una punizione di Carletto . . . violenta e spietata! 10 ore fa
Franco: Like a free kick of Carletto [probably the nickname of a former soccer player of the team A. C. Milan] . . . *violent and cruel! 10 hours ago*

→ 7 Francesca: mi piace!!! 7 ore fa
Francesca: I like it!!! 7 hours ago

[. . .]

→ 13 Antonia: bella! la [*sic*] copio subito! 6 ore fa
Antonia: nice! I'll copy it straight away! 6 hours ago

[. . .]

While this extract will be analyzed in full in Chapter 8, certain features are relevant here. In the comment at Post 1, Elisa performs her first action in this interaction: she provides a quote from a book (*Forse c'è qualcosa di peggio dei sogni svaniti: la non voglia di sognare ancora. Fabio Volo*). The actions accomplished by two Friends in the comments at Posts 7 and 13 indicate that they have interpreted this comment in a "serious" way. In the comment at Post 7, Francesca says she likes the quote (*mi piace!!!*); at Post 13, Antonia similarly indicates that she likes the quote (*bella! la copio subito!*). However, the action performed by Franco in the comment at Post 2, where he responds to Elisa's initial contribution by applying it to the supporters of the soccer team F.C. Inter (*Già . . . poveri interisti*), generates a humorous discussion, with Franco mocking Elisa for being cruel and Elisa accepting his words.

Humor was found to be a very frequent feature of FB comment threads throughout the corpus of this book. Of the 205 threads opened by first-post tellings, 147 of the tellings are overtly or covertly humorous—and that count excludes examples such as 5.18 above, where the humor is only found in responses. Performing humor so frequently in first-post tellings appears to be connected once again with the desire of FB users to secure responses from Friends. Whether overt or covert, the action of posting humorous first-post tellings tends to lead to other actions which result in longer interactions, with stronger participation by more Friends.

An example of this was seen above in Extract 5.16 about Mauro dressing up as Metroman. Mauro returns to the theme of Metroman in another humorous comment thread, Extract 5.19, which is unusually long, with thirty-nine comments. Only a short version of this interaction is presented here; a full version of this comment thread is available in Appendix A. It seems that this interaction has received multiple responses from Friends because of the intended humorous approach suggested by Mauro in the textual message in the comment at Post 1. In the initial unit of this contribution, Mauro uses an exaggerated statement to introduce his initial hyperlink-telling.

Extract 5.19 Metroman

1 Mauro: Cmq [*sic*] ormai siamo arrivati ad un Livello Superiore. L'anno prossimo partecipa agli EMA's [Mauro publishes a hyperlink about Metroman]
Mauro: by the way it's clear that he has reached a higher Level. Next year he will participate in the European Music Awards

A 5 persone piace questo
5 people like this

2 Mauro: Parola d'ordine: SUBBBLIMARE [term probably created by Metroman which is impossible to translate] Metroman . . . mannagia a te . . .
Mauro: password: SUBBBLIMARE damn you Metroman . . .

3 Mauro: Gianni Zaira Valeria Amelia Claudia Sara Aldo [Nicknames of Mauro's Friends]

→ 4 Vanessa: hahahahhahahhahahaahahhahaahhaahhahhahaahhaah sto piangendo
Vanessa: hahahahhahahhahahaahahhahaahhaahhahhahaahhaah I'm crying

5 Mauro: Alessio Chiara Auron

[. . .]

→ 7 Alessio: quella mattina a cascina gobba [*sic*] [metro station] mi ha cambiato la vita . . . lo ammetto . . .
Alessio: that morning at Cascina Gobba he changed my life . . . I have to admit

[. . .]

→ 15 Valeria: A livello di completezza io mi ritengo un artista completo [quote taken from the video published within the hyperlink at Post 1].
Valeria: As far as completeness is concerned I consider myself a complete artist.

[. . .]

18 Mauro: Minuto 2.30 "INQUADRAMI IL SALTO MORTALE" [quote taken from the video published within the hyperlink at Post 1]
Mauro: Minute 2.30 "FRAME THE SOMERSAULT"

[. . .]

→ 23 Amelia:—gnahahahah ma infatti ti vedi mentre gli fai il video lì seduta o sbaglio? (il vecchio in imbarazzo in primo piano:voto [*sic*] mille)
Amelia:—gnahahahah that's right you can see yourself seated while filming him or am I wrong? (the embarrassed old man on the video looks amazing)

[. . .]

→ 29 Daniele: AHAHA vale [*sic*], dovevi alzarti e fargli il controcoro come fai con gli Into ;)
Daniele: AHAHA valeria, you should have stood up and sang harmonies as you generally do with the Into [probably the name of Valeria's band] *;)*

[. . .]

→ 32 Vanda: faccio effetto solo Milano, capito?????? [quote taken from the video published within the hyperlink at Post 1] ero sulla banchina della metro e l'ho sentito da fuori. peccato [*sic*] che non ho fatto in tempo a entrare in quel vagone :)
Vanda: I make sense only in Milan, do you understand?????? I was waiting on the subway bench and I heard him from the outside. Such a shame I had no time to catch that carriage:)

→ 33 Zaira: io ho provato questa emozione e ne sono orgogliosa cazzo.
Zaira: I've experienced this emotion and fuck I'm proud of it.

[. . .]

→ 36 Giorgio: . . . mi vergogno di essere vissuto in quella citta!
Giorgio: . . . I'm ashamed of having lived in that city!

→ 37 Riva: AHAHAHAHAHAHAHAAAAAAAAAAAAHHHHHHHHHHH!!!!!!!!!

→ 38 Aldo: Ha una nomination garantita x best underground artist
Aldo: he will definitively receive a nomination for best underground artist

→ 39 Pietro: l'altro giorno l'ho beccato per la terza volta!!!
Pietro: the other day I saw him for the third time!!!

In the comment at Post 1 Mauro performs the first action in this interaction; he uses an overstatement to introduce his hyperlink-telling, saying that Metroman is likely to participate in the next European Music Awards (EMAs) and then he posts a hyperlink-telling about this "singer" (*Cmq ormai siamo arrivati ad un Livello Superiore. L'anno prossimo partecipa agli EMA's*). The humor in this comment is clear, as Metroman is a busker, not someone who would be participating in the commercial EMAs. Then, in the comment at Post 2 Mauro performs another action; he seems to continue with the previous contribution by commenting on his own telling and quoting Metroman (*Parola d'ordine: SUBBBLIMARE Metroman . . . mannagia a te . . .*).

Eleven Friends respond to Mauro's initial telling. The actions performed by Friends in these responses show that they have interpreted the comment at Post 1 as humorous and seem to be triggered by the ironic intention of Mauro's initial narrative. Moreover, it appears that Friends need some previous knowledge of Metroman, the character of the video in the comment at Post 1, in order to understand the irony embedded in this telling. It is likely that Friends have responded to the comment at Post 1 because they want to show other Friends that they got Mauro's initial "joke." Hence, it is possible that Friends have responded to Mauro's narrative because it enhances a sense of affiliation among them.

The actions performed by Friends in their responses at Posts 4, 7, 15, 23, 29, 32, 33, 36, 37, 38, and 39 suggest that they have understood Mauro's humorous approach. In the comment at Post 4 after laughing at the video at Post 1, Vanessa continues with the exaggerated tone, adopted by Mauro in the textual message at Post 1, publishing an unlikely statement in which she tells Mauro that his video has moved her to tears (*hahahahhahahhahahaahahhahaahhaahhahhahaahhaah sto piangendo*). In the comment at Post 7 Alessio publishes an overstatement when he tells Mauro that encountering Metroman at Cascina Gobba (metro station) has changed his life (*quella mattina a cascina gobba mi ha cambiato la vita . . . lo ammetto . . .*). The actions in the comments at Post 4 as well as Post 7 suggest that Vanessa and Alessio have interpreted Mauro's initial telling as humorous.

In the comment at Post 15 Valeria performs another action in this interaction: she publishes a quote from the video at Post 1 (*A livello di completezza io mi ritengo un artista completo*). Although the precise intent of this comment is unclear, it seems a humorous comment on Mauro's initial telling. After laughing at the video-telling at Post 1, in the comment at Post 23 Amelia asks Valeria to confirm if she appears in the video published by Mauro in the comment at Post 18 (*- gnahahahah ma infatti ti vedi mentre gli fai il video lì seduta o sbaglio (il vecchio in imbarazzo in primo piano:voto mille)*). The action performed by Valeria in the comment at Post 15, and the action accomplished by Amelia in the comment at Post 23, suggest that these two Friends have understood the humorous intention embedded in Mauro's initial telling.

After laughing at the beginning of the contribution at Post 29, Daniele performs another action in this comment thread: he comments on the video in which Valeria appears (*AHAHA vale, dovevi alzarti e fargli il controcoro come fai con gli Into ;)*). In the comment at Post 32 Vanda publishes another quote probably taken from the video in the comment at Post 1 (*faccio effetto solo Milano, capito??????*); then, she accomplishes another action when she shares a personal anecdote about the day she saw Metroman performing live on the underground (*ero sulla banchina della metro e l'ho sentito da fuori. peccato che non ho fatto in tempo a entrare in quel vagone :)*). The emoticons at the end of the comments at Posts 29 and 32, which represent two smiles, both signal that Daniele and Vanda have treated Mauro's initial telling as humorous.

In the comment at Post 33 Zaira performs another action: she responds to Vanda's previous contribution with another exaggerated positive evaluation of Metroman's live performance, which is concluded with an expletive to further enhance the exaggeration (*io ho provato questa emozione e ne sono orgogliosa cazzo*). In the comment at Post 36, Giorgio publishes an ironic comment when he says that after having watched the videos in previous comments, he is ashamed of having lived in Milan (*. . . mi vergogno di essere vissuto in quella citta!*), while in the comment at Post 37 Riva laughs at Mauro's video-telling (*AHAHAHAHAHAHAHAAAAAAAAAAAAAHHHHHHHHHHH!!!!!!!!!*), and in the contribution at Post 38 Aldo maintains the exaggerated tone of previous comments when he tells Mauro that Metroman's nomination in the next European Music Awards should be as best underground artist (*Ha una nomination garantita x best underground*). The actions performed by Zaira, Giorgio, Riva, and Aldo in the comments at Posts 33, 36, 37, and 38 suggest that these Friends have interpreted Mauro's initial telling as humorous, while contributing to the general tone of exaggerated evaluations of the video in the comment at Post 1.

In the comment at Post 39, Pietro accomplishes another action in this interaction when he seems to play along with previous contributions published by Friends in this comment thread. Indeed, Pietro states that he saw Metroman for the third time a couple of days ago (*l'altro giorno l'ho beccato per la terza volta!!!*). The series of exclamation marks at the end of this comment (*!!!*), which might represent the emotional component of this contribution, suggests that the action performed by Pietro in this contribution is intended to be humorous, though it might have either a positive or negative overtone due to the ambiguous term "*beccato*." "*Beccato*" might be translated into English in two different ways: the first, which is slightly negative and means "to get caught"; while the second, which is to some extent positive means "to meet" or "to run into" someone. As mentioned earlier, it is likely that Pietro is telling Friends that he ran into Metroman for the third time.

While it is possible that the action of naming in the comments at Posts 3 and 5 also has had a role in securing Friends' responses (comment at Post 3 addressed to "*Gianni Zaira Valeria Amelia Claudia Sara Aldo*"; comment at Post 5 addressed to "*Alessio Chiara Auron*"), it is likely that the first-post telling has received multiple responses because of the implicit enjoyment and sense of affiliation generated by the humor used in this narrative. It seems that Friends performed the actions in the responses to the comment at Post 1 because they wanted to show to other Friends that they understood Mauro's "joke" and they wanted to build on that humor. Thus, the action of structuring a telling in order to be humorous might generate a sense of enjoyment, playfulness, and affiliation among Friends, who seem to be more likely to perform other actions and participate in a comment thread.

While on a much smaller scale, the use of humor to create affiliation can be seen in Extract 5.20, where a covert humorous telling receives responses from three Friends.

Extract 5.20 Soundgarden

1 Mauro: finitela di postare i Soundgarden . . . bastardi.
Mauro: stop posting Soundgarden . . . you bastards.

→ 2 Elvira: ahahahahah

3 Elvira: e tu vai a vedere gli off al magnolia, no?
Elvira: but're you going to see the off [possibly the name of a band] *at magnolia* [possibly the name of a club], *aren't you?*

→ 4 Alfredo: . . .

→ 5 Denise: prrrrrrrrrrrr :)

Although the action performed in the final unit of the comment at Post 1, the mock-insult (*bastardi*), might signal the apparent humorous approach of this contribution, the telling in this comment is not obviously humorous (*finitela di postare i Soundgarden . . . bastardi*). However, the actions performed in the comments at Posts 2, 4, and 5 show that Friends have interpreted the comment at Post 1 in a facetious way. Given the semi-public nature of FB it is possible that Friends have responded to the comment at Post 1 because they wanted to show to other Friends that they have understood Mauro's mocking "insult."

As discussed in Chapter 3, in the comment at Post 1 Mauro requests Friends to stop posting messages about Soundgarden, an American band (*finitela di postare i Soundgarden . . . bastardi*). This contribution is responded to by the comments at Posts 2, 4, and 5, with all these messages suggesting that Friends have interpreted the telling at Post 1 in a humorous way. More precisely, while in the comments at Posts 2 and 5 Elvira and Denise laugh and mock Mauro by posting a raspberry followed by a smiling emoticon addressed to his telling (Comment at Post 2: *ahahahahah*. Comment at Post 5: *prrrrrrrrrrrr :)*), at Post 4 Alfredo publishes a series of suspension points (. . .) which might represent a pause or silence oriented to the contribution at Post 1. The actions in the comments at Posts 2, 4, and 5 suggest that Elvira, Alfredo, and Denise have treated Mauro's initial comment as humorous.

It is argued here, on the basis of the analyses of Extracts 5.19 and 5.20, that the action of performing first-post tellings which are humorous or which can be interpreted in a humorous way or which can be commented on using humor is generally more likely to trigger other actions from Friends and therefore secure their responses. Friends seem more likely to respond to humorous tellings because they are playful and enhance a sense of affiliation.

Overall, it appears that humor is frequently used by FB users in order to secure responses from Friends. It can be argued that humorous first-post tellings stimulate actions from Friends and thus secure their responses. This is because they trigger a sense of in-group understanding (Baym, 1995) and knowing participation (Georgakopoulou, 2016). This can be clearly seen in Extracts 5.19 and 5.20. In Extract 5.19, by responding to Mauro's humorous telling, Friends perform actions which show that they have some previous knowledge of Metroman, thus displaying that they belong to a specific "group." This is also the case in Extract 5.20, where by responding to Mauro's initial telling, Friends accomplish actions that display that they have some knowledge of Mauro's offline activities, more precisely, that he missed the concert by Soundgarden and intends to go to another concert, thereby showing that they are part of what seems to be a restricted "group." In general, therefore, it seems that humorous first-post tellings are more likely to secure responses from Friends because they trigger a sense of playfulness and in-group understanding among them.

Conclusions

After showing in Chapter 4 that the majority of comment threads included in the corpus of this study are opened by first-post tellings, this chapter has discussed the interactional problems that may arise when an FB user opens a comment thread with a telling, and the techniques he or she might use to overcome these problems.

After pointing out that securing the space for a first-post telling is a problem that does not affect FB comment threads, this chapter has found that securing recipients for a telling is problematic for first-post tellers. This is clear from the actions FB users perform in their initial tellings. Naming the intended recipients of a telling, providing recipients with enough information to interpret a telling, and using humor are the most common actions or techniques utilized by FB users to secure responses to first-post tellings. Humor, even when not overt, is a particularly common action performed by first-post tellers to secure recipients for initial tellings; this is probably because humor generates a sense of playfulness, affiliation, and in-group understanding among Friends, who are therefore more likely to accomplish other actions in a comment thread, for example, responding to these tellings.

Having now established that FB comment threads are commonly opened by first-post tellings, and having discussed the interactional problems that may affect these tellings and the actions or techniques deployed to overcome them, the following chapter will briefly look at non-initial tellings.

6

Non-initial Tellings

Introduction

In Chapter 4 it was shown that FB comment threads are generally opened by tellings. Following this, Chapter 5 has focused on the interactional problems that may arise when an FB user opens a comment thread by using a telling, and the actions that he or she may undertake to overcome these problems.

The present chapter turns to investigate non-initial tellings, and shows the fundamental difference in status between first-post tellings and other tellings occurring in FB comment threads. After defining non-initial tellings, this chapter discusses the role of non-initial tellings in FB comment threads, and the very different position they have in the *sequence organization* of these interactions.

Defining non-initial tellings

In this book the term *non-initial tellings* refers to tellings which occur in comments that are not initial, such as the telling in the comment at Post 7 in Extract 6.1. In this contribution, Elisa performs an action that orients to Mauro's previous telling about Kaki King, an American guitarist; accordingly she posts a non-initial telling about her own plans for the evening.

Extract 6.1 Kaki King's concert

1 Mauro: Questa volta ti lascio andare va . . . (forse) [Mauro publishes a hyperlink containing the video of one of the songs of the artist Kaki King]
Mauro: this time I will give you a miss . . . (perhaps)

2 Elisa: suona stasera al bloom [probably the name of a club]
Elisa: she's playing tonight at the bloom

3 Elisa: ah vai?
Elisa: are you going?

4 Mauro: ahahahah "questa volta ti lascio andare va . . . (forse)"
Mauro: ahahahah "this time I will give you a miss . . . (perhaps)"

5 Elisa: bah
Elisa: bah

6 Mauro: lineare: ciao Elisa, penso di non andare, anche se un po' mi dispiace . . . alla fine della fiera sono sempre andato a vederla in passato. Ma stasera vorrei essere più pantofolaio.
Mauro: clear: hi Elisa, I reckon I won't go, although I'm a little bit disappointed because . . . in the past I always ended up going and seeing her. But tonight, I would like to stay at home.

→ 7 Elisa: io aperitivo e poi casa. se [*sic*] mi riprendo, domani battles [possibly the name of a band], se no sticazzi :D
Elisa: I'll have a happy hour and then home. If I feel better, tomorrow I'll go to the battles, if not fuck it :D

8 Mauro: gran gruppo gli StiCazzi! Spaccano sempre!
Mauro: wonderful group the fuck it! They always rock!

9 Elisa: sìsìl [*sic*] sono grandissimi!
Elisa: yeahyeah they're great!

10 Milena: peccato. se [*sic*] ci andavi . . . forse stavolta venivo anch'io
Milena: it's a shame. if you went . . . I would have gone too

After Mauro begins this comment thread with a series of comments where he hesitantly tells Friends that he does not really want to go to the concert of Kaki King and talks about what he will do instead, Elisa in the comment at Post 7 performs her fourth action in this interaction. She responds to Mauro's telling with a non-initial telling about her own activities.

In the comment at Post 1, Mauro performs a couple of actions which are unclear. He posts a hyperlink-telling that contains one of the songs of Kaki King. He also publishes a textual message which is unclear; Mauro tells Friends that perhaps he will give Kaki King a miss (*questa volta ti lascio andare va . . . (forse)*), but does not explicitly mention that she is giving a concert. The actions performed by Elisa in the comments at Posts 2 and 3, where she seems to initiate two *repair sequences*, show that she may not have understood Mauro's initial telling. In fact, in the comment at Post 2 Elisa tells Mauro that Kaki King will perform live tonight at the "*bloom*," presumably the name of a club (*suona stasera al bloom*) and in the comment at Post 3 she asks Mauro if he is planning to go to the concert (*ah vai?*).

In the comment at Post 4 Mauro performs another action in this interaction: he responds to Elisa by republishing the contribution in the comment at Post 1 preceded by a representation of laughter (*ahahahah* "*questa volta ti lascio andare va . . . (forse)*"). Then, in the comment at Post 5 Elisa posts "*bah*," which seems to express her problem in understanding Mauro's comments at Posts 1 and 4. Finally, in the comment at Post 6 Mauro accomplishes an action that is relevant to this interaction. He greets Elisa and then responds to her previous question in the comment at Post 3 by explaining that although he has been to all the previous concerts of Kaki King, this time he will probably stay home and relax (*lineare: ciao Elisa, penso di non andare, anche se un po' mi dispiace . . . alla fine della fiera sono sempre andato a vederla in passato. Ma stasera vorrei essere più pantofolaio*).

This comment triggers another action from Elisa; more precisely, a second telling. In the comment at Post 7 Elisa responds to Mauro's comment at Post 6 with a non-initial telling about her own plans for a relaxing evening—having a drink and then going home in order to be rested for "*Battles*," which is likely to be the name of another band, the following day (*io aperitivo e poi casa. se mi riprendo, domani battles, se no sticazzi :D*). Elisa's action in the comment at Post 7, her non-initial telling, is closed by an expletive (*se no sticazzi*). This is followed by a smiling emoticon (*:D*) which seems to positively assess Elisa's own plans for the evening and the following day.

The expletive "*sticazzi*" stimulates another action from Mauro, a joke in the comment at Post 8, where he plays with the word "*sticazzi*" by supposing that "*sticazzi*" is the name of the band Elisa is going to see live the following day (*gran gruppo gli StiCazzi! Spaccano sempre!*). This joke is responded to by the action accomplished by Elisa in the humorous comment at Post 9, where she responds to Mauro with an unlikely statement about the "*sticazzi*" band (*sìsìl sono grandissimi!*).

This comment thread ends with Milena's action in the comment at Post 10, where she tells Mauro that she might have gone to Kaki King's concert, if Mauro had attended it (*peccato. se ci andavi . . . forse stavolta venivo anch'io*).

So, Extract 6.1 begins with an extended discussion of Mauro's plans for the evening, which then triggers Elisa's action in the comment at Post 7, her non-initial telling about her own activities.

Another non-initial telling is evident in Extract 6.2, where the action performed by Marco in the comment at Post 8 orients to Elisa's initial telling on her future travel plans and consists of a non-initial telling about his own future activities.

Extract 6.2 Bologna

1 Elisa: . . . valigia pronta :-) destinazione Bologna!!!
Elisa: . . . the suitcase is ready :-) destination Bologna!!!

A 6 persone piace questo
6 people like this

2 Marco: BELLO!
Marco: AWESOME!

3 Elisa: si marchino [*sic*] . . . faccio il tour Ferrara, Bologna, e Parma . . . hi hi hi!smack
Elisa: yes marchino . . . I will go to Ferrara, Bologna, and Parma [Italian cities] . . . *hi hi hi!smack*

4 Marco: A FERRARA CI HO VISSUTO!! BELLA!
Marco: I USED TO LIVE IN FERRARA!! IT'S WONDERFUL!

5 Elisa: davvero?non [*sic*] lo sapevo!si [*sic*] dicono che sia stupenda . . . !quando [*sic*] torno ti dico!
Elisa: really?I didn't know!people tell me that it's impressive . . . !when I get back I'll let you know!

6 Marco: il marchino [*sic*] !! mah [*sic*] quante cose ha fatto!!! divertiti [*sic*] !!
Marco: marc!! well he has done so many things!!! have fun!!

7 Elisa: bravo marc . . . hai fatto bene!grazie [*sic*] . . . smack!
Elisa: well done marc . . . you did well!thanks . . . smack!

→ 8 Marco: io "invece" a fine mese inizio il corso per conseguire la qualifica di mediatore civile nelle cause giudiziarie!figata [*sic*]!
Marco: on the other hand, at the end of the month I'll be starting a course to become a civil mediator in lawsuit!cool!

9 Elisa: figooo!
Elisa: cool!

This comment thread is opened by a telling articulated over several comments, where Elisa and Marco perform several actions to discuss Elisa's trip to Bologna. This discussion triggers a non-initial telling about Marco's professional activities, which contrasts with Elisa's travel plans.

In the comment at Post 1 Elisa performs her first action in this comment thread; she tells Friends about her travel plan. Elisa has prepared her suitcases because she is going to the city of Bologna (. . . *valigia pronta :-) destinazione Bologna!!!*). Both the emoticon (*:-)*) in the middle of this comment, and the series of exclamation marks (*!!!*) that closes it, suggest Elisa's excitement for the trip. This excitement seems to have been understood by Marco, who in the comment at Post 2 uses a positive evaluation to accomplish another action in this comment thread: a response to the initial telling (*BELLO!*). In the comment at Post 3 Elisa continues with her telling by providing Marco with more details about her trip, and the news that she is, in fact, planning to visit various cities including Ferrara, Bologna, and Parma (*si marchino . . . faccio il tour Ferrara, Bologna, e Parma . . . hi hi hi!smack*). In the comment at Post 4 Marco performs another action in this interaction; he tells Elisa that he lived in Ferrara (*A FERRARA CI HO VISSUTO!! BELLA!*).

The announcement in the comment at Post 4 triggers the actions in the comments at Posts 5 and 6, where Elisa tells Marco that she did not know that he lived in Ferrara and Marco responds to it with an ironic comment followed by what seems to be an apparent closing "*divertiti!!*" (have fun!!) (Liddicoat, 2011; Schegloff and Sacks, 1973) (Comment at Post 5: *davvero?non lo sapevo!si dicono che sia stupenda . . . !quando torno ti dico!*. Comment at Post 6: *il marchino!! mah quante cose ha fatto!!! divertiti!!*). After commenting on the contribution at Post 6, in the comment at Post 7 Elisa thanks Marco for his previous comment and seems to accept the closure by posting "*smack*" (*bravo marc . . . hai fatto bene!grazie . . . "smack!"*).

However, in the comment at Post 8 Marco performs another action in this comment thread by posting a non-initial telling about his future professional activities, which are work oriented rather than leisure oriented. This telling is followed by an ironic assessment. After telling Elisa that he will attend a course to become a mediator in civil lawsuits, Marco assesses his own telling by using the term "*figata*!" (cool). This comment is potentially humorous, where Marco seems excited about this course, when in reality he is probably not (*io* "invece" *a fine mese inizio il corso per conseguire la qualifica di mediatore civile nelle cause giudiziarie!figata!*). The apparently humorous approach embedded in Marco's non-initial telling seems to have been understood by Elisa, who responds to it in the comment at Post 9 where she performs another action in this comment thread when she says that Marco's plan is cool (*figooo!*).

Extract 6.2 contains two tellings: the initial telling articulated over two comments, Posts 1 and 3, where Elisa discusses her forthcoming trip, and the second telling in the comment at Post 8, where Marco talks about his professional plans. The topics of those two tellings are completely different: the first is about Elisa's personal life, while the second is about Marco's professional life. However, the non-initial telling seems to have been occasioned by the initial telling. In fact, the second telling seems to be a response to the first telling, where Marco tells Elisa that while she will be traveling he will be working. Therefore, the action performed by Elisa in her first-post telling has occasioned the action accomplished by Marco in his non-initial telling as a kind of ironic contrast.

Another non-initial telling occurs in Extract 6.3, where Renzo's first-post telling is responded to by Angela with a non-initial telling about her future plan of buying a new phone.

Extract 6.3 iPhone

1 Renzo: non ce l'ho fatta . . . alla fine l'ho preso!!! il [*sic*] mio primo iphone!!!!
Renzo: I couldn't resist . . . at the end I bought it!!! my first iphone!!!!

A Loris, Mauro e altre 4 persone piace questo elemento
Loris, Mauro, and other 4 people like this

2 Sara: io ancora resisto . . .
Sara: I still resist . . .

3 Linda: che emozione!!! domani [*sic*] smanettiamo!!!
Linda: how exciting!!! tomorrow we'll play with it!!!

4 Renzo: ssiiiiiiiIiiiiii!!! non [*sic*] so se riuscirò a dormire!!
Renzo: yeahahahahahha!!! I don't know, whether I'll be able to sleep!!

5 Linda: auhaha noooo!! devi [*sic*] essere riposato . . . se no nn [*sic*] riesci as [*sic*] usarlo poi!!!
Linda: auhaha noooo!! You need to rest . . . otherwise, you won't be able to use it!!!

6 Mauro: Ti abbiamo detto di aspettare!
Mauro: We told you to wait!

7 Alberto: renz [*sic*] non darlo in mano alla linda [*sic*] . . . ;) e nemmeno a ferrò che se no lo usa come sasso da far rimbalzare sull'acqua . . .
Alberto: renz don't give it to linda . . . ;) or to ferrò [probably the nickname of one of Renzo's Friends] *otherwise he'll use it as a stone to bounce on the water . . .*

8 Linda: ooohhh . . . Albe problemi!?!? Renz [*sic*] t [*sic*] capisco . . . avevi la scimmietta . . .
Linda: ooohhh . . . Albe do you have a problem!?!? Renz I understand you . . . you had to have it ["*scimmietta*" is a slang term which means to strongly desire something] . . .

9 Alberto: io no . . . l'iphone di renzo [*sic*] si se lo da in mano a te . . .!
Alberto: I don't . . . but renzo's iphone does, if he gives it to you . . .!

→ 10 Angela: spendaccione! ma [*sic*] fa bene coccolarsi a volte, no? io [*sic*] "invece" mi sa che ormai devo proprio decidermi a cambiare cell e a prenderne uno che almeno abbi [*sic*] la fotocamera, che dici? :)

Angela: spendthrift! but sometimes we have to spoil ourselves, don't we? Instead I reckon that I need to make up my mind and buy a new mobile with a camera, what do you reckon? :)

11 Linda: CANE!!
Linda: Dog!!

12 Alberto: a cuccia!
Alberto: sit!

13 Renzo: In effetti l'intento era quello di aspettare a prenderlo ma . . . non ho resistito . . . mi farò regalare il 5 per natale in caso!!
Renzo: actually the idea was to wait before buying it but . . . I couldn't resist . . . I'll ask someone to buy me the 5 for Christmas just in case!!

14 Piera: ma non avevamo convinto salvo [*sic*] a prenderlo??????
Piera: but didn't we persuade salvo [probably the name of another of Renzo's Friends] *to buy it??????*

15 Fabiana: il mio primo?? ma [*sic*] perchè ci sarà un secondo eo [*sic*] un terzo? io [*sic*] posso prendere il tuo rottamato poi
Fabiana: my first?? does that mean that there'll be a second and a third one? So then I can have your old one

16 Giulia: mani bucate! ;P
Giulia: spendthrift! ;P

As noted in Chapter 3, Renzo launches this comment thread by talking about his new iPhone. After a series of comments in which Friends respond to the initial telling and mock each other, in the comment at Post 10 Angela performs her first action in this interaction. She publishes a non-initial telling about her own idea of changing her phone.

The action performed by Renzo in the comment at Post 1 consists of an announcement; he tells Friends that he has bought his first iPhone (*non ce l'ho fatta . . . alla fine l'ho preso!!! il mio primo iphone!!!!*). The series of exclamation marks at the end of the comment at Post 1 indicate the emotional component of this contribution; Renzo seems excited for his purchase. In the comment at Post 2 Sara performs an action in this comment thread; she responds to Renzo by telling him that she is resisting the temptation of buying an iPhone (*io ancora resisto . . .*). The excitement in Renzo's initial telling seems to have been understood by Linda in the comment at Post 3, where she tells Renzo that the following day they will play with his new phone (*che emozione!!! domani smanettiamo!!!*).

Linda's action, the positive evaluation in the comment at Post 3, is responded to by Renzo in the comment at Post 4. The action performed by Renzo in this contribution seems ironic and in fact Renzo tells Linda that he will probably not fall asleep because of the excitement generated by the idea of playing with his new iPhone (*ssiiiiiiiIiiiiii!!! non so se riuscirò a dormire!!*). The humorous approach embedded in Renzo's response in the comment at Post 4 is understood by Linda who performs another action in this comment thread when in the comment at Post 5 she publishes a representation of laughter followed by a suggestive joke about Renzo's sexual performance. Linda says that Renzo needs to be rested, if he wants to be able to use "it" properly, leaving the term "it" open to interpretation (*auhaha noooo!! devi essere riposato . . . se no nn riesci as usarlo poi!!!*). In the comment at Post 6 Mauro accomplishes another action in this interaction; he seems to join the playful framework proposed by Renzo and Linda in previous comments as he publishes a playful negative evaluation of Renzo's telling. Mauro tells Renzo that they told him to wait before buying the new phone (*Ti abbiamo detto di aspettare!*).

The action performed by Alberto in the comment at Post 7 contributes to the general humorous tone proposed by the facetious comments at Posts 4, 5, and 6. In this contribution Alberto plays along with Linda. He seems to evaluate Linda's joke in the comment at Post 5 by telling Renzo that he should not give his new phone to Linda or "*ferrò*," which is probably the nickname of another Friend, because "*ferrò*" will use the phone to make ripples on the water (*renz non darlo in mano alla linda . . . ;) e nemmeno a ferrò che se no lo usa come sasso da far rimbalzare sull'acqua . . .*). In the comment at Post 8 Linda first responds to Alberto by continuing to play along with him; she asks Alberto if he has any problems, then she seems to positively evaluate Renzo's action of having bought the iPhone; Linda tells Renzo that he had a strong desire and he could not resist it (*ooohhh . . . Albe problemi!?!? Renz t capisco . . . avevi la scimmietta . . .*). The idiomatic expression "*avevi la scimmietta*" in the comment at Post 8 means "you could not resist it." Therefore, it is possible that Linda tells Renzo that he bought the phone because he could not resist it.

The action performed by Alberto in the comment at Post 9 orients to Linda's previous ironic question in the comment at Post 8. Alberto posts another "joke" where he tells Linda that he does not have any problem with her, but Renzo's new phone might have some, if he gives it to her (*io no . . . l'iphone di renzo si se lo da in mano a te . . .!*).

In the comment at Post 10, after publishing the playful negative evaluation "*spendaccione!*" (spendthrift), Angela tells Renzo that although he looks like a person who spends a lot of money, he has done well, because sometimes people should reward themselves (*spendaccione! ma fa bene coccolarsi a volte, no?*). The action at the beginning of the comment at Post 10 is a negative evaluation and it is followed by a comment that seems to mitigate it. Angela approves of Renzo's choice because sometimes one has to spoil oneself. After this mitigation Angela accomplishes another action in this comment thread. She publishes a non-initial telling; Angela tells Renzo about her own idea of buying a new phone which has at least a camera (*io* "invece" *mi sa che ormai devo proprio decidermi a cambiare cell e a prenderne uno che almeno abbi la fotocamera, che dici? :)*). This non-initial telling is closed by the tag question "*che dici?*" (what do you reckon?), which is likely to be directed to Renzo due to the second-person singular conjugation of the verb "*dire*" (to say).

However, the actions performed by Renzo and Friends in the comments that follow Angela's non-initial telling seem to ignore this contribution and continue to refer to the initial telling. In the comments at Posts 11 and 12 Linda and Alberto mock each other. In the comment at Post 11 Linda humorously tells Alberto that he is a dog (*CANE!!*), then in the comment at Post 12 Alberto continues to play along with the theme of dogs and tells Linda to calm down and stay in her place (*a cuccia!*) (sit).

The action performed by Renzo in the comment at Post 13 ignores Angela's non-initial telling and Linda and Alberto's jokes in the comments at Posts 10, 11, and 12 and it seems to be directed to Mauro's previous contribution in the comment at Post 6. Renzo tells Mauro that he wanted to wait, but he could not resist. Renzo closes the comment at Post 13 by telling Mauro that he might buy the upcoming model of iPhone, the iPhone 5, for Christmas, if he likes his new phone (*In effetti l'intento era quello di aspettare a prenderlo ma . . . non ho resistito . . . mi farò regalare il 5 per natale in caso!!*).

The actions performed by Piera, Fabiana, and Giulia in the comment at Posts 14, 15, and 16 also ignore Angela's non-initial telling and orient to Renzo's initial telling in the comment at Post 1. Piera tells Renzo that she thought that they had persuaded Salvo to buy Renzo an iPhone (*ma non avevamo convinto salvo a prenderlo??????*). Instead in the comment at Post 15 Fabiana comments on Renzo's choice of words in his telling at Post 1; she asks him to give her his new iPhone, if he decides to buy a second one (*il mio primo?? ma perchè ci sarà un secondo eo un terzo? io posso prendere il tuo rottamato poi*). Then, in the comment at Post 16, Giulia negatively evaluates Renzo and the initial telling in the comment at Post 1 by saying that he is a spendthrift (*mani bucate! ;P*).

It seems that after a series of comments in which Friends discuss Renzo's initial telling about the iPhone, Angela responds to this telling with a non-initial telling about her own future plan of buying a new phone. Although the non-initial telling published by Angela in the comment at Post 10 is closed by a tag question directed to Renzo, neither he nor the other Friends who participate in this comment thread respond to it. Thus, it seems that even when a non-initial teller performs a specific action, such as posting a tag question, to elicit responses to his or her non-initial telling, it is not always the case that this action generates any another action from either the initial teller or Friends who participate in the comment thread.

In general, therefore, it seems that FB comment threads can contain non-initial tellings, narratives which occur in comments that are not initial and appear to be occasioned by first-post tellings. This makes non-initial tellings similar to second stories in spoken conversation. Moreover, one of the functions of second stories is to show an understanding of previous stories. Specifically, a teller may utter a second story in order to demonstrate how he or she has interpreted the previous story (M. Goodwin, 1990; Jefferson, 1978, 1984; Liddicoat, 2011; Sacks, 1986, 1992). This is similar to what seems to happen in Extracts 6.1, 6.2, and 6.3 where Elisa, Marco, and Angela have performed three non-initial tellings to show their understanding of the initial tellings that open these interactions.

FB comment threads thus clearly contain non-initial tellings as well as first-post tellings. These non-initial tellings occur after a previous narrative, and show what the poster's understanding is of the first-post telling.

Non-initial tellings and *sequence organization*

While it may be hypothesized that non-initial tellings would be similar to first-post tellings, it turns out that this is not the case. As will be shown in this section, first-post tellings are frequent while non-initial tellings are rare; first-post tellings often trigger other actions which may result in extensive responses, while non-initial tellings generate minimal or no action and in fact they normally receive minimal or no responses from Friends. Therefore, the first-post telling clearly holds a special significance in FB interactions.

In Chapter 4 it was noted that almost all the comment threads in the corpus of this book begin with a telling—205 of the 213 comment threads were launched by tellings with only 8 comment threads having a first contribution which was not a telling. This contrasts sharply with non-initial tellings. Of the 205 comment threads which are opened by first-post tellings, only 6 are responded to with non-initial tellings.[1] Non-initial tellings are extremely rare in the corpus of this book. Not only are non-initial tellings rare, but they stimulate few actions from Friends. They in fact receive limited or no responses from Friends, in contrast to first-post tellings. The analysis of Extract 6.3 given above showed that the action performed by Angela in her non-initial telling did not stimulate any other action from Friends. In fact, it received no responses at all, being ignored by all participants, including the original poster, despite ending with the tag question "*che dici?*" which was directed back to him (wouldn't you say?).

A similar pattern of minimal response to non-initial tellings can be seen in analyzing another two of the remaining examples. For example, in Extract 6.4, a non-initial telling receives only one response from the original teller, while it seems to be ignored by other Friends.

Extract 6.4 Volleyball

1 Elisa: In Galles è più facile trovare il Sacro Graal che delle ginocchiere da pallavolo.
Elisa: In Wales it's easier to find the Holy Grail than volleyball knee pads.

A 5 persone piace questo
5 people like this

→ 2 Maria: consolati ieri ho girato per 2 negozi sportivi di londra [*sic*] e ho trovato solo cuffie da piscina in silicone (bleah!)
Maria: I'm with you yesterday I went to 2 shops in london and I only found swimming caps made of silicone (bleah!)

3 Elisa: nuuu, tirano i capelli un casino. usssh che fastidio!
Elisa: nuuu, they pull your hairs a lot. usssh so annoying!

4 Elisa: io "invece" ho girato almeno 15 negozie [*sic*] nel raggio di 200 metri (e non sto esagerando, sono numeri reali) a cardiff [*sic*]. Alla facciazza di mission impossible!
Elisa: instead I went to at least 15 shops in a 200 m range (and I'm not exaggerating these are correct numbers) in cardiff. Talking about mission impossible!

5 Eleana: quindi usi il sacro graal come ginocchiere da pallavolo?
Eleana: so are you using the holy grail as volleyball knee pads?

6 Auro: Quindi a che ti servono le ginocchiere nel Galles? Per scavare alla ricerca del sacro graal?
Auro: So what are you using the volleyball pads for in Wales? To look for the holy grail?

7 Elisa: le ginocchiere servono per problemi di acrobazie in uno spettacolo.
Elisa: I need the volleyball pads to perform a stunt during a show.

8 Auro: Prendi la gomma piuma di in cuscino oppure le protezioni per i rollerblade. Sennò adatti una conchiglia da rugby
Auro: you can use some cushion foam or the rollerblade pads. Otherwise, you can adapt a protective rugby shell

9 Elisa: ma non devono essere rigide! (1) sono [*sic*] scomode (2) fanno rumore quando cadi! . . . cmq [*sic*] alla fine le abbiamo trovate!
Elisa: but they don't have to be rigid! (1) they are uncomfortable (2) they make noise when you fall! . . . anyway, in the end we found them!

In the comment at Post 2 Maria performs her first action in this interaction; she responds to the telling about the volleyball pads in the comment at Post 1 with a non-initial telling about the swimming cap she was looking for in London. This action receives minimal response; in fact, only Elisa, the first-post teller, responds to this telling in her comment at Post 3 before continuing on with her own telling in the comment at Post 4.

Specifically, Elisa opens this interaction with an initial telling that is intended to be humorous. She tells Friends that in Wales it is easier to find the holy grail than some volleyball pads (*In Galles è più facile trovare il Sacro Graal che delle ginocchiere da pallavolo*). The facetious tone embedded in Elisa's initial telling seems to have been understood by Maria. In fact, in the comment at Post 2 she performs an action that shows her understanding of the telling in the comment at Post 1. Maria responds to Elisa with another telling about similar difficulties she had in finding a swimming cap in London. Maria's non-initial telling is about a coherent topic—the swimming cap she was looking for in London, having gone to two sports stores and only being able to find a silicone swimming cap (*consolati ieri ho girato per 2 negozi sportivi di londra e ho trovato solo cuffie da piscina in silicone (bleah!)*).

Although Maria's telling shows understanding and affiliation with Elisa's previous telling, and is in fact about a similar experience, this telling receives minimal response, with only Elisa's response in the comment at Post 3. After the contribution at Post 3 where Elisa tells Maria that silicone caps are annoying because hairs get caught in them (*nuuu, tirano i capelli un casino. usssh che fastidio!*), in the comment at Post 4 Elisa performs another action in this interaction. She returns to her initial telling by providing Friends with more details about her own telling. This action is achieved by using what seems to be a topic shifter (Schiffrin, 1987), "*invece*" (instead), which takes the attention back to Elisa's first-post telling (*io* "invece" *ho girato almeno 15 negozie nel raggio di 200 metri (e non sto esagerando, sono numeri reali) a cardiff. Alla facciazza di mission impossible!*). In the comment at Post 4 Elisa says that she was in Cardiff and she went into fifteen shops without finding any volleyball pads. The action performed by Eleana at Post 5 ignores Maria's non-initial telling and orients to Elisa's initial telling; she ironically asks Elisa, if she is considering using the holy grail as a volleyball pad (*quindi usi il sacro graal come ginocchiere da pallavolo?*).

The playful tone generated by the initial telling seems to have been picked up by Auro in the comment at Post 6, where he performs another action in this interaction and posts a comment that orients to Elisa's initial telling. Auro asks her if she needs the volleyball pads in order to dig for the holy grail (*Quindi a che ti servono le ginocchiere nel Galles? Per scavare alla ricerca del sacro graal?*). The action performed by Elisa in her response in the comment at Post 7 shows that she has interpreted Auro's ironic request in a serious way; she provides him with an explanation for her search for the volleyball pads saying that she needs them for an acrobatic stunt during a show (*le ginocchiere servono per problemi di acrobazie in uno spettacolo*).

Auro responds in the comment at Post 8, where after suggesting to Elisa possible solutions for her problem, he seems to continue with the playful framework introduced in the comments at Posts 5 and 6. Auro tells Elisa to use some cushion foam or rollerblade pads for her stunt; then he seems to mock Elisa by saying that if she is not able to find any foam or pads, she can adjust some rugby protective shells (*rendi la gomma piuma di in cuscino oppure le protezioni per i rollerblade. Sennò adatti una conchiglia da rugby*). In the comment at Post 9, after telling Auro that his options are not suitable, Elisa closes her telling by performing another action in this comment thread; she says to Friends that in the end they found the volleyball pads (*ma non devono essere rigide! 1) sono scomode 2) fanno rumore quando cadi! . . . cmq alla fine le abbiamo trovate!*).

In Extract 6.4 it can be seen that although the action performed in the non-initial telling shows affiliation with the first-post teller, as Maria has told Elisa that she had a similar experience, this does not seem to secure responses from Friends. In fact, after having commented on the non-initial telling, in the comment at Post 4 Elisa, the original teller, returns the conversation to her own telling.

The same relative lack of response to a non-initial telling also occurs in Extract 6.5 about the purse snatching Alberta witnessed while driving her car. This interaction has been discussed in Chapters 4 and 5 and it is reproduced here for convenience. Although the autobiographical telling is not completely clear, it seems that Alessia responds to it with a non-initial telling that receives only one response from the original teller.

Extract 6.5 The purse snatching

1 Alberta: Ma che bella giornata di merda . . . iniziata bene ma finita stramalissimo con tanto di scippo in diretta!
Alberta: What a crappy day . . . . It has started well but it ended terribly and included a live purse snatching

→ 2 Alessia: e delle mie 700 euro per riparare la macchina . . . ne vogliamo parlare!!!! ufff
Alessia: tell me about it!!! what about me and the 700 euros I had to pay to fix my car . . .!ufff

3 Alberta: Fidati! noi [*sic*] ci andiamo vicino . . .
Alberta: Trust me! I know what you mean . . .

4 Chiara: bhe finita stramalissimo . . . e della telefonata con me che mi dici?!? ho [*sic*] pure seguito lo scippo in diretta! =)
Chiara: ok so it ended terribly . . . and what about our phone conversation? I also witnessed the purse snatching live!=)

5 Alberta: No comment!!!!!!! Arrivo al corso e racconto lo scippo, e poi mi chiedono ma poi com'è finite [*sic*]? Niente mi hanno suonato e me ne sono andata, ma non ho detto che tu mi ha suggerito: SCAPPAAAAAA!
Alberta: No comment!!!!!!! I arrived at the class and I told people about the snatching and people asked me how it all ended? Nothing I said, someone beeped me and I had to drive on, but I didn't mention what you suggested to me: RUUUUN!

6 Lucia: ma Alberta che cavolo e [*sic*] successo?
Lucia: but Alberta what the hell happened?

The autobiographical telling in the comment at Post 1 is responded to by Alessia with a non-initial telling in the comment at Post 2. Although those tellings share similar topics, as they are about Alberta and Alessia's recent terrible experiences, the initial telling receives multiple responses from Friends, while the non-initial telling secures only one response from Alberta, the first-post teller.

At Post 1 Alberta tells Friends that she had a terrible day because she witnessed a purse snatching (*Ma che bella giornata di merda . . . iniziata bene ma finita stramalissimo con tanto di scippo in diretta!*). As already mentioned in previous chapters, this telling is responded to by Alessia's action in the comment at Post 2, where she publishes a non-initial telling about the problem she had with her car. Alessia tells Alberta that she spent seven hundred euros to fix her own car (*e delle mie 700 euro per riparare la macchina . . . ne vogliamo parlare!!!! ufff*). Although this telling seems to promote affiliation—Alessia shares a story about a problematic experience, this non-initial telling receives minimal response. Only

Alberta in the comment at Post 3 performs an action that orients to this telling; she comments on Alessia's previous telling by saying that their stories are similar (*Fidati! noi ci andiamo vicino . . .*), while other Friends seem to ignore it.

The action performed by Chiara in the comment at Post 4 ignores Alessia's telling in the comment at Post 2 and responds to Alberta's telling in the comment at Post 1. Chiara agrees with Alberta's negative evaluation about the purse snatching (*bhe finita stramalissimo*). Then, she asks Alberta to comment on the phone conversation they had when Alberta was witnessing the snatching (*e della telefonata con me che mi dici?!? Ho pure seguito lo scippo in diretta! =)*). This question is responded to in the comment at Post 5, where Alberta accomplishes another action in this comment thread and tells Chiara that she prefers not to comment on their phone conversation (*No comment!!!!!!!*). After responding to Chiara in the comment at Post 5, Alberta seems to continue with her own telling about the purse snatching by telling Friends what happened when she arrived at the course she was attending. Alberta told people about the purse snatching she witnessed while driving her car and they asked her to explain what happened after the snatching; she told them that she had to move her car because someone was beeping her (*Arrivo al corso e racconto lo scippo, e poi mi chiedono ma poi com'è finite? Niente mi hanno suonato e me ne sono andata, ma non ho detto che tu mi ha suggerito: SCAPPAAAAAA!*). This interaction ends with the action performed by Lucia in the comment at Post 6, where she requests Alberta to provide her with more information about the purse snatching (*ma Alberta che cavolo e successo?*).

In general, non-initial tellings seem less likely to secure responses from Friends than initial tellings. Furthermore, even when a response occurs, this is minimal and generally from the first-post teller. So, even if a Friend wants to show affiliation by publishing a non-initial telling which is topically coherent with the initial telling, this action generally receives minimal or no response from other Friends. Therefore, although non-initial tellings might show affiliation, what happens further on in a comment thread suggests that Friends are generally more likely to return to comment on the original telling, rather than to respond to the non-initial one. This is different from what normally happens in spoken conversation, where the number of responses received by a telling does not seem to be affected by its position in the interaction (Liddicoat, 2011; Sacks, 1992).

This chapter has dealt with five of the six examples of non-initial tellings in the corpus of this book, showing that non-initial tellings are rare in FB comment threads. A possible explanation for this is that although the action of posting a non-initial telling may be used by an FB user to show affiliation with an initial teller, it seems more likely that FB users introduce new tellings in new comment threads rather than post them in already existing threads. Indeed, it is possible that FB users are aware that the action of posting a non-initial telling secures few or no other actions from Friends.

The lack of responses might relate to a technical constraint of the system. In fact, while Friends can always see the first and the four or five most recent comments in a comment thread, they cannot automatically see any other comment published in a comment thread. Depending on how their system is set up, to see these other comments they have to click on a message such as *View 2 more comments*, where the precise message depends on the number of hidden comments (in this case two).

Whether the lack of responses to non-initial tellings is related only to this technical constraint, or to other social factors, it is nonetheless true that non-initial tellings receive few responses if any, compared with tellings in first comments. Thus, FB users seem to prefer to tell a new "story" in a new comment thread rather than to publish it in an existing interaction, presumably because in this way they are more likely to secure responses from Friends.

Conclusions

Having looked at first-post tellings in Chapters 4 and 5, this chapter has turned to non-initial tellings.

Non-initial tellings—that is, narratives that occur in comments other than the first comment in a comment thread—are found in the corpus of this book. They are used in a way similar to second stories in spoken conversation, showing that the person posting the telling has understood the first-post telling, and is signaling his or her affiliation with the poster of the first-post telling.

However, there is a big difference between first-post tellings and non-initial tellings. While the actions performed in first-post tellings often trigger multiple actions from Friends, non-initial tellings stimulate very few or no actions at all from them. They sometimes trigger one or two comments from the first-post teller, but, generally speaking, the actions performed by FB users in later comments normally ignore the non-initial telling, and orient back to the first telling. In fact, perhaps because of this strong focus on first-post tellings, non-initial tellings are very rare, with only six occurring in the corpus of this book. It would seem that if Friends have a story to tell, they prefer to post it in a new comment thread, perhaps because of the minimal response given to non-initial tellings.

The limited number of non-initial tellings in the data may relate to the way FB is framed. While a Friend can see all the comments that begin comment threads, this is not the case with contributions that follow them; when a comment thread consists of multiple contributions, only the first and the four or five most recent comments posted in the comment thread are automatically visible to Friends. It is possible that the minimal response received by non-initial tellings may depend on their position in comment threads. These tellings are not always visible to Friends, who therefore cannot respond to them.

The first comment in a comment thread thus clearly has a special status, both within the FB system itself, but more importantly within the social interaction underlying the organization of comment threads. This issue is explored further in the following chapter, which looks more generally at comments that follow a first-post telling, in terms of how they fit into the *sequence organization* of comment threads.

7

Responses to Tellings

Introduction

The previous three chapters have focused on tellings in FB comment threads. It has been demonstrated that the vast majority of FB comment threads are opened by tellings, while tellings other than first-post tellings are rare in this type of interactions.

However, FB comment threads may contain many contributions after an initial telling, as was seen in Chapter 3. This chapter turns to look at these contributions in more detail, focusing on the first comment made by each Friend in a comment thread opened by a telling. The following chapter moves to later comments, that is, contributions made by the person posting the original comment and Friends who have already posted an earlier comment to a comment thread. The way that these two types of comments are organized sequentially turns out to be quite different.

Friends' first comments

A new comment thread is opened by a first comment, from the FB user posting the opening comment.[1] Once that first comment has been posted, the comment thread is then visible on the FB Home of Friends of that FB user. From that point on, Friends may contribute to the comment thread. The first time that a Friend publishes a contribution to a comment thread will be discussed here as a first comment; if at a later point a Friend publishes again in the same comment thread, that will be referred to as a later comment. It will be argued here that there is an important difference in *sequence organization* between first comments and later comments, so they are discussed separately in this and the following chapter.

Friends' first comments respond to the first comment

As mentioned before in the previous section the first comment posted by a Friend in a comment thread which is opened by a telling almost always responds to the telling. Indeed, 337 out of the 369 first comments analyzed in this book consist of responses to initial tellings.

Moreover, first comments posted by Friends commonly orient to and show understanding of the first-post telling. This is similar to what happens in spoken conversation, where turns that follow tellings normally orient to and show understanding of these narratives (C. Goodwin, 1986; M. Goodwin, 1993; Jefferson, 1984; Liddicoat, 2011; Mandelbaum, 1989; Norrick, 1993, 1994; Pomerantz, 1984; Sacks, 1974, 1992; Terasaki, 2004). Stories and announcements are commonly responded to with second stories (Liddicoat, 2011; Sacks, 1992) and assessments (C. Goodwin, 1986; M. Goodwin, 1993; Jefferson, 1984; Mandelbaum, 1989; Pomerantz, 1984; Terasaki, 2004), jokes are generally responded to with laughter, assessments, other jokes, or topical talk (Norrick, 1993, 1994; Sacks, 1974). Thus, although FB comment threads and spoken conversation are two different exchange systems,[2] where the first is a speech and the second is a textual exchange system, tellings occurring in both these types of interactions are responded to in similar ways.

An example demonstrating how first comments posted by Friends generally orient to and show understanding of the telling they refer to can be seen in Extract 7.1, where the first comments published by Elia, Alessia, and Piera in this comment thread orient to and show understanding of the initial humorous telling in the comment at Post 1.

Extract 7.1 Lying in the sun

1 [Vanessa publishes a photo-telling which portrays herself and her colleagues lying in the sun during working hours]

A Roberto piace questo
Roberto likes this

→ 2 Elia: AH MA BRAVI è COSì CHE SI PRODUCE !!!
Elia: AH WELL DONE THIS is THE WAY YOU PRODUCE!!!

3 Vanessa: erano le 15.30 e approfittavamo del sole!!!
Vanessa: it was 3:30 P.M. and we were making the most of the sun!!!

→ 4 Alessia: ke [*sic*] belli ke [*sic*] siete!!!!
Alessia: what a spectacle you are!!!!

5 Vanessa: Eravamo tanti [*sic*] stanchi è stata una settimana dura!!!!
Vanessa: We were really tired, it's been a busy week!!!!

→ 6 Piera: ah però! devo [*sic*] cambiare ufficio... ho deciso
Piera: wow! I've got to move to your office... I've made up my mind

As already noted in Chapter 4, in the comment at Post 1 Vanessa launches this comment thread by accomplishing her first action in this interaction; she performs a telling. More precisely, she posts a selfie that shows herself and her colleagues lying in the sun during working hours. This telling is intended to be humorous, and in fact it seems that Vanessa is using the photo-telling in the comment at Post 1 to mock her Friends by "saying" that she is enjoying the sun while they are working.

The actions performed by Elia, Alessia, and Piera in the comments at Posts 2, 4, and 6 orient to Vanessa's initial telling. Although the first comments published by those Friends are different—where the comments at Posts 2 and 4 are positive evaluations, while the comment at Post 6 is an unlikely and humorous statement—they are all directed to the photo-telling in the comment at Post 1. Moreover, the actions accomplished by Elia, Alessia, and Piera in these comments show understanding of the facetious tone embedded in Vanessa's initial telling. Specifically, in the comment at Post 2 Elia publishes an ironic positive evaluation of the productivity of Vanessa and her colleagues (*AH MA BRAVI è COSì CHE SI PRODUCE !!!*), ironically saying that Vanessa and her colleagues are productive workers. The way the comment at Post 2 is written indicates its facetious tone; Elia uses capital letters as well as a series of exclamation marks to indicate that he is shouting this contribution.

The action performed by Vanessa in the comment at Post 3 shows that she has understood the humorous approach embedded in the comment at Post 2. She responds to this comment by providing a mocking justification for her own action in the comment at Post 1 saying that she and her colleagues were lying in the sun because it was 3:30 p.m. (*erano le 15.30 e approfittavamo del sole!!!*). The tone embedded in this justification shows the original intention of the telling in the comment at Post 1, which is to tease Friends who would be working during the normal working hours, unlike Vanessa and her colleagues.

In the comment at Post 4 Alessia performs an action in this comment thread: a positive humorous evaluation of the initial telling in the comment at Post 1. Alessia says that Vanessa and her colleagues look wonderful (*ke belli ke siete!!!!*). By ironically commenting on the physical appearance of Vanessa and her colleagues (*ke belli ke siete!!!!*), Alessia shows that she has understood the humorous intention embedded in the comment at Post 1. Once again, the action accomplished by Vanessa in the comment at Post 5 shows that she has interpreted the comment at Post 4 in a facetious way. Vanessa publishes another mocking justification for the comment at Post 1, ironically saying that she and her colleagues were tired after a long week at work (*Eravamo tanti stanchi è stata una settimana dura!!!!*).

Interestingly, the action performed by Alessia in the comment at Post 4 ignores the actions performed by Elia and Vanessa in the contributions at Posts 2 and 3, while it explicitly responds to the initial telling in the comment at Post 1. Alessia comments neither on the humorous positive evaluation in the comment at Post 2 nor on the mocking justification in the comment at Post 3; instead she clearly refers back to the first-post telling. In the comment at Post 6 Piera performs her first action in this comment thread. She posts another response to the comment at Post 1 and ignores the actions accomplished by Friends in previous contributions. Specifically, the comment at Post 6 is an unlikely statement, oriented to the initial telling and referring to an event that is not likely to occur. Piera ironically tells Vanessa that after seeing her photo, she is considering moving office (*ah però! devo cambiare ufficio . . . ho deciso*). In other words, Piera expresses in a humorous way that she is envious because Vanessa is lying in the sun, while she is working.

Extract 7.1 bears out the hypothesis that although Friends may respond to a first-post telling in different ways, the first action they accomplish in a comment thread regularly orients to and shows understanding of the initial telling. The comments at Posts 2 and 4 are two positive evaluations, while the comment at Post 6 is an unlikely statement; however, all the actions performed in these contributions clearly orient to and show understanding of the first-post telling. Moreover, the actions performed by Elia, Alessia, and Piera in their first comments are similar to the actions performed by conversationalists in turns that commonly follow jokes told in spoken conversation. Previous research has pointed out that recipients of a joke commonly respond to it with assessments, laughter, other jokes, and topical talk (Norrick, 1993, 1994; Sacks, 1974, 1992). Conversationalists use those types of responses to show how they have interpreted the joke. Therefore, it seems that despite the system in which an interaction occurs, people perform similar actions after humorous tellings. They in fact appear to use positive evaluations and unlikely statements to respond to tellings that are intended to be humorous.

First comments that orient to and show understanding of the initial telling are also present in Extract 7.2. In this comment thread Mauro's initial humorous telling is responded to by five Friends. Each Friend posts a first comment that clearly orients to and shows understanding of the comment at Post 1, apparently ignoring the actions that other Friends have done in previous comments.

Extract 7.2 Walruses

1 Mauro: Applausi
[Mauro publishes a photo of two walruses] Cosa fanno due trichechi davanti a un panificio? Aspettano le focacce.
Mauro: Applause
There are two walruses in front of a bakery. What are they doing there? They are waiting for the ugly seals.

A 5 persone piace questo
5 people like this

→ 2 Elisa: [Elisa publishes a hyperlink containing a video of people who are laughing]

→ 3 Sara: non l ho [*sic*] capitaaaaaaaa
Sara: I don't get iiiiiiit

→ 4 Rosa: AHAHAHAHAHAH ANCHE TUUUUUUUUUUUUUUUUUUUUUUU
Rosa: AHAHAHAHAHAH YOU TOOOOOOOOOOOOOOOOOO

→ 5 Raffaele: in pratica vanno a puttane!
Raffaele: they're actually looking for prostitutes!

→ 6 Roberto: scrivila sulla porta d'ingresso del panificio, sai dopo come attiri i clienti? :D
Roberto: write it on the front door of your bakery, imagine how many clients you'll attract? :D

This comment thread is launched by Mauro's action in the comment at Post 1, where he posts a riddle which is based on a word play on the term "*focacce*." The noun "*focacce*" has two different meanings in Italian; it could potentially mean ugly seals as well as focaccia bread. Specifically, in the comment at Post 1 Mauro asks for applause, publishes a photo of two walruses, and presents a riddle where he asks what two walruses are doing in front of a bakery, and then he responds to it with the punch line, saying that they are waiting for some "*focaccia*." This term is the result of the combination of the noun "*foca*" (seal) and the suffix "*acce*" (ugly), thus meaning ugly seals. In other words, in this comment Mauro is relying on his Friends to interpret the term "*focacce*" as both bread (hence the bakery) and ugly seals (hence the walruses) (*Cosa fanno due trichechi davanti a un panificio?Aspettano le focacce*). This riddle is responded to by the actions performed by Elisa, Sara, Rosa, Raffaele, and

Roberto in the comments at Posts 2, 3, 4, 5, and 6. Although those comments contain different first comments, the actions they perform all clearly orient to the original telling.

In the comment at Post 2 Elisa accomplishes her first action in this comment thread. She posts a contribution that explicitly orients to and shows understanding of Mauro's initial telling. This comment contains a hyperlink which shows a video of people who are laughing. In the comment at Post 3 Sara performs another action in this interaction; she responds to the comment at Post 1 by expressing that she does not understand Mauro's riddle (*non l ho capitaaaaaaaa*). This comment could be understood as being intended as the *first pair part* of a *repair sequence*; therefore, it clearly orients to and shows a problem in understanding the comment at Post 1. However, even if the action performed in this comment projects a response, none of the Friends who participate in this comment thread respond to it. In fact, the comments that follow the contribution at Post 3 show that Friends have ignored Sara's clarification request, while they have responded to Mauro's initial telling in the comment at Post 1. So, although the comments at Posts 2 and 3 contain different types of first comments, the actions performed in these contributions explicitly orient to and show understanding (or lack of understanding) of the comment at Post 1.

It is the same for the comments at Posts 4, 5, and 6. After an initial representation of laughter which appears to respond to the comment at Post 1, in the comment at Post 4 Rosa publishes a shouted contribution "you too" that is unclear in terms of how it should be interpreted (*ANCHE TUUUUUUUUUUUUUUUUUUUUUU*). However, the action accomplished by the initial laughter clearly shows its orientation to the comment at Post 1. In the comment at Post 5 Raffaele performs another action in this interaction; he publishes a *second pair part* which responds to the "question" component of the riddle published by Mauro in the comment at Post 1, where he asked what two walruses are doing in front of a bakery (*Cosa fanno due trichechi davanti a un panificio?*). Raffaele responds to this "question" by saying that walruses are actually looking for prostitutes (*in pratica vanno a puttane!*).

The fact that the action performed in the comment at Post 5 is a response to the "question" in the comment at Post 1 indicates that this contribution explicitly refers to and shows understanding of this comment, while it clearly ignores the actions performed by Friends in previous contributions posted in this interaction. It is the same for the comment at Post 6, where Roberto publishes a first comment that positively, although perhaps ironically, evaluates Mauro's initial riddle. Roberto suggests to Mauro that he should write this joke on the front door of his own bakery in order to verify whether it will attract more clients (*scrivila sulla porta d'ingresso del panificio, sai dopo come attiri i clienti? :D*).

As seen with the comments in Extract 7.1, the comments in Extract 7.2 have shown that the first comment posted by a Friend in a comment thread commonly responds to the original telling, even when other comments have already been published in the comment thread. This is because the first action performed by a Friend in a comment thread normally orients to the telling that opens the interaction, and it apparently ignores all the other actions performed by Friends in the comment thread.

This is also evident in Extract 7.3 where the first comments published by Friends in this comment thread orient to and show understanding of the opening telling.

Extract 7.3 Saturday night

1 Claudio: I'm sorry, but Saturday night in London is not for me O_o[3]

A 3 persone piace questo
3 people like this

→ 2 Arturo: It's the same for me and includes friday [*sic*] too :(

→ 3 Silvio: Someone is getting old . . .!!!!!lol

→ 4 Silvia: if you were here . . . sagra del marone di castel del rio [*sic*]. . . :))

→ 5 Robert: Don't worry Claudio, you find out these things as you get old ;p

6 Claudio: Lol maybe u [*sic*] guys r [*sic*] right :p But the important thing is that ppl [*sic*] r [*sic*] still asking for my ID :p P.S. Oh Silvy, such an envy!!!!

7 Martin: Fake ID

This comment thread is opened by the initial telling in the comment at Post 1, where Claudio tells Friends about how he feels about going out on Saturday nights in London. This telling receives four responses from Arturo, Silvio, Silvia, and Robert in the comments at Posts 2, 3, 4, and 5, which all orient to and show understanding of the first-post telling. However, in the comment at Post 7 Martin publishes a first comment which does not orient to the initial telling. In this comment, Martin responds to the comment at Post 6, which is the most recent contribution in this comment thread. Thus, although the majority of the first comments posted by Friends in this comment thread orient to the contribution at Post 1, the comment at Post 7 does not.

In the comment at Post 1 Claudio performs his first action in this interaction; a telling where he says to Friends that he does not like to go out on Saturday nights in London (*I'm sorry, but Saturday night in London is not for me O_o*).

This telling is responded to by Arturo in the comment at Post 2, where he shows affiliation with Claudio by indicating that he likes neither Saturday nights nor Friday nights in London (*It's the same for me and includes friday too :(*). The actions performed by Silvio and Silvia in the comments at Posts 3 and 4 orient to Claudio's initial telling. These comments show how Silvio and Silvia have interpreted the contribution at Post 1. Specifically, the action performed by Silvio in the comment at Post 3, is a humorous negative evaluation of Claudio's initial telling; Silvio says that Claudio is getting old (*Someone is getting old . . .!!!!!lol*). In the comment at Post 4, on the other hand, Silvia says to Claudio that in Castel del Rio, an Italian town, he could be attending the chestnut festival which is currently on (*if you were here. . . sagra del marone di castel del rio . . . :)))*). It seems that Silvia is mocking Claudio; perhaps she knows that Claudio loves chestnuts, but because he is in London, he cannot go to the chestnut festival. Alternatively, Silvia may simply be teasing Claudio by suggesting that a rural festival is clearly more in his line of interests than London's nightlife.

In the comment at Post 5 Robert performs his first action in this comment thread; a response to the comment at Post 1. In this comment he shows understanding of both the initial telling and the comments that have been posted by Friends in this interaction. Robert picks up the theme of age introduced by Silvio's ironic negative evaluation in the comment at Post 3 and humorously confronts Claudio by telling him that "wisdom" comes with age (*Don't worry Claudio, you find out these things as you get old ;p*).

The actions performed by Claudio in the comment at Post 6 seem to orient to all the actions performed by Friends in previous contributions, specifically those in the comments at Posts 3 and 4. In fact, after an initial representation of laughter, Claudio responds to Silvio's comment on his age at Post 3 by jokingly claiming that security guards at clubs still ask him for an identification card, which ironically suggests that Claudio looks younger (*Lol maybe u guys r right :p But the important thing is that ppl r still asking for my ID*). Then, after a smiling emoticon, Claudio performs another action in this comment when he responds to Silvia's previous comment at Post 4 about the chestnut festival by ironically telling her that he is envious (*:p P.S. Oh Silvy, such an envy!!!!*).

As mentioned above, Martin performs his first action in this comment thread in the comment at Post 7. This action does not orient to the comment at Post 1; Martin explicitly responds to the comment at Post 6, where Claudio has told Silvio that security is still asking him to provide his identification card for entering clubs. In his response Martin suggests that Claudio use a fake ID card in order to enter clubs (*Fake ID*). The comment at Post 7 shows that the first comment posted by a Friend in a comment thread does not always respond to the initial telling. This is because the first action performed by a Friend in a comment thread does not always orient to the action performed in the initial telling, but it can also orient to the most recent action performed in a comment thread (as it will be clearly discussed in the following section).

In general, therefore, it has been demonstrated that the first comment published by a Friend in a comment thread generally orients to and shows understanding of the initial telling. Moreover, the actions performed by Friends in the first comments that come after an initial telling are similar to the actions performed by conversationalists after spoken tellings; they in fact consist of evaluations, representations of laughter, second tellings, and unlikely statements. In addition, these comments show affiliation with the original poster. Therefore, it is likely that Friends have adapted the way they respond to humorous tellings in spoken conversations to FB comment threads. They in fact perform similar actions in the contributions that follow tellings occurring in these two types of interactions.

The examples so far have been relatively short, with most contributions being first comments. A lengthier example, a short version of which has already been discussed in Chapter 3, shows exactly the same phenomenon, however.

Extract 7.4 Music discussion-Bancale

1 [Mauro publishes a hyperlink which contains a video of one of the songs of Bancale] 10:56 a.m.

A 3 persone piace questo
3 people like this

2 Mauro: eccolo, questo è il nuovo Guru—Il Neubauten Italiano [*sic*] che sembra TufKad (e molti altri—meno che un cantante diciamo . . .) Alessia, Zaira, Claudia, Chiara, Bono, Cinzia 10:56
Mauro: here he is, the new Guru—The Italian Neubauten who looks like TufKad [names of two singers] *(and many others—apart from a singer shall we say . . .) Alessia, Zaira, Claudia, Chiara, Bono, Cinzia* *10:56 a.m.*

3 Dario: sopra tutto [*sic*] . . . la cariola [*sic*]! 11:15
Dario: especially . . . the wheelbarrow! *11:15 a.m.*

4 Gianni: E MI CHIEDI CHE COS'E' IL MIO VUOTO!?!?!? 19:41
Gianni: AND YOU ASK ME WHAT IS MY EMPTINESS!?!?!? *7:41 p.m.*

5 Alessia:—oddio, ma è il numero uno O_ò 20:25
Alessia:—oh my god, but he is the best O_ò *8:25 p.m.*

6 Claudia: Mi piace! Vorrei che mi parlasse di notte, seduto per terra accanto al mio letto.
Io lo so da che libro vengo. 22:00
Claudia: I like him!
I wish he would talk to to me at night, sitting on the floor close to my bed.
I know from which book I come from. *10 p.m.*

7 Mauro: io porto Torce 22:00
Mauro: I'll bring Torce [the term *Torce* could refer to the Human Torch, one of the characters of the comic book Fantastic Four] *10 p.m.*

8 Cinzia: tenerezza quando salutava con la manina, io cmq [*sic*] voglio dare loro una seconda chance. 3:13
Cinzia: how sweet when he waved goodbye with his little hand, in any case I want to give them a second chance. *3:13 a.m.*

→ 9 Sara: io no 3:13
Sara: I don't *3:13 a.m.*

10 Cinzia: L'idea iniziale è quella di scrivere canzoni in cui il blues delle origini incontri le rispettive influenze dei tre componenti del gruppo per raccontare sia nei testi che nelle atmospfere [*sic*] dei brani la provincia bergamasca come luogo geografico, sociale ed esistenziale. 3:16
Cinzia: The initial idea was to write songs in which the original blues was mixed with the respective influences of the three members of the band in order to be able to tell of the province of Bergamo as a geographical, social and existential place in both the texts and the atmospheres of the songs. *3:16 a.m.*

11 Cinzia: = non venite mai a bergamo [*sic*] 3:16
Cinzia: = don't ever come to bergamo *3:16 a.m.*

12 Mauro: Poeta e Maniaco, Ragioniere e Muratore. Credo inizi ed essere perfetto. 3:18
Mauro: Poet and Maniac, Accountant and Bricklayer. I think that it/he/they [either the situation, the singer, or more members of the band] *is/are starting to be perfect.* *3:18 a.m.*

13 Rosanna: dai che sti [*sic*] qua sono dei frantuma-cojones! 5:31
Rosanna: please these people are a pain in the arse! *5:31 a.m.*

14 Mauro: questo di sicuro . . . anche a colpi di mazza! ☺ 5:57
Mauro: absolutely . . . a huge pain in the arse! [original play on words on the term *"rompere"* (to break) in the comment at Post 13 which is not translatable]*!* ☺ *5:57 a.m.*

15 Rosanna: e a colpi di carriola! 6:25
Rosanna: a mega pain in the arse [another comment that refers to the play on words started in the comment at Post 13]*!* *6:25 a.m.*

16 Mauro: e di cazzuola! 10:33
Mauro: a super mega pain in the arse [another comment that refers to the play on words in the comments at Posts 13, 14, and 15]*!* *10:33 a.m.*

17 Veronica: La R moscia non l'avevo notata! 11:07
Veronica: I hadn't previously noticed his French R! *11:07 a.m.*

18 Mauro: le tettine si però . . . 5 ore fa
Mauro: but you noticed the tits . . . *5 hours ago*

As noted in Chapter 3, Extract 7.4 is launched by the action performed by Mauro in the comment at Post 1 where he posts an initial hyperlink-telling. Seven Friends publish a first comment which responds directly to this telling, in the contributions at Posts 3, 4, 5, 6, 8, 13, and 17.[4]

After publishing the hyperlink-telling in the comment at Post 1,[5] containing one of the songs of Bancale, an Italian band, in the comment at Post 2 Mauro ironically evaluates the singer of this band. Although the action performed in the comment at Post 2 is not completely clear, Mauro seems to mock the lead singer of Bancale. He makes a comparison by ironically suggesting to Friends that the singer of this band is the new guru, the Italian Neubauten, who looks like Tufkad (where Neubauten and Tufkad are the names of a band and a singer respectively) and many other singers, but in the end Mauro humorously says that apart from this he does not consider the lead singer of Bancale to be a proper singer (*eccolo, questo è il nuovo Guru—Il Neubauten Italiano che sembra TufKad (e molti altri—meno che un cantante diciamo . . .)*). After the comment on the singer of Bancale, in the final unit of the comment at Post 2, Mauro performs another action in this interaction: he selects the intended recipients of his telling by explicitly naming them (*Alessia, Zaira, Claudia, Chiara, Bono, Cinzia*).

The actions accomplished by Dario, Gianni, Alessia, Claudia, Cinzia, Rosanna, and Veronica in their first comments in the contributions at Posts 3, 4, 5, 6, 8, 13, and 17 respond to Mauro's initial telling. Specifically, in the comment at Post 3, Dario, who has not been included among the recipients selected by Mauro in the comment at Post 2, shows an understanding of the humorous tone embedded in the comment at Post 1 when he posts a comment that refers to the wheelbarrow contained in the video published in this contribution (*sopra tutto . . . la cariola!*). The action performed by Gianni in the comment at Post 4, another Friend who is not one of the recipients selected in the comment at Post 2, orients to Mauro's initial telling and apparently ignores Dario's previous contribution in the comment at Post 3. After watching the video in the comment at Post 1, Gianni rhetorically asks Mauro why he has asked him to explain what is his emptiness

(*E MI CHIEDI CHE COS'E' IL MIO VUOTO!?!?!?*). The way the comment at Post 4 is written, using capital letters, indicates that Gianni is "shouting" this contribution. Despite the shouting, the intention of the action performed in this comment is unclear, and in fact Gianni is perhaps referring to a previous conversation he had with Mauro.

In the comment at Post 5 Alessia, one of the recipients selected by Mauro in the comment at Post 2, ignores the contributions published by other Friends and performs her first action in this comment thread. She responds to the first-post telling with a comment that is intended to be humorous; Alessia tells Friends that the lead singer of Bancale is the best (*—oddio, ma è il numero uno O_ò*), disagreeing with Mauro who in the comment at Post 2 says that he does not consider the singer of Bancale to be a proper singer (*meno che un cantante diciamo . . .*).

In the comment at Post 6, Claudia, another recipient identified by Mauro in the comment at Post 2, participates in the playful framework introduced by Mauro, Dario, and Alessia in the comments at Posts 2, 3, and 5. After saying that she likes the video at Post 1 (*Mi piace!*), Claudia publishes an unlikely statement that she would like to have the singer of Bancale sitting on the ground close to her bed, talking to her at night time (*Vorrei che mi parlasse di notte, seduto per terra accanto al mio letto*). The comment at Post 6 is closed by an action which is unclear, with Claudia claiming that she knows the book from which she comes (*Io lo so da che libro vengo*). This statement apparently refers to a specific line of the song included in the video at Post 1. Although the action performed in the final unit of the comment at Post 6 is unclear, the actions accomplished in the first unit of this comment explicitly orient to the telling at Post 1. Moreover, the action performed by Mauro in the comment at Post 7 shows that he has understood the intention of the comment at Post 6; in this contribution he responds to Claudia by telling her that he will bring "*Torce*" (*io porto Torce*). This comment is not completely clear, but it is possible that Mauro is commenting on the hypothetical scene described by Claudia in the comment at Post 6, with Mauro suggesting that he will bring a torch to light Claudia while she is on her bed with the singer of Bancale talking to her. "*Torce*" could be the plural form of the noun "*torcia*," but with the capitalization, it is equivocal; it could refer to the name of another band or to the Human Torch,[6] one of the characters of the comic book *Fantastic Four*.

In the comment at Post 8, Cinzia, another of the recipients selected by Mauro in his comment at Post 2, responds to Mauro's telling while clearly ignoring the previous contributions posted by other Friends in the comments at Posts 3, 4, 5, 6, and 7. Cinzia says that the scene in the video at Post 1 where the main character says goodbye by shaking his hand inspires tenderness (*tenerezza quando salutava con la manina*). Then, Cinzia ends the comment at Post 8 by telling Friends that she wants to give Bancale a second chance (*io cmq voglio dare loro una seconda chance*).

Another response to the first-post telling at Post 1 which explicitly ignores the actions performed by Friends in previous contributions is posted by Rosanna in the comment at Post 13, where she comments on the original telling in the comment at Post 1 by publishing an ironic negative evaluation of Bancale. Rosanna claims that the band is boring. She uses the expletive "*frantuma-cojones*" (pain in the arse) followed by an exclamation mark in order to express her facetious negative evaluation of Bancale (*dai che sti qua sono dei frantuma-cojones!*). Finally, in the comment at post 17, Veronica performs her first action in this comment thread, which once again orients to the comment at Post 1. She posts another response to Mauro's initial hyperlink-telling; Veronica says that she watched the video several times before noticing the French "r" of the lead singer (*La R moscia non l'avevo notata!*). Therefore, the actions performed by Dario, Gianni, Alessia, Claudia, Cinzia, Rosanna, and Veronica in the comments at Posts 3, 4, 5, 6, 8, 13, and 17 are all responses to Mauro's initial telling.

It is interesting that the first contribution published by a Friend in a comment thread often responds to the original telling even though it may occur several comments after it, because this contrasts with what regularly happens in spoken conversation. In spoken conversation, the *conditional relevance property* establishes that the *second pair part* of an *adjacency pair* sequence has to occur immediately after the *first pair part* that precedes it. This is because the actions performed in the *first* and *second pair part* of an *adjacency pair sequence* are tied together and make sense only when they occur one after the other. In other words, the action accomplished in the *first pair part* of an *adjacency pair sequence* projects the action that will be performed in the *second pair part* of this sequence. Moreover, these two actions make sense only when interpreted together. Even when other turns at talk do occur between a *first* and a *second pair part*, they are limited in number and perform interactional work which is relevant to the *second pair part* that completes the sequence (Liddicoat, 2011; Schegloff, 1972, 2007).

However, the comments at Posts 13 and 17 in Extract 7.4 do not follow this pattern. They explicitly respond to the first-post telling even though they occur twelve and sixteen comments after it. The action performed by Rosanna in the comment at Post 13 clearly orients to the telling in the comment at Post 1 (*dai che sti qua sono dei frantuma-cojones!*); she says that Bancale is a pain in the arse.

This is similar to what Veronica does in the comment at Post 17, where she refers to the comment at Post 1 when she comments on the French pronunciation of the letter "r" by the lead singer of Bancale (*La R moscia non l'avevo notata!*). Thus, although the comments at Posts 13 and 17 are not adjacently positioned after the first-post telling, they are responding to it. This is clear from the actions performed by Friends in these contributions; Rosanna in the comment at Post 13 evaluates the band Bancale, and Veronica in the contribution at Post 17 publishes a comment on the lead singer of this band.

The fact that first comments may respond to an initial telling even when they occur several contributions after it may depend on the written nature of comments posted in FB comment threads. This nature allows Friends a longer space to respond to a contribution in a comment thread, like "split" (Tudini, 2010) or, as Herring (1999) called them, "disrupted" *adjacency pairs*. These comments, which normally occur in online chats, are "separated in linear order from a previous message [that they are] responding to" (Herring, 1999), but they do not create any interactional problem to participants in an interaction.

The phenomenon of first comments which respond to first-post tellings although they occur several contributions after them may also depend on similar constraints that characterize the allocation of turns at talk and the positioning of comments in spoken conversation and FB comment threads. In fact, similar to spoken interaction where conversationalists do not have control over the positioning of their turns in a conversation, and they generally compete for the floor, Friends do not have control over the positioning of their first comments in a comment thread. In other words, when a Friend publishes a first comment in an already existing comment thread, this is automatically positioned after the most recent comment published in the comment thread. Therefore, even if Rosanna and Veronica wanted to publish the contributions at Posts 13 and 17 immediately after the comment at Post 1, they could not. This is because of the system, which, as already noted in Chapter 2, does not allow Friends to have control over the positioning of first comments in comment threads.

Thus, even though there is the *Comment* button, which is positioned directly after the first comment in a comment thread, when a Friend clicks on it and posts his or her first comment in a comment thread, this contribution is published after the most recent comment in the comment thread. In other words, even though Rosanna and Veronica may have read the comment at Post 1 and clicked on the *Comment* button positioned immediately after it, possibly not even reading other comments, their first comments were not positioned immediately after the comment at Post 1 when published. As will be discussed in the final section of this chapter, this is not the case for first comments that respond to contributions that are not the first comments in FB comment threads.

Therefore, Extract 7.4 has demonstrated that the *conditional relevance property* that characterizes the *sequence organization* of turns at talk in spoken conversation does not apply to first comments posted in FB comment threads. The *conditional relevance property* refers to the requirement that responses must be relevant to an immediately prior turn (Liddicoat, 2011; Schegloff, 1972, 2007), and its absence in FB may depend on the different ways spoken conversation and FB comment threads are organized. In fact, while the *turn-taking system* organizes turns at talk in spoken conversation, this system does not affect the *sequence organization* of first comments in FB comment threads.

In addition, what is interesting about first-post tellings in FB comment threads is that they generally receive multiple responses from Friends with no extra actions performed by the FB user posting the original comment to establish who may perform the next action in a comment thread. This is once again different from what regularly happens in spoken conversation. There are cases in spoken conversation where multiple *second pair parts* may follow a single *first pair part* without the initial speaker being required to perform any action to establish who has the floor; however, these are limited and generally depend on highly restricted contexts. For example, in both greeting and "howareyou" sequences occurring in multiparty conversations (Schegloff, 2007) or in teacher's talk (Liddicoat, 2011), several answers may follow one after the other without the initial speaker performing a specific action to allocate the floor.

However, even though in spoken conversation there are a few cases where a string of *second pair parts* containing several actions may follow a single *first pair part* without requiring the initial speaker to perform any other action, this is not what regularly happens in everyday talk. What commonly happens in conversations that involve multiple participants, such as in formal meetings occurring in institutional settings, is that the speaker (e.g., the chair of the meeting) performs an action, that is, he or she allocates the floor (Larrue and Trognon, 1993; Mondada, 2012, 2013b). Hence, in cases of multiple responses to a single prompt, the chair performs a specific action to establish who has the right to produce the next action in the interaction.

Instead in FB comment threads opened by a first-post telling, generally one response follows another, without the user posting the original comment performing any other action to establish who has the right to post the next contribution in a comment thread—as has been seen in Extract 7.4—where the original telling has received seven responses from Friends without the initial poster accomplishing any additional action to secure them.

The analysis of the extracts in this section has found that FB comment threads have a different organization from spoken conversation. Following a first-post telling, it is commonly the case that the first comment made by a Friend responds to the original telling. This is the case regardless of whether the first comment occurs immediately following the first comment (i.e., as the comment at Post 2), or is separated from it by other comments. While the actions performed in the responses themselves are similar to the actions performed in the turns that come after tellings in spoken conversation—evaluations, laughter, second tellings, and unlikely statements as jokes, for example—it seems that the property of conditional relevance does not necessarily apply to first comments in FB comment threads. Reasons for this will be explored later on in this chapter.

Friends' first comment responds to the most recent comment

While it has been argued in the previous section that the first comment from a Friend normally responds to the original telling, two responses have already been seen which do not fit this pattern. First comments commonly respond to the first comment of a comment thread, but they may also respond to the most recently published comment. These types of first comments from Friends are rare in my data; indeed, only 32 out of the 369 first comments analyzed for this book were not responses to initial tellings.

In Extract 7.3, it was shown that four of the first comments from Friends responded directly back to Claudio's first comment. The actions performed by Friends in these contributions oriented to the action performed by Claudio in the telling in the comment at Post 1. However, in the comment at Post 6, Claudio (the original poster) posted another comment, and following that, Martin gave his first contribution to this comment thread, the comment at Post 7 (*Fake ID*). The action performed by Martin in this comment oriented to the action accomplished by Claudio in the comment at Post 6, where he discussed being asked for ID. Similarly, it was argued that in Extract 7.4, seven Friends gave first comments that responded to the comment at Post 1. However, in the comment at Post 9, Sara posted a first comment (*io no*) that contained an action which clearly oriented to the immediately preceding comment—the comment at Post 8, where Cinzia suggested that she would like to give the band a second chance, and Sara said she would not.

Other examples of first comments which respond to the most recent comments rather than the first contribution of a comment thread can be seen in Extract 7.5, where Mauro's initial hyperlink-telling in the comment at Post 1 is responded to by a Friend, who publishes a first comment which responds to the initial telling, while three other Friends post a first comment that clearly responds to the most recent comment in the comment thread.

Extract 7.5 Music discussion-The Smashing Pumpkins[7]

1 Mauro: Zero Compromessi
[Mauro publishes a hyperlink containing a video of the band The Smashing Pumpkins] 21 ore fa
Mauro: Zero Compromises *21 hours ago*

A 3 persone piace questo
3 people like this

2 Mauro: o quasi. 21 ore fa
Mauro: or almost. *21 hours ago*

3 Claudio: piaciuto? A me no . . . 21 ore fa
Claudio: did you like it? I didn't . . . *21 hours ago*

4 Auro: piaciuto :)? 21 ore fa
Auro: liked it :)? *21 hours ago*

→ 5 Petra: Mauro non deludermi 21 ore fa
Petra: Mauro please don't disappoint me *21 hours ago*

[. . .]

11 Petra: allora è un altro discorso e posso capire se ti è piaciuto . . . (sospettavo di una tua teoria mauriana).ma [*sic*] come direbbe qualcuno,"chi vuole andare in gita,non [*sic*] sa non sa non sa!" (il mio billy [*sic*] resta il mio billy [*sic*],solo [*sic*] nella mia testa,ora [*sic*] su quel palco c'è un fuori di testa che cerca ancora di "vendere musica") 21 ore fa
Petra: in this case it's a different story and I can understand why you liked it . . . (I suspected a maurian theory).but as someone would say, "who ever wants to go on tour, doesn't know doesn't know doesn't know!" (my billy remains my billy,only in my head, on that stage right now there's a fool who's still trying to "sell music") *21 hours ago*

→ 12 Roberta: e il fatto che non gliene frena nulla di compiacere gli altri lo rende un vero artista . . . 21 ore fa
Roberta: and it's the fact that he couldn't care less about gratifying others that makes him a real artist . . . *21 hours ago*

13 Petra: si ma roberta [*sic*] fare musica di merda al giorno d'oggi solo per andare ancora in giro in tour a suonare zero ai pochi fan accaniti e nostalgici che veramente ci stanno sotto è un offesa [*sic*] nel profono [*sic*] anche a quello [*sic*] che fu l'era dei GRANDi 1 [possibly the name of one of the songs of The Smashing Pumpkins or a typo] 21 ore fa
Petra: ok roberta but to make crappy music nowadays just because you want to go on tour to play nothing for a few nostalgic, obstinate fans is a deep offence to what used to be the era of the GREAT ONES 1 *21 hours ago*

[. . .]

25 Mauro: Claudia non mi dire che ti sei persa il finale . . . 11 ore fa
Mauro: Claudia don't tell me that you've missed the final song . . .
11 hours ago

→ 26 Claudia: c'eravamo, dietro. poi [*sic*] la nebbia. 9 ore fa
Claudia: we were there, at the back. and then the fog. *9 hours ago*

Extract 7.5 is opened by the telling in the comment at Post 1 where Mauro performs his first action in this comment thread by publishing a hyperlink containing a song of the American band The Smashing Pumpkins. In the contribution at Post 3 Claudio publishes a first comment that contains an action which orients to the first-post telling. On the other hand, the actions performed by Petra, Roberta, and Claudia in the comments at Posts 5, 12, and 26 explicitly orient to the most recent comments in this comment thread: the comments at Posts 4, 11, and 25, respectively.

After introducing and then posting the hyperlink-telling in the comment at Post 1, in the comment at Post 2 Mauro performs another action in this comment thread when he seems to play with the title of the song contained in the video at Post 1. Mauro says that this song has no compromises or almost none (Comment at Post 1: *Zero Compromessi.* Comment at Post 2: *o quasi*). In the comment at Post 3 Claudio publishes a first comment which apparently responds to the initial telling in the comments at Posts 1 and 2. The action performed by Claudio in this contribution shows that he has understood Mauro's comment at Post 2; he asks Mauro if he liked "it" (*piaciuto? A me no . . .*). Although the referent of the question in the comment at Post 3 is unclear, the following comments show that Claudio is alluding to a concert by The Smashing Pumpkins that he, Mauro, and other Friends have recently attended and that Claudio did not like.

After the comment at Post 4, where Auro repeats exactly what Claudio says in the comment at Post 3 (*piaciuto :)?*), thereby performing an action that seems to orient to the comment at Post 1, in the comment at Post 5 Petra publishes her first comment in this comment thread. The action performed in this comment explicitly refers to the most recent comments in this comment thread, which are the contributions at Posts 3 and 4. Petra asks Mauro to not disappoint her (*Mauro non deludermi*). Petra is clearly referring back to the action performed by Claudo in the comment at Post 3 and repeated by Auro in the comment at Post 4, where they have asked Mauro if he liked the concert by The Smashing Pumpkins.

Therefore, while the actions performed in the first comments published by Claudio and Auro in the comments at Posts 3 and 4 orient to the first-post telling, the action accomplished by Petra in her first contribution, the comment at Post 5, clearly refers to the most recent comment in this comment thread. It is the same for the actions performed in the first comments posted by Roberta and Claudia in the contributions at Posts 12 and 26. In the comment at Post 12 Roberta publishes a first comment which consists of a response to the comment at Post 11, the most recent contribution in this comment thread. In this comment Roberta explicitly disagrees with the action performed by Petra in the final component of the comment at Post 11, where she has told Mauro that she does not like the singer of The Smashing Pumpkins anymore because he acts like a fool who plays music simply because he wants to sell "it" (*il mio billy resta il mio billy,solo nella mia testa,ora su quel palco c'è un fuori di testa che cerca ancora di "vendere musica"*). Roberta disagrees with Petra's negative evaluation by saying that Billy Corgan, the singer of The Smashing Pumpkins, is a proper artist because he makes music without being interested in pleasing people (*e il fatto che non gliene frena nulla di compiacere gli altri lo rende un vero artista . . .*).

The action performed by Petra in the comment at Post 13 shows that the comment at Post 12 clearly orients to the action performed in the contribution at Post 11, the most recent comment in this comment thread. In fact in the comment at Post 13, Petra continues talking about the singer of The Smashing Pumpkins. She tells Roberta that Billy Corgan making crappy music simply because he wants to go on tour is an offence against his nostalgic fans (*si ma roberta fare musica di merda al giorno d'oggi solo per andare ancora in giro in tour a suonare zero ai pochi fan accaniti e nostalgici che veramente ci stanno sotto è un offesa nel profono anche a quello che fu l'era dei GRANDi 1*).

Another first comment which contains an action that clearly orients to the action performed in the most recent comment in this comment thread is the comment at Post 26, where Claudia responds to Mauro's request in the comment at Post 25. In this comment Mauro explicitly asks Claudia (who has not so far participated in this comment thread) if she saw the end of the concert (*Claudia non mi dire che ti sei persa il finale . . .*), and in the comment at Post 26 Claudia responds to him. Claudia says that she saw the end of the concert and that then she was in the fog (*c'eravamo, dietro. poi la nebbia*). Even if the action performed by Claudia in the final unit of the comment at Post 26 is unclear, the action contained in the initial unit of this comment explicitly responds to the request published by Mauro in the comment at Post 25, which is the most recent comment in this comment thread.

The analysis of Extract 7.5 once again demonstrates that the actions performed by Friends in first comments orient either to the action performed in the first telling or less frequently to the action accomplished in the most recent comment posted in a comment thread. This somewhat odd circumstance appears to arise from the system of FB itself, as will be discussed in the next section.

Other actions performed by Friends in first comments

So far it has been argued that the actions Friends perform in first comments orient to either the first-post telling or the action performed in the most recent comment posted in a comment thread. There are cases where the actions accomplished in first comments orient to the actions performed in other comments. However, in order to do this, the person posting the comment must do extra interactional work.

An example of this can be seen in the comment at Post 6 in Extract 7.6, where a Friend names the recipient of her comment in order to explicitly select the contribution she is responding to.

Extract 7.6 Alberta's photo

1 [Alberta publishes a photo that shows herself and Silvia] 6:39 a.m.

2 Alberta: cazzo sta foto nn [*sic*] fa cagare no no di piùùùùùùùùùùùùùùù ùùùùùùùù!!! 6:39
Alberta: fuck crappy is not enough to describe this photoooooooooooooo!!! 6:39 a.m.

3 Silvia: oh ma io non ci sono ancora tra le ex fatine della Yoe!!!! dovevo [*sic*] mandarle qualcosa mi sento esclusa!!!! e [*sic*] poi è bellissima!!! 6:41
Silvia: oh but I'm not included in Yoe's ex-fairies!!!! I had to send her something I feel excluded!!!! by the way it's awesome!!! 6:41 a.m.

4 Alberta: si si tu sei venuta bene io sembra che ho neanche [*sic*] gli cchi [*sic*] storti!!! 6:43
Alberta: yeah you look alright but it seems that I'm cross-eyed!!! 6:43 a.m.

5 Silvia: ma vaaaaaaaaaaaaaaaaaaaaaa non è vero 6:43
Silvia: come oooooooooon now this isn't true 6:43 a.m.

→ 6 Yoe: SILVIA SCUSAMI, NON VOLEVO ESCLUDERTI, HAI RAGIONE, CMQ [*sic*] APPENA CI SI VEDE SI SCATTANO LE FOTO PER L'ALBUM 23 ore fa
Yoe: SILVIA I'M SORRY, I DIDN'T WANT TO EXCLUDE YOU, YOU'RE RIGHT NEXT TIME WE CATCH UP WE HAVE TO TAKE SOME PHOTOS FOR THE ALBUM 23 hours ago

7 Yoe: Albe, come faccio a mettere questa foto nel album? 9 ore fa
Yoe: Albe, is it possible to add this photo to the album? 9 hours ago

After a series of comments in which Alberta and Silvia discuss the photo-telling in the comment at Post 1, which is a selfie of these two users that show them hugging each other, Yoe publishes her first comment in this comment thread. The action performed in this comment refers neither to the action accomplished in the first-post telling nor to the action performed in the most recent comment in the comment thread, instead it is a response to the comment at Post 3.

The photo-telling in the comment at Post 1 launches the interaction in Extract 7.6. In the comment at Post 2 Alberta performs another action in this interaction when she evaluates her own photo-telling, and in fact she tells Friends that it is horrible (*cazzo sta foto nn fa cagare no no di piùùùùùùùùùùùùùùùùùùùùùùùù!!!*). The initial expletive "*cazzo*" as well as the series of "*ù*" and the exclamation marks at the end of the comment at Post 2 show the intended humorous approach of this contribution. The comment at Post 3 is Silvia's response to the comments at Posts 1 and 2. The action performed in this comment is hard to interpret without insider knowledge; this contribution begins with an initial complaint about Silvia's exclusion from the group "*le ex fatine della Yoe*" (Yoe's ex-fairies); following this Silvia disagrees with Alberta's negative evaluation of the photo in the comment at Post 1 and tells Alberta that her photo is wonderful (*oh ma io non ci sono ancora tra le ex fatine della Yoe!!!! dovevo mandarle qualcosa mi sento esclusa!!!! e poi è bellissima!!!*).

In the comment at Post 4 Alberta responds to Silvia's comment at Post 3 by suggesting to her that while Silvia looks fine in the photo at Post 1, she seems to be cross-eyed (*si si tu sei venuta bene io sembra che ho neanche gli cchi storti!!!*). In the comment at Post 5 Silvia performs another action in this interaction when she once again explicitly disagrees with Alberta's previous negative evaluation in the comment at Post 4 by saying that she is wrong (*ma vaaaaaaaaaaaaaaaaaaaaaa non è vero*).

In the comment at Post 6 Yoe publishes her first comment in this comment thread. The action performed by Yoe in this contribution is neither directed to the photo-telling in the comment at Post 1 nor to the action performed by Silvia in the contribution in the comment at Post 5, the most recent comment in this comment thread. Yoe explicitly responds to the comment at Post 3, where Silvia has complained about her exclusion from Yoe's group. Yoe apologizes to Silvia by telling her that she did not mean to exclude her, that she is right, and that they will take some photos for the album when they catch up again (*SILVIA SCUSAMI, NON VOLEVO ESCLUDERTI, HAI RAGIONE, CMQ APPENA CI SI VEDE SI SCATTANO LE FOTO PER L'ALBUM*). Thus, the action performed in the comment at Post 6 clarifies the action performed by Silvia in her previous comment at Post 3. It is likely that "*le ex fatine della Yoe*" is the name of a photo album created by Yoe on FB, which contains images of a group of Friends that does not include Silvia.

In addition, the comment at Post 6 shows that the action performed by a Friend in the first comment of a comment thread may orient to a previous action performed by another Friend in a comment which is neither the initial telling nor the most recent comment in the interaction. Although the action performed in the comment at Post 6 acts as the *second pair part* of the complaint-apology sequence launched by Silvia in the comment at Post 3 (*oh ma io non ci sono ancora tra le ex fatine della Yoe!!!! dovevo mandarle qualcosa mi sento esclusa!!!!*), Yoe, the author of this comment, performs the extra action of explicitly selecting the addressee of her comment; she names Silvia (*SILVIA SCUSAMI*). It seems here that the action of naming is done in order to avoid the potential for communicative problems which could arise when a Friend publishes a first comment which contains an action that does not orient to the action performed in either the initial telling or the action accomplished in the most recent comment in the comment thread.

It is also possible that Yoe performed the action of naming because at the time at which data were collected for this book the *Reply* button was not available on FB. As mentioned in Chapter 2, this button, which is available under every comment posted in a comment thread, allows Friends to post a first or a later comment immediately after another comment that has already been posted in a comment thread. Moreover, it also allows Friends to position this comment immediately after the comment they are responding to, thus avoiding any potential for communicative problems. It is possible that Yoe selected Silvia as the recipient of the comment at Post 6 because at the time of the publication of this contribution the *Reply* button was not available on FB and therefore she could not post this comment immediately after Silvia's comment at Post 3. In other words, it seems that Yoe named Silvia as the recipient of the comment at Post 6 to make sure that her contribution was interpreted as a response to the comment at Post 3.

First comments that contain an action that neither orients to the original telling nor to the action performed in the most recent comment posted in the comment thread also occur in Extract 7.7, where the actions performed by Daniele and Roberta in the comments at Posts 11 and 13 orient to the actions accomplished by Mina and Daniele in the comments at Posts 9 and 11, respectively.

Extract 7.7 Metroman-Carnevale

1 Mauro: ho Deciso . . . A CARNEVALE MI VESTO DA METROMAN
Mauro: I have decided . . . AT THE NEXT CARNEVALE PARTY I'LL DRESS UP AS METROMAN

A Elisa ed altre 12 persone piace questo
Elisa and other 12 people like this

2 Auro: non dormo più!
Auro: I can't sleep anymore

3 Filippo: io da banana
Filippo: and I will dress up like a banana

4 Aria:—ti prego fallo davvero, non illudermi/ci.
Aria:—please do it, don't let us down.

5 Mina: Oltre a vestirti come lui, però dovrai cantare tutta la sera sennò non vale!! ;D
Mina: If you dress up like him [Metroman], *you will have to sing all night long or otherwise it won't count!! ;D*

[. . .]

9 Mina: Lo so che è ovvio . . . purtroppo ti conosco :D
Mina: I know it's obvious . . . unfortunately I know you :D

10 Richard: sexy
Richard: sexy

→ 11 Daniele: @Mina: purtroppo ti conosco è un insulto gravissimo . . . io non ti parlerei + a vita ;) @Mauro: io mi vesto da palo della metro, così puoi attaccarti al palo e girare!!!
Daniele: @Mina: unfortunately "I know you" is a terrible offence . . . I feel like not talking to you anymore;) @Mauro: I will dress up as an underground pole, so you can attach yourself to the pole and swing around me!!!

12 Mauro: e li salto! sicuro [*sic*]?
Mauro: and then I'll jump! Are you sure?

→ 13 Roberta: UAHAHAHAHAHAHH SCUSA DANI ALLORA PASSERò IL TEMPO AD APPICCICARTI STICKERS ADDOSSO! E anche appendere annunci pubblicitari!!!!
Roberta: UAHAHAHAHAHAHH I'M SORRY DANI BUT I WILL SPEND MY TIME STICKING STICKERS ON YOU! And hang posters as well!!!!

[...]

This comment thread has already been discussed in this book, more precisely in Chapters 4 and 5 and is about Metroman. In the comment at Post 1 Mauro performs an action in this interaction when he announces his humorous plan for the next Carnevale party, which is to dress up as Metroman (*ho Deciso . . . A CARNEVALE MI VESTO DA METROMAN*). Once again the first-post telling in the comment at Post 1 receives six responses from Friends, without the person posting the original comment performing any additional action to secure them. Specifically, in the comment at Post 2 Auro ironically tells Mauro that he will not be able to sleep, because of the anticipated excitement of watching Mauro dressed up as Metroman during the next Carnevale party (*non dormo più!*). In the comment at Post 3 Filippo mocks Mauro by saying that he will dress up as a banana, if Mauro dresses up like Metroman (*io da banana*).

In the comment at Post 4 Aria responds to the first-post telling by teasing Mauro, he must dress up like Metroman if he does not want to disappoint her and his Friends (*ti prego fallo davvero, non illudermi/ci*). The action performed by Mina in the comment at Post 5 shows that she has understood the humorous tone embedded in previous comments by stating that if Mauro dresses up as Metroman, he will also have to sing as Metroman usually does on the underground (*Oltre a vestirti come lui, però dovrai cantare tutta la sera sennò non vale!! ;D*). In the comment at Post 10 Richard performs another action in this interaction when he comments on Mauro's initial telling by saying that if Mauro dresses up as Metroman, he will be sexy (*sexy*).

The actions performed by Auro, Filippo, Aria, Mina, and Richard in their first comments orient to the original telling in the comment at Post 1. However, one of the actions performed in the comment at Post 11, which is the first comment published by Daniele in this comment thread, orients to the action performed by Mina in the contribution in the comment at Post 9. The comment at Post 11 is made of two units that contain two actions which are directed to two other actions which have been previously performed in this comment thread. Moreover,

Daniele selects the recipients of his actions by using the @ symbol. He responds to Mina's previous action in the comment at Post 9, where Mina has told Mauro that she knows that he is serious about his plan of dressing up as Metroman (*Lo so che è ovvio . . . purtroppo ti conosco :D*) and then he comments on Mauro's initial telling (*ho Deciso . . . A CARNEVALE MI VESTO DA METROMAN*). Therefore, while the intention of the action contained in the initial unit of the comment at Post 11 is not clear, it seems to orient to the action performed in the comment at Post 9. Daniele seems to mock Mina because of the expression "*ti conosco*" (I know you) which she used in the comment at Post 9. Daniele tells Mina that he considers "*ti conosco*" to be a terrible offence (*@Mina: purtroppo ti conosco è un insulto gravissimo . . . io non ti parlerei + a vita ;)*).

On the other hand, in the second unit of the comment at Post 11 Daniele performs another action in this interaction when he comments on the original telling at Post 1. He says that if Mauro dresses up as Metroman, he will dress up as an underground pole, so Mauro can swing around him (*@ Mauro: io mi vesto da palo della metro, così puoi attaccarti al palo e girare!!!*). Thus, although the action performed in the final unit of the comment at Post 11 orients to the initial telling, the action performed in the initial unit of this comment explicitly orients to the action performed in the comment at Post 9.

After the comment at Post 12, where Mauro responds to Daniele's comment at Post 11 by saying that he will jump if Daniele will dress up as underground pole (*e li salto! sicuro?*), in the comment at Post 13, two comments later, Roberta performs her first action in this comment thread, which is a response to the comment at Post 11. Roberta comments on Daniele's idea of dressing up as an underground pole, explicitly addressing him by name (*DANI*) and telling him that if he dresses up as underground pole, she will put stickers and classified advertisements on him during the Carnevale party (*UAHAHAHAHAHAHH SCUSA DANI ALLORA PASSERò IL TEMPO AD APPICCICARTI STICKERS ADDOSSO! E anche appendere annunci pubblicitari!!!!*).

Therefore, while the actions performed in the first comments published by Auro, Filippo, Aria, Mina, and Richard orient to the initial telling, the actions performed by Daniele and Roberta in their first comments orient to the actions performed in previous contributions posted in this comment thread. Interestingly Daniele and Roberta, just like Yoe in Extract 7.6, have selected the addressees of their first comments by explicitly naming them. Hence, naming the intended recipient of a first comment seemed to be a common technique utilized by Friends (before the introduction of the *Reply* button) to publish a first comment which oriented to the action performed in another contribution that was neither the initial telling nor the most recent comment in the comment thread.

The use of an extra action to mark a comment as not following the normal conventions can also be seen in Extract 7.8, where one Friend publishes a first comment that contains an action that refers back to all the actions performed in this interaction.

Extract 7.8 Learning English in Berlin

1 Mauro: Berlino in primavera è bellissima.
Ed io sono esigente, educato per rispetto formale, senza troppe aspettative.
Ho sogni grandi ma poco coltivati . . . se non impruvo [*sic*] l'inglisc [*sic*] entro tre anni sono un coglione. 8 ore fa
Mauro: Berlin in Spring is awesome.
And I'm demanding, polite for etiquette, without too many expectations.
I have big dreams but not nurtured enough . . . if I don't improve my English I'm a dickhead. *8 hours ago*

A 14 persone piace questo
14 people like this

2 Elena: 1. cazzo fai a berlino [*sic*]?
2. per English lessons sono a disposizione (€ 10.00/ora)
3. posso anche insegnarti il tedesco, stessa tariffa
4. improving english a berlino [*sic*], è come imparare l'italiano a scampia [*sic*] . . . Sì dai ciao 8 ore fa
Elena: 1. what the fuck are you doing in Berlin?
2. I'm available for English lessons at € 10.00/per hour
3. I can teach you German too, for the same price
4. improving english in berlin, is like learning Italian in Scampia [Italian town] . . . *yeah right forget it* *8 hours ago*

3 Arturo: ti lancio l'idea, organizziamo l'aperitivo in inglese con insegnanti madrelingua e spritz [name of a cocktail] 8 ore fa
Arturo: I have an idea, we can organize a happy hour with native speaker English teachers and spritz *8 hours ago*

4 Mauro: Ok io non bevo. ho [*sic*] già una capacità mnemonica scandalosa da sano, figurarsi da bevuto. 8 ore fa
Mauro: Ok but I won't drink. I already have limited learning abilities when I'm sober, imagine when I'm drunk. *8 hours ago*

5 Roberta: con un americano (in entrambi i sensi) cambierebbe tutto ♥ 8 ore fa
Roberta: with an american [name of a cocktail] *everything will change* ♥ *8 hours ago*

6 Mauro: io mi chiedo come cazzo faccio a farmi capire sapendo 9 parole in croce . . . questo è un miracolo. però [*sic*] mi sento come un pc durante il MillenniunBug [*sic*]. Forse gli stranieri mi trattano come categoria protetta e fanno finta di capirmi per non demoralizzarmi. le [*sic*] più merde sono quelli che mi dicono "Wow You speak well." Come dire ad un bambino "Bravvvoooo . . . sai fare la caraaaaa sulla guancina!!!Bravooo" 8 ore fa
Mauro: I wonder how the fuck I'm able to communicate knowing only 9 words . . . this is a miracle. but I'm feeling like a computer during the MillenniunBug. Maybe foreigners treat me as a protected species and pretend to understand me to avoid demoralizing me. The worst ones are those who say "Wow You speak well." Like telling a child "Well donnneeee . . . you know how to blow raspberries!!!Good boy" *8 hours ago*

7 Elena: sono solo più elastici di noi . . . mentalmente 8 ore fa
Elena: they're more flexible than us . . . mentally speaking *8 hours ago*

→ 8 Chiara: quindi ricapitolando . . . vuoi imparare l'inglese per trasferirti a berlino [*sic*]? 3 ore fa
Chiara: so to summarize . . . you want to learn English because you want to move to Berlin? *3 hours ago*

9 Mauro: ma no, io non mi trasferisco. vado [*sic*] e torno. se [*sic*] imparo l'inglese vado, capisco e faccio [*sic*] capire bene, e torno. 3 ore fa
Mauro: no, I won't move. I'll go and come back. If I improve my English, I'll go, understand and make myself understood clearly and then I'll come back. *3 hours ago*

Mauro opens this comment thread with a report on his activities in Berlin followed by an unclear action, though it appears to be a telling about his future plan of learning the English language in three years (*Berlino in primavera è bellissima. Ed io sono esigente, educato per rispetto formale, senza troppe aspettative. Ho sogni grandi ma poco coltivati . . . se non impruvo l'inglise entro tre anni sono un coglione*). This telling is responded to by two comments that contain actions that clearly orient to it. In the comment at Post 2, after asking Mauro why he is in Berlin, Elena offers him some English tuitions; then she mocks his idea of improving his knowledge of the English language while in Berlin by saying that learning English in Berlin is like learning Italian in Scampia, a town where inhabitants generally do not speak standard Italian (*1. cazzo fai a berlino? 2. per English lessons sono a disposizione (€ 10.00/ora) 3. posso anche insegnarti il tedesco, stessa tariffa 4. improving english a berlino, è come imparare l'italiano a scampia . . . Sì dai ciao*).

In the comment at Post 3, Arturo performs another action in this comment thread when he continues with the playful framework introduced by Elena in the comment at Post 2; he responds to Mauro's initial telling in the comment at Post 1 about learning English in Berlin by proposing that they should organize a happy hour with English tutors (*ti lancio l'idea, organizziamo l'aperitivo in inglese con insegnanti madrelingua e spritz*). After the comment at Post 4, where Mauro responds to the comment at Post 3 by saying that he will not drink because alcohol might affect his learning abilities (*Ok io non bevo. ho già una capacità mnemonica scandalosa da sano, figurarsi da bevuto*), in the comment at Post 5 Roberta publishes her first comment in this comment thread. She continues to play along with the theme of drinks by responding to Mauro's comment at Post 4 and telling him that an "*americano*" (American) will help him to improve his English (*con un americano (in entrambi i sensi) cambierebbe tutto* ♥). The action in the comment at Post 5 is a play on words; the term "*americano*" is either the name of a cocktail or a person from the United States. Therefore, the action performed by Roberta in the comment at Post 5 is a telling; she says to Mauro that drinking alcohol as well as talking with an American man may improve his knowledge of the English language.

In the contribution at Post 8 Chiara publishes her first comment in this comment thread. The action performed in this comment neither orients to the action performed in the comment at Post 1 nor specifically to the action accomplished in the contribution at Post 7, the most recent comment in this comment thread; instead it refers back to all the actions performed by Friends in this interaction. Chiara begins the comment at Post 8 by using the expression "*quindi ricapitolando*" (so in summary); "*quindi*" appears to be similar to the English discourse marker "so," a marker commonly used to introduce a turn at talk which refers back to the entire discourse that has preceded it (Rendle-Short, 2003; Schiffrin, 1987). Chiara is applying a device which is commonly used in spoken conversation to an FB comment thread. Moreover, she posts "*ricapitolando*" (to summarize) immediately after "*quindi*," the verb reinforcing the recapitulatory function of "*quindi*" and introducing the action performed in the final part of this comment: the clarification request that concludes the contribution at Post 8 (*vuoi imparare l'inglese per trasferirti a berlino?*), where Chiara explicitly and jokingly asks Mauro if he wants to learn English because he wants to move to Berlin. Therefore, in the comment at Post 8 Chiara is using "*quindi ricapitolando*" to perform an extra action that signals to Friends that her contribution does not orient specifically to the action accomplished in either the first-post telling or to the action performed in the most recent comment in this comment thread.

So, first comments from Friends commonly contain actions that orient to the action performed in the first-post telling or alternatively the action performed in the most recent comment. Interestingly, when a Friend publishes a first comment in a comment thread he or she does exactly what the system is set up for him or her to do. In fact, the button *Comment* (which immediately follows the first comment) and the dialogue box *Write a comment* (which follows the last comment in a comment thread) invite Friends to post contributions which can be understood as containing actions that orient to either the initial telling or actions performed in response to the most recent comment posted in a comment thread. Those features allow Friends to publish a contribution in an existing comment thread and they are positioned respectively after the first comment and the most recent comment in the comment thread. Hence, Friends can select one of those features to post a contribution on a comment thread. However, regardless of the features they select, when a Friend clicks on the *Enter* button on his or her keyboard this contribution is automatically positioned after the most recent comment in the comment thread. In other words, even though a Friend may select the button *Comment* positioned immediately after the initial telling, when he or she publishes his or her contribution in the comment thread this is visualized on the screen after the most recent comment in the interaction.

Moreover, as already noted in Chapter 6, if a comment thread consists of multiple comments, Friends can only see the first and the four or five most recent comments, while they cannot see all the other contributions published in interaction, and must click on a message to see the other comments published in the comment thread. Thus, when a Friend publishes a first comment that contains an action that orients to either the initial or the most recent comment in a comment thread, he or she does exactly what the system encourages him or her to do.

Comments in Extracts 7.6 to 7.8 indicate that the actions performed in some first comments do not follow the pattern mentioned above. When this happens the Friend, who publishes the first comment that contains an action which orients neither to the action performed in the initial telling nor to the action performed in the most recent comment in the comment thread, seems to explicitly select the recipient of the contribution to which this action is orienting to—as has been done in Extract 7.6 and in Extract 7.7—or uses some other technique involving additional interactional work, such as Chiara's use of "*quindi ricapitolando*" in Extract 7.8.

The action of naming a user to select him or her as the intended recipient of a comment has stopped with the introduction of the *Reply* button. However, this button is not available after the first comment of a comment thread. Instead this comment is followed by the *Comment* button which, as already mentioned in Chapter 2, allows Friends to post comments that respond to first contributions in comment threads and position them after the most recent comment posted in a comment thread. In other words, while when a Friend uses the *Reply* button he or she has control over the positioning of a comment in a comment thread, this is not case when he or she utilizes the *Comment* button. This button in fact does not give a Friend the control over the positioning of his or her comment in a comment thread. All of this indicates the fundamental difference in status between the first and other comments posted in FB comment threads. While Friends can have control over the positioning of comments that respond to comments which have already been posted in a comment thread, they do not have control over the positioning of comments that respond to the first comment of a comment thread.

This chapter has demonstrated that the action performed by a Friend in the first comment he or she makes to a comment thread generally orients to either the action performed in the original telling or the action performed in the most recent comment posted in a comment thread.

Conclusions

The actions performed by Friends in the comments that follow first-post tellings are similar to the actions performed by conversationalists after spoken tellings. Evaluations, representations of laughter, second tellings, and unlikely statements are in fact the prototypical actions performed by Friends in the comments that come after first-post tellings in FB comment threads.

A first comment published by a Friend in a comment thread does exactly what the system is set up for him or her to do. This contribution in fact contains an action that orients to either the action performed in the initial telling or the action performed in the most recent comment posted in a comment thread, even though other comments may have already been published in the comment thread.

The following chapter will discuss the prototypical patterns that characterize the way initial posters and Friends publish later contributions in a FB comment thread opened by a first-post telling.

8

Later Comments

Introduction

Chapter 7 discussed first comments posted by Friends in FB comment threads opened by a telling. This chapter, on the other hand, focuses on later comments made by Friends and original posters and analyzes the impact of these contributions on the organization of FB interactions.

Later comments from Friends and original posters

After defining what is meant by a later comment, the following sections demonstrate that the persons posting the original comments and Friends follow similar patterns for publishing later comments in FB comment threads opened by an initial telling.

A later comment is defined here as being a contribution posted by either the initial poster or a Friend, which is not their first comment in that comment thread. As examples, consider the comments by Elisa and Claudia in the contributions at Posts 3, 4, 5, and 7 in Extract 8.1.

Extract 8.1 Terrible Monday

1 Elisa: lunedì = giorno di merda!!! 18 ore fa
Elisa: Monday = shitty day!!! 18 hours ago

A 11 persone piace questo
11 people like this

2 Claudia:—soprattutto questo lunedì :-(((18 ore fa
Claudia:—especially this Monday :-(((18 hours ago

→ 3 Elisa: Claudiaaa!ieri [*sic*] non ti ho vista,c'era [*sic*] troppo casino :-(((in ufficio non funzionano i riscaldamenti 18 ore fa

Elisa: Claudiaaa!yesterday I didn't see you,it was such chaos :-(((in the office the heating system isn't working *18 hours ago*

→ 4 Claudia: Ciao Elisa!! io [*sic*] ti ho visto passare ma non ho fatto in tempo a chiamarti!!!! . . . senza [*sic*] riscaldamento e malaticcia???!!! Si il tuo è decisamente un lunedi di M . . .!!!! ;-) 18 ore fa

Claudia: Hi Elisa!! I saw you go by but I didn't have the time to call you!!!! . . . without the heating system and sick???!!! Yeah, yours is definetly a S . . . Monday!!!! ;-) *18 hours ago*

→ 5 Elisa: adesso per fortuna è uscito il tecnico :-) 18 ore fa

Elisa: finally the technician has arrived :-) *18 hours ago*

6 Gaia: Hahahaha verissimo tatina 15 ore fa

Gaia: Hahahaha you are right darling *15 hours ago*

→ 7 Elisa: eheheeh che capperi!!!hi [*sic*] hi hi 15 ore fa

Elisa: eheheeh what the hell !!!hi hi hi *15 hours ago*

Extract 8.1 is opened by the action performed by Elisa in the comment at Post 1, where she posts an initial telling. After Claudia posts her first contribution in the comment at Post 2, she and Elisa post a series of later comments where they discuss the previous day as well as Elisa's problem with the heating system.

In the comment at Post 1 Elisa's use of the expletive "*giorno di merda*" (shitty day) is followed by a series of exclamation marks to complain to Friends that Mondays are terrible days (*lunedì* = *giorno di merda!!!*). In the comment at Post 2 Claudia performs her first action in this interaction; she responds to the statement in the comment at Post 1 by publishing her first contribution in this comment thread. Claudia shows affiliation with Elisa by telling her that her statement is true, specifically if it refers to this Monday (*—soprattutto questo lunedì :-(((*). In the contribution at Post 3 Elisa publishes a later comment, her second contribution in this comment thread. Specifically, Elisa performs an action that orients to the action performed by Claudia in the comment at Post 2; she names Claudia in her greeting and says that the day before being very chaotic, she could not see Claudia that day (*Claudiaaa!ieri non ti ho vista,c'era troppo casino :-(((*). Then, Elisa concludes the comment at Post 3 by performing another action in this interaction; she changes the topic[1] and tells Claudia that the heating system in her office is not working (*in ufficio non funzionano i riscaldamenti).*

In the comment at Post 4 Claudia publishes a later comment in this comment thread, her second contribution in this interaction. After responding to the comment at Post 3 by greeting Elisa, in the comment at Post 4 Claudia performs another action in this interaction; she tells Elisa that she saw her the day before, but she did not have time to talk to her (*Ciao Elisa!! io ti ho visto passare ma non ho fatto in tempo a chiamarti!!!!*). Then, Claudia concludes the comment at Post 4 by commenting on Elisa's problem with the heating system and telling her that being sick at work with this extra issue definitely makes Elisa's Monday terrible (*. . . senza riscaldamento e malaticciа???!!! Si il tuo è decisamente un lunedi di M . . .!!!! ;-)*). In the contribution at Post 5 Elisa posts another later comment in this comment thread. She responds to Claudia's comment at Post 4 by telling her that the technician has finally arrived and he is fixing the heating system (*adesso per fortuna è uscito il tecnico :-)*).

Thus, in the comments at Posts 3, 4, 5, and 7 Elisa and Claudia, the initial poster and a Friend who participates in this comment thread, post a series of later comments in this interaction. The actions performed in these contributions indicate that this part of the comment thread is a dyadic interaction between Elisa and Claudia.[2] Strong evidence that this is the case comes from the second-person singular pronouns "*ti*" and "*tuo*" (you, your) utilized in the comments at Posts 3 and 4, which explicitly select a single participant as a recipient of a comment.

In the comment at Post 6 Gaia joins this comment thread by publishing her first contribution in this interaction. The action performed in this comment clearly orients to the action performed in the comment at Post 1, and in fact is a positive evaluation of Elisa's initial statement about Mondays. After an initial representation of laughter, Gaia explicitly agrees with Elisa's statement by saying that she is right about Mondays being terrible days (*Hahahaha verissimo tatina*). In the contribution at Post 7 Elisa performs another action in this interaction; she responds to the comment at Post 6 by posting another later comment in this comment thread. After initially expressing laughter, she posts the expletive "*che capperi*" (damn it) which shows agreement with Gaia's previous evaluation in the comment at Post 6 (*eheheeh che capperi!!!hi hi hi*).

Extract 8.1 has exemplified later comments to a comment thread, those which are not the first contributions published by either the original poster or a Friend in a comment thread. One feature which can be seen in Extract 8.1 is that persons posting the original comments and Friends seem to follow similar patterns for publishing later comments in an FB comment thread opened by a first-post telling. Specifically, in the comments at Posts 3, 4, 5, and 7, Elisa (original poster) and Claudia (Friend) post four later comments that contain actions which clearly orient to the actions performed in the most recent contributions posted in this comment thread.

Moreover, the analysis of Extract 8.1 has pointed out that a user beginning a comment thread and a Friend may use later comments to create a private dyadic exchange within an ongoing comment thread. When this happens they use specific devices, such as personal pronouns, to explicitly select the recipients of their contributions, while potentially excluding other Friends from the interaction.

The following section discusses patterns for publishing later comments in FB comment threads opened by initial tellings. The final part of this chapter looks at cases where something else takes place, before returning to focus on dyadic interactions.

Later comments orient to the most recent comment

In Chapter 7 it was demonstrated that the first comment posted by a Friend in a comment thread generally contains an action that orients to the action performed in either the initial telling or the most recent comment in the comment thread. In contrast, the data presented in Extract 8.1 suggest that a later comment generally contains an action that orients to the action performed in the most recent contribution published in a comment thread only. This can be confirmed in Extracts 8.2 to 8.5, where the later comments published by either the person making the initial comment or Friends contain actions that always orient to the actions performed in the most recent comments in those comment threads.

Extracts 8.2 and 8.3 discuss later comments published by original posters, while Extracts 8.4 and 8.5 analyze later comments posted by Friends.

Extract 8.2 Movie discussion

1 Ciro: Mercoledi sera andiamo a vedere Benvenuti al nord con Bisio [Ciro publishes a hyperlink containing a review of this movie] Sempre all'Orfeo in via Coni Zugna, ci troviamo alle 19:40! Gennaio 23 alle 3:16
Ciro: Wednesday night we're going to see Benvenuti al nord [title of a movie] *at the Orfeo cinema in via Coni Zugna* [address of the cinema], *see you there at 7:40 p.m.* *January 23 at 3:16 a.m.*

A 2 persone piace questo
2 people like this

2 Maria: Noi l'abbiamo già visto, carino! Gennaio 23 alle 4:13
Maria: we've already seen it, it's nice! *January 23 at 4:13 a.m.*

3 Marcello: ci vediamo alle 7:40 dentro l'atrio prima delle casse? forse [*sic*] verrà anche mia madre. Martedì alle 3:53

Marcello: see you at 7:40 p.m. in the hall in front of the cash registers? my mother may come too *Tuesday at 3:53 p.m.*

→ 4 Ciro: ok attenzione che inizia alle 19:55! Mercoledì alle 12:22
Ciro: ok keep in mind that it starts at 7:55 p.m. *Wednesday at 12:22 p.m.*

In the comment at Post 1 Ciro performs his first action in this comment thread: he posts an invitation to watch the movie *Benvenuti al nord* at the cinema. After saying that they are planning to go to the cinema on Wednesday, Ciro concludes the comment at Post 1 by posting the arrangements for the evening, which include the session time as well as the address of the cinema (*Sempre all'Orfeo in via Coni Zugna, ci troviamo alle 19:40*).

In the comments at Posts 2 and 3 Maria and Marcello post two first contributions that contain actions that orient to the invitation posted in the comment at Post 1. Specifically, after declining Ciro's invitation because she has already watched the movie, in the comment at Post 2 Maria performs another action in this interaction: she publishes a positive evaluation of the movie *Benvenuti al nord* (*Noi l'abbiamo già visto, carino!*). On the other hand, in the comment at Post 3, Marcello launches a *repair sequence*. It seems that Marcello is not clear about the arrangements for the evening, and explicitly requests that Ciro confirm the time and the location of the appointment by asking if they will meet in the hall of the cinema in front of the counters at 7:40 p.m. (*ci vediamo alle 7:40 dentro l'atrio prima delle casse?*). Then, in the final unit of the comment at Post 3 Marcello performs another action in this comment thread: he tells Ciro that his mother will probably come to the cinema too (*forse verrà anche mia madre*).

In the comment at Post 4 Ciro publishes a later comment, his second contribution in this comment thread. The action performed in this comment clearly orients to one of the actions contained in the comment at Post 3, the most recent comment in this interaction. Ciro completes the *repair sequence* launched by Marcello in the comment at Post 3. He confirms to Marcello the arrangements for the evening by posting the acceptance token *ok*, then he concludes the comment at Post 4 by reminding Marcello to be on time because the movie will start at 7:55 p.m. (*ok attenzione che inizia alle 19:55!*).

Even though in Chapter 7 we have seen that the action contained in the *first pair part* of an *adjacency pair sequence* (when it is the first comment in a comment thread) projects a *second pair part* which may not necessarily occur immediately after it, the comment at Post 4 suggests that this is perhaps not the case for all contributions in a comment thread. In fact, here we see that the *second pair part* of the *adjacency pair sequence* (the comment at Post 4) occurs immediately after the *first pair part* that precedes it (the comment at Post 3). Thus, the comment at Post 4 is a later comment which contains an action that orients to the action performed in the most recent comment posted in this comment thread.

The analysis of Extract 8.2 suggests that later comments published by the FB user initiating the comment thread generally contain actions that orient to the actions performed in the most recent comments posted in comment threads.

The same feature characterizes Extract 8.3, where Claudio, the person who posts the first telling, publishes several later comments which contain actions that clearly orient to the actions performed in the most recent comments posted in this comment thread.

Extract 8.3 Tiramisù[3]

1 Claudio: Doesn't look very nice now??? :P
[Claudio publishes a photo which shows him and a bowl that contains half of a tiramisù cake] Yesterday at 6:08 a.m.

A 2 persone piace questo
2 people like this

[. . .]

5 Alex: that's mineeeeeeeeeeeeeeeeeee Yesterday at 6:41 a.m.

→ 6 Claudio: run run ;) Yesterday at 6:42 a.m.

7 Jorge: poor tiramisù . . . didn't do anything to you . . . yet xD
Yesterday at 7:06 a.m.

→ 8 Claudio: it did! it [*sic*] was saying "you can't have meeeee . . . you're on a diet . . ." So I showed you that for me the diet doesn't start on Monday :P
Yesterday at 7:09 a.m.

9 Jorge: it's weird . . . some chocolate cookies said the same thing to me in the morning . . . is the word coming to an end? . . . Show that tiramisù who's the boss xD Yesterday at 7:11 a.m.

→ 10 Claudio: 2012 is very close yep ;) Yesterday at 7:20 a.m.

As already noted in Chapter 5, Extract 8.3 is included in a series of comment threads where Claudio posts several photos of a tiramisù cake, which are a series of snapshots over several days of him eating the entire cake.

Extract 8.3 is opened by the actions performed by Claudio in the comment at Post 1, where he posts an initial photo-telling of him with the leftover portion of a tiramisù cake. After a series of first contributions where Friends comment on the photo-telling, in the comments at Posts 6, 8, and 10 Claudio publishes three later comments which contain actions that explicitly orient to the actions performed in the most recent comments posted in this comment thread at that time.

The comment at Post 6 is a later comment which contains an action that orients to the action performed in the contribution at Post 5—the most recent comment in this comment thread—where Alex has humorously told Claudio that what is left is his portion of the tiramisù cake (*that's mineeeeeeeeeeeeeeeeeee*). The smiling emoticon at the end of the comment at Post 6 shows that Claudio has understood the facetious tone embedded in Alex's comment, and in fact Claudio tells Alex that he needs to hurry if he wants to eat some of the leftover tiramisù cake (*run run ;)*). Two other later comments which contain actions that explicitly orient to the actions performed in the most recent comments posted in this comment thread are the contributions at Posts 8 and 10. More precisely, in these two comments Claudio performs actions that orient to the actions performed in the contributions published by Jorge in the comments at Posts 7 and 9. In the comment at Post 7 Jorge humorously asks Claudio if the tiramisù cake did anything to him, and in the comment at Post 8 Claudio ironically responds to Jorge saying that the cake provoked him; specifically, it challenged him by saying that he could not eat it because he was on a diet (*it did! it was saying "you can't have meeeee . . . you're on a diet . . ." So I showed you that for me the diet doesn't start on Monday :P*).

Similarly, the action performed by Claudio in the comment at Post 10 orients to the action performed in the comment at Post 9, where Jorge ironically tells Claudio that the phenomenon of talking sweets may symbolize the arrival of the end of the world (*it's weird . . . some chocolate cookies said the same thing to me in the morning . . . is the word coming to an end? . . . Show that tiramisù who's the boss xD*). In the comment at Post 10 Claudio shows that he has understood the irony of this contribution; he says to Jorge that 2012 (year of the supposed end of the world) is indeed nearing (*2012 is very close yep ;)*).

In general, later comments published by original posters in comment threads opened by an initial telling seem to contain actions that orient to the actions performed in the most recent comments posted in those interactions.

The Extracts 8.4 and 8.5 focus on later comments posted by Friends. These extracts demonstrate that the same pattern of a later comment containing an action that generally orients to the action performed in the most recent comment posted in a comment thread applies not only to the person publishing the original comment, as seen above, but also to later comments published by Friends. Extract 8.4 is opened by a humorous telling, about Claudio and his stay in a hostel in Malaga, a Spanish city. After publishing a first contribution that contains an action that orients to the initial telling, in the comment at Post 4, Martino, a Friend who participates in this comment thread, publishes a later comment which contains an action that clearly orients to the action performed in the then most recent comment in this interaction.

Extract 8.4 Hostel in Malaga

1 Claudio: Ostello a Malaga. 10 letti, 8 pieni e tutte fighe tranne me. Punizione divina????? Ho già prurito!!! (E il bagno è chiaramente il loro regno—non c'è un centimetro libero per appoggiare il sapone). Fortuna resto solo 2 notti :-P circa un'ora fa
Claudio: Hostel in Malaga. 10 beds, 8 full of hot chicks except for me. Divine punishment????? I'm already itchy!!! (And the bathroom it's clearly their kingdom—there's not even a centimeter for my soap). Luckily I'll only stay for 2 nights :-P Almost an hour ago

A 5 persone piace questo
5 people like this

2 Martino: un grande . . . facciamo cambio circa un'ora fa
Martino: you're the best . . . do you wanna swap Almost an hour ago

3 Claudio: Magari! Fanno un pollaio da sgozzarle proprio!!! circa un'ora fa
Claudio: If only! They make so much noise that the place sounds like a henhouse, makes me want to slaughter them!!! Almost an hour ago

→ 4 Martino: mucha suerte . . . circa un'ora fa
Martino: good luck . . . Almost an hour ago

[. . .]

In the comment at Post 1 Claudio performs his first action in this interaction; he posts a report on his stay in Malaga. The way this comment is written shows the humorous approach of this telling; after saying that eight of the ten beds available in his room are taken by girls, Claudio, who is gay, rhetorically asks Friends if this is a divine punishment (*Ostello a Malaga. 10 letti, 8 pieni e tutte fighe tranne me. Punizione divina????? Ho già prurito!!!*). Then, Claudio continues his report by saying that the bathroom is the girls' kingdom and is so full that it is impossible to find space even for his soap (*E il bagno è chiaramente il loro regno—non c'è un centimetro libero per appoggiare il sapone*). Claudio closes the comment at Post 1 by saying that fortunately he will stay in this hostel for two nights only (*Fortuna resto solo 2 notti :-P*).

In the comment at Post 2 Martino posts his first contribution to this comment thread. The action performed in this comment shows that Martino has understood the humorous tone embedded in Claudio's initial telling. Martino posts an invitation, where he proposes to Claudio that they swap their accommodations (*un grande . . . facciamo cambio*). In the comment at Post 3 Claudio ironically tells Martino that he would be happy to accept his invitation to stay with the girls, because they make the place seem like a henhouse which makes him want to slaughter them (*Magari! Fanno un pollaio da sgozzarle proprio!!!*). In the comment at Post 4 Martino publishes a later comment in this comment thread (his first). The action performed in this contribution clearly orients to the action accomplished in the comment at Post 3, the most recent comment in this interaction. In the comment at Post 4 Martino ironically wishes Claudio good luck with the situation (*mucha suerte . . .*). Although the comment at Post 4 is written in Spanish, the action performed in it explicitly orients to the action performed in the contribution at Post 3, the most recent comment posted in this comment thread.

Here in Extract 8.4 we see a later comment published by a Friend that contains an action that orients to the action performed in the most recent comment posted in this interaction. This is also evident in Extract 8.5, where Maria, a Friend who participates in this comment thread, posts two later comments which contain actions that clearly orient to the actions performed in the most recent contributions published by Claudio in this interaction.

Extract 8.5 Weather discussion

1 Claudio: Tira un'aria che pela . . . Domenica alle 5:15
Claudio: The wind is so cold that it chills you to the bone . . . Sunday at 5:15 a.m.

2 Maria: io sono stata a Parigi il febbraio scorso . . . che freddo porco che faceva . . . ti sono vicina ;) Domenica alle 6:43
Maria: last February I went to Paris . . . the cold was bloody freezing . . . I'm close to you ;) Sunday at 6:43 a.m.

3 Claudio: Stammi davvero vicino perchè qui ci rimango. Tra placche e febbriciattola, più st'aria [*sic*] . . . spero di rientrare nella nebbiosa Londra alive :) Domenica alle 6:45
Claudio: Stay really close to me because I'm going to die here. What with a sore throat and a fever, and this wind . . . I hope to return alive to foggy London :) Sunday at 6:45 a.m.

→ 4 Maria: tra londra [*sic*] e parigi [*sic*] . . . meglio l'aria di bologna [*sic*]! :** (solo l'aria temo) Domenica alle 6:46
*Maria: between london and paris . . . better the air of bologna! :** (the air only I'm afraid) Sunday at 6:46 a.m.*

5 Claudio: Ve che a Bologna fa più freddo che a Londra. Però ci sono i ristoranti con ogni ben di dio! Domenica alle 6:47
Claudio: fact is that Bologna is colder than London. But there are restaurants full of delicacies! Sunday at 6:47 a.m.

→ 6 Maria: caza vi! ;) e [*sic*] soprattutto . . . ci sono le none [*sic*] !! ;) :) Domenica alle 6:49
Maria: caza vi! [probably an idiomatic expression in Emilian dialect which might work as an expletive] *;) and more importantly . . . there are the grandmothers!! ;) :) Sunday at 6:49 a.m.*

7 Claudio: Merda l'hai detto! Domenica alle 6:51
Claudio: Shit well said! Sunday at 6:51 a.m.

8 Nives: Va a let e po cruvet! Così ti scaldi Domenica alle 10:13
Nives: Go to bed and stay warm! Sunday at 10:13 a.m.

This comment thread has already been mentioned in Chapter 2 and is opened by an initial telling followed by several comments that orient to it. In the contributions at Posts 4 and 6, Maria publishes two later comments which contain actions that explicitly respond to the actions performed in the most recent comments posted in this comment thread.

At Post 1 Claudio launches the comment thread by performing a telling; he says to Friends that in Paris the wind is so cold that it chills him to the bone (*Tira un'aria che pela . . .*). Maria responds to this comment at Post 2, where she shows affiliation by saying to Claudio that last February when she was in Paris the weather was terribly cold (*io sono stata a Parigi il febbraio scorso . . . che freddo porco che faceva . . . ti sono vicina ;)*). In the comment at Post 3 Claudio performs another action in this interaction; he publishes a later comment (his first) which orients to the action performed in the comment at Post 2. Then in the contribution at Post 4 Maria posts her first later comment in this comment thread. This comment clearly contains an action that refers to the action performed in the final unit of the comment at Post 3, the then most recent comment in this comment thread, where Claudio has said that he is so sick that he can only hope to make it back to London (the city where he is currently living) alive. Maria ironically says that out of London and Paris she prefers the air of Bologna (Claudio's hometown) (*tra londra e parigi . . . meglio l'aria di bologna! :** (solo l'aria temo)*).

In the comment at Post 5 Claudio performs another action in this interaction; he responds to the action performed in the comment at Post 4. Then, in the contribution at Post 6 Maria posts another later comment (her second) which contains an action that explicitly orients to the action performed in the comment at Post 5, the then most recent comment. After an initial statement which is unclear, probably an expletive in *Romagnolo* dialect (*caza vi! ;)*), in the final unit of the comment at Post 6 Maria clearly refers back to the action performed in the comment at Post 5, where Claudio has said that Bologna is better than London because of its restaurants. Maria explicitly agrees with Claudio's positive evaluation of Bologna; she states that Bologna is better than London not just for its restaurants, but specially because their grandmothers live there (*e soprattutto . . . ci sono le none!! ;) :)*).

The contributions at Posts 4 and 6 in Extract 8.5 are examples of further later comments published by a Friend which contain actions that orient to the actions performed in the most recent comments posted in the interaction.

So, the analysis of Extracts 8.2 to 8.5 has demonstrated that original posters and Friends publish later comments which generally contain actions that orient to the actions performed in the most recent comments posted in a comment thread.

Other later comments

Further evidence that later comments generally orient to the actions performed in the most recent comments posted in a comment thread comes from the extra interactional work that is commonly performed by either the original poster or a Friend when they publish a later comment which contains an action that is not orienting to the action performed in the most recent contribution posted in the comment thread. An example of this can be seen in Extract 8.6, given here in an abbreviated form as it was earlier discussed in Chapter 7 (it is available in a full version in Appendix A).

Extract 8.6 Music discussion—The Smashing Pumpkins

1 Mauro: Zero Compromessi [Mauro publishes a hyperlink containing a video of the band The Smashing Pumpkins] 21 ore fa
Mauro: Zero Compromises *21 hours ago*

[. . .]

13 Petra: si ma roberta [*sic*] fare musica di merda al giorno d'oggi solo per andare ancora in giro in tour a suonare zero ai pochi fan accaniti e nostalgici che veramente ci stanno sotto è un offesa [*sic*] nel profono [*sic*] anche a quello [*sic*] che fu l'era dei GRANDi 1 [possibly the name of one of the songs of The Smashing Pumpkins or a typo] 21 ore fa

Petra: ok roberta but to make crappy music nowadays just because you want to go on tour to play nothing for a few nostalgic, obstinate fans is a deep offence to what used to be the era of the GREAT ONES 1 *21 hours ago*

14 Auro: concordo con roberta [*sic*].a [*sic*] anche qui a londra [*sic*], fatte salve le aspettative, è stato dal punto di vista musicale molto bello!però [*sic*] concorderei anche col malumore di quelli che avrebbero voluto vedere e sentire QUEI pezzi di QUEGLI smashing [*sic*] . . .!insomma [*sic*] un po' d'amaro a me lo ha lasciato comunque. 21 ore fa

Auro: I agree with roberta.even here in london, apart from the exceptions, from a musical point of view it was fantastic!but I agree with the discontent of those who were hoping to see and hear songs from THOSE smashing . . .!actually the concert left me with a bitter-taste in any case. *21 hours ago*

15 Mauro: non credo che voglia per forza vendere, tanto è vero che non fa nemmeno musica di facile presa . . . penso sia l'unica cosa che gli rimane . . . e nella musica che fa penso ci metta proprio la rabbia e la sfida del o mi ami o mi odi, gli Smashing Pumpkins sono sempre stato io ecc . . . ecc . . . senza Sacralizzarlo [*sic*] e sapendo cosa sarebbe un concerto con 1979, Perfect,Ava [*sic*] Adore [names of some of the songs of The Smashing Pumpkins] ecc ecc ecc . . . credo però di preferire che sia così, se facesse un concerto di singoloni con questa bandnonband, risulterebbe caricaturale e ridicolo. Preferisco che sia acido e sincero e mandi a fanculo la buon costume ed il [*sic*] Greatest hits. 21 ore fa

Mauro: I don't think that he necessarily wants to sell, in fact he's not making music which is popular . . . I reckon this is the only thing that he has left . . . and in his music he is putting the rage and the challenge of either love me or hate me, The Smashing Pumpkins have always been me etc . . . etc . . . without I idolizing him and knowing what a concert would have been like with 1979, Perfect, Ava Adore etc etc etc . . . yet I think that it is better this way, if he gave a concert of huge singles with this bandnoband, he would seem ridiculous and a caricature. I prefer him to be brutal and honest and that he tells the police and the Greatest hits to fuck off. *21 hours ago*

16 Mauro: ah lo capisco Auro . . . davvero. basta [*sic*] l'inizio di Tonight [name of a song of The Smashing Pumpkins] per aprire una voragine . . . forse è bello rimaner con l'Utopia, piuttosto che con l'edulcorazione [*sic*] del prodotto originale, boh, mi piglia così. Ovvio se ci penso a cosa sarebbe averli visti 12 anni fa . . . ciao . . . 21 ore fa

Mauro: ah Auro I understand you . . . really. The opening of Tonight is enough to open an abyss . . . maybe it's better to stick to Utopia, rather than sugar coating the original product, well, that's what I think. Obviously I wonder what it would have been like to see them 12 years ago . . . bye . . . *21 hours ago*

→ 17 Mauro: Petra come intitolavi . . . ai nostalgici regala un cazzo. Zero Compromessi . . . e di questo ne andre [*sic*] fiero. 21 ore fa
Mauro: Petra as you said . . . he doesn't give shit to nostalgic people. Zero Compromises . . . and he should be proud of this. *21 hours ago*

[. . .]

After a series of comments where Mauro (the initial poster) and his Friends discuss a concert by The Smashing Pumpkins and then talk about the band, in the contribution at Post 17 Mauro publishes a later comment which contains an action that does not orient to the action performed in the most recent comment in this comment thread. In this contribution Mauro performs an action that orients to the action performed by Petra in the comment at Post 13, where she has told Roberta (another Friend who participates in this interaction) that making "crappy" music to go on tour is an offence Billy Corgan commits against his nostalgic fans. In the comment at Post 17 Mauro seems to show affiliation with Petra, when he says that Billy Corgan is uncompromising, indeed he (Billy Corgan) does not play for his nostalgic fans (*Petra come intitolavi . . . ai nostalgici regala un cazzo. Zero Compromessi . . . e di questo ne andre fiero*). Moreover, in the comment at Post 17 Mauro performs an extra action, he selects the intended recipient of his contribution by naming her (Petra). It therefore seems that here the action of naming is done to avoid the potential for communicative problems which could arise because the action performed by Mauro in this comment does not orient to the action performed in the most recent comment posted in this comment thread.

However, as already discussed in Chapter 7, it is likely that Mauro selected the recipient of the comment at Post 17 because at the time of the data collection the *Reply* button was not available on FB. It is therefore possible that Mauro has selected Petra as the intended recipient of the comment at Post 17 because without the *Reply* button he could not position his contribution after the comment at Post 13.

What the data demonstrates is that even though the pattern for publishing later comments in a comment thread looks similar to the pattern followed by Friends when they publish a first comment in an interaction, they are not the same. In fact, while the first contribution posted by a Friend in a comment thread generally contains an action that orients to either the initial telling or the action performed in the most recent comment posted in a comment thread, a later comment contains an action that can only orient to the action performed in the most recent comment posted in a comment thread. This makes sense especially given the structure of FB comment threads. Once a Friend has posted a first comment in a comment thread, and therefore responded to the initial telling, he or she will probably not publish another comment that contains an action that orients to the same contribution. This poster will therefore presumably post a later comment which contains an action that orients to the action performed in either the most recent comment or an action performed in a contribution which has responded to the action he or she has performed in his or her first comment in the comment thread. This is particularly true for first-post tellers, who are unlikely to publish later comments which contain actions that orient to their own tellings.

As with first contributions, it seems that when an FB user publishes a later comment in a comment thread he or she does exactly what the system encourages him or her to do, but with the additional factor of not responding again to a comment which contains an action to which he or she has already responded. That is, the user will not use the *Comment* button positioned immediately after the first comment to make a later comment, since he or she has already responded to that contribution; the only ways of responding in a comment thread are through the dialogue box *Write a comment* and the *Reply* button. While the dialogue box *Write a comment* is positioned immediately after the "last" comment posted in a comment thread, thus seeming to invite a user to publish a contribution that contains an action that orients to the action performed in the most recent comment posted in a comment thread, the *Reply* button is positioned after every comment posted in a comment thread (with the exception of the first comment) and it seems to invite an FB user to post a comment that contains an action that orients to another action which has already been performed.

In any comment thread then, as a result of the FB system, FB users publishing their second or later comments are guided to orient to the action performed in the most recent comment posted in a comment thread. Where they wish to respond to another action that has already been performed in another comment instead, they can use the *Reply* button. However, this is not used in the current dataset.

Dyadic exchanges within FB comment threads

Some of the data presented above have shown that the person posting the original comment and a Friend may begin a private dyadic exchange within an ongoing comment thread when they publish a series of later comments that contain actions which orient to the actions contained in their most recent contributions in the comment thread. This can be clearly seen in Extract 8.7, which has already been presented in a brief version in Chapter 5 and reproduced here. Three separate dyadic exchanges take place between the original poster and Friends who participate in this interaction.

Extract 8.7 Fabio Volo's quote

1 Elisa: Forse c'è qualcosa di peggio dei sogni svaniti: la non voglia di sognare ancora. Fabio Volo [quote taken from a book of Fabio Volo, an Italian radio presenter] 10 ore fa
Elisa: Maybe there is something worst than vanished dreams: the desire to no longer dream. Fabio Volo *10 hours ago*

A 11 persone piace questo
11 people like this

→ 2 Franco: Già . . . poveri interisti. 10 ore fa
Franco: yeah . . . poor interisti [nickname for F. C. Inter supporters]. *10 hours ago*

3 Elisa: :-) 10 ore fa
Elisa: :-) *10 hours ago*

4 Franco: Però anche tu infierisci . . . sei cattiva! 10 ore fa
Franco: but you like to rub salt into a wound . . . you're mean! *10 hours ago*

5 Elisa: ahhaha . . . si si cattivissima . . . ! 10 ore fa
Elisa: ahhaha . . . yeah yeah really mean . . . ! *10 hours ago*

6 Franco: Come una punizione di Carletto . . . violenta e spietata! 10 ore fa
Franco: Like a free kick of Carletto [probably the nickname of a former soccer player of the team A. C. Milan] . . . *violent and cruel!* *10 hours ago*

→ 7 Francesca: mi piace!!! 7 ore fa
Francesca: I like it!!! *7 hours ago*

8 Elisa: l'ho copiata dall'ultimo libro . . . lo voglio!!!!:-) 6 ore fa
Elisa: I copied it from his latest book . . . I want it!!!!:-) *6 hours ago*

9 Francesca: ma ce l'ho!te [*sic*] lo passo se vuoi! 6 ore fa
Francesca: I have it! I can give it to you! *6 hours ago*

10 Elisa: già comprato?:-) 6 ore fa
Elisa: have you already bought it?:-) *6 hours ago*

11 Francesca: e già letto! 6 ore fa
Francesca: and I've already read it! *6 hours ago*

12 Elisa: beneeee . . . si grazie,se [*sic*] me lo presti mi fai un favore!hi [*sic*] hi hi 6 ore fa
Elisa: well doneeee . . . yes please,if you can give it to me I'll really appreciate it!hi hi hi *6 hours ago*

→ 13 Antonia: bella! la [*sic*] copio subito! 6 ore fa
Antonia: nice! I'll copy it straight away! 6 hours ago

14 Elisa: copia pure cara! 6 ore fa
Elisa: you can copy it darling! 6 hours ago

15 Antonia: L'ho già comprato anche io il libro!! Non vedo l'ora di iniziarlo! 6 ore fa
Antonia: I have already bought it too!! I can't wait to start reading it! 6 hours ago

16 Elisa: bene!!!mi [*sic*] piace un sacco 6 ore fa
Elisa: well done!!!I love him so much 6 hours ago

The quote in the comment at Post 1 opens this comment thread and is responded to in the comments at Posts 2, 7, and 13 by three different Friends. The actions performed in these comments, in turn, provoke three separate dyadic exchanges between Elisa and Franco, Elisa and Francesca, and Elisa and Antonia, who publish a series of later comments that contain actions which orient to the actions performed in their most recent contributions in this comment thread.

The first dyadic exchange is between Elisa and Franco. As mentioned above, in the comment at Post 1 Elisa publishes a quote taken from the most recent book of Fabio Volo, a radio presenter, which states that there is something worse than vanished dreams, which is the desire to no longer dream (*Forse c'è qualcosa di peggio dei sogni svaniti: la non voglia di sognare ancora. Fabio Volo*). In the comment at Post 2 Franco publishes his first contribution in this comment thread. This comment is intended to be humorous; Franco reinterprets the comment at Post 1 as being a humorous comment on the supporters of the soccer team F. C. Inter. Franco explicitly mocks F. C. Inter supporters by suggesting that they are desperate because they support a mediocre team and can no longer even dream (*Già . . . poveri interisti*).

This contribution starts a dyadic exchange of later comments that continues until the comment at Post 6. In the comments at Posts 3, 4, 5, and 6, Elisa and Franco alternately post comments that contain actions that orient to the actions performed in the most recent comments of the other in this comment thread. In the comment at Post 3, Elisa shows understanding of the humorous tone embedded in Franco's comment at Post 2 by posting a later comment which contains a representation of laughter (:-)). In the comment at Post 4, Franco continues to play with the theme of soccer by publishing a later comment (his first) that is a humorous negative evaluation of Elisa. He suggests that Elisa is mean because she has mocked F. C. Inter supporters by publishing the quote in the comment at Post 1 (*Però anche tu infierisci . . . sei cattiva!*).

Then, in the comment at Post 5 Elisa publishes another later comment which orients to the action performed by Franco in the contribution at Post 4; she agrees with the previous humorous negative evaluation proposed by Franco by stating that she is really mean (*ahhaha . . . si si cattivissima . . . !*). The action performed in the comment at Post 5 is responded to by the action performed in another later comment (the second) posted by Franco in the contribution at Post 6, where he says that Elisa is mean like a free kick of Carletto, which is probably the nickname of a former soccer player of A. C. Milan, the team supported by Elisa (*Come una punizione di Carletto . . . violenta e spietata!*).

In the comments at Posts 3, 4, 5, and 6, Elisa and Franco post several later comments which contain actions that orient to the actions performed in their most recent contributions in this comment thread and create a private dyadic exchange (the first) within the ongoing comment thread. This occurs again in the comment at Posts 8, 9, 10, 11, and 12, where Francesca and Elisa start a private dyadic exchange (the second) by publishing a series of later comments in this comment thread. In the comment at Post 7 Francesca posts her first contribution in this interaction. This comment contains an action that clearly orients to the action performed in the comment at Post 1; Francesca positively evaluates Elisa's quote by saying that she likes it (*mi piace!!!*). In the comment at Post 8, Elisa responds to Francesca by posting another later comment (her third) which orients to the contribution at Post 7. Elisa concludes the comment at Post 8 by saying that she wants to buy Fabio Volo's book (*l'ho copiata dall'ultimo libro . . . lo voglio!!!!:-)*).

In the comment at Post 9 Francesca responds to Elisa's previous comment at Post 8 by posting her first later comment in this comment thread. Francesca tells Elisa that she has already bought Fabio Volo's book and she invites Elisa to borrow it (*ma ce l'ho!te lo passo se vuoi!*). In the comment at Post 10 Elisa performs another action that orients to the action contained in Francesca's previous comment at Post 9. This action initiates a *repair sequence*, Elisa wants to verify if she has understood the comment at Post 9. She explicitly asks Francesca if she has already bought the book (*già comprato?:-)*). The action performed by Francesca in the comment at Post 11 orients to Elisa's question about the purchase of the book. Francesca says that she has already read it (*e già letto!*). After a positive evaluation of the comment at Post 11, in the comment at Post 12 Elisa performs another action in this interaction; she accepts the invitation to borrow Francesca's copy of the book (*beneeee . . . si grazie,se me lo presti mi fai un favore!hi hi hi*).

Therefore, in the comments at Posts 8, 9, 10, 11, and 12 Elisa and Francesca post five later comments containing actions that clearly orient to the actions performed in their most recent contributions in this interaction and create a private dyadic exchange (the second) within this comment thread. A third dyadic exchange occurs in the comments at Posts 14, 15, and 16, where after the action performed by Antonia in her first contribution in the comment at Post 13, she and Elisa begin a private interaction by exchanging several later comments. As mentioned above, in the comment at Post 13 Antonia publishes her first comment in this comment thread, and this contribution clearly orients to the action performed in the initial telling. After positively evaluating the quote in the comment at Post 1, Antonia tells Elisa that she will copy it (*bella! la copio subito!*). In the comment at Post 14 Elisa responds to Antonia by saying that she can use the quote (*copia pure cara!*). In the comment at Post 15 Antonia performs another action in this interaction; she seems to refer back to the invitation to borrow the book introduced by Francesca in the comment at Post 9, and she tells Elisa that she has a copy too, but she still has to read it (*L'ho già comprato anche io il libro!! Non vedo l'ora di iniziarlo!*). After a positive evaluation of the comment at Post 15, in the contribution at Post 16 Elisa posts a statement where she says that she likes Fabio Volo (*bene!!!mi piace un sacco*).

In the contributions at Posts 14, 15, and 16 Elisa and Antonia post three later comments which contain actions that orient to the actions performed in their most recent comments in this interaction and create a private dyadic exchange (the third) within this comment thread.

Private dyadic exchanges may occur within an FB comment thread opened by a first-post telling, when an initial poster and a Friend publish a series of later comments which contain actions clearly oriented to the actions performed in their most recent contributions in the comment thread. Strong evidence of the private nature of those exchanges comes from the way in which participants use second-person singular pronouns and verbs in these dyadic interactions.

Moreover, the analysis of this extract has also suggested that dyadic exchanges may begin when the person initiating the comment thread and a Friend are simultaneously online and therefore available to interact. The times of publication of the comments included within the three dyadic exchanges in Extract 8.7 suggest that they occurred when Elisa and Franco, Elisa and Francesca, and Elisa and Antonia were simultaneously online. Two other dyadic exchanges made up of later comments occur in Extract 8.8.

Extract 8.8 Tattoo

1 Alberta: Ho in mente un tatuaggio strafigo . . . . Valeria, domenica buttiamo giù qche [*sic*] idea . . . Novembre 26 alle 4:57
Alberta: I'm thinking about a cool tattoo . . . . Valeria, on Sunday we can discusssome ideas . . . November 26 at 4:57 a.m.

A Silvia piace questo
Silvia likes this

→ 2 Silvia: tipo??? Novembre 26 alle 5:01
Silvia: what kind??? November 26 at 5:01 a.m.

3 Alberta: due sposi teschi!!! ahahahahahah Novembre 26 alle 5:01
Alberta: two married skulls!!! ahahahahahah November 26 at 5:01am

4 Silvia: nooooo copiona quello è il miooooo!!!! Novembre 26 alle 5:02
Silvia: nooooo copycat that one is mineeeee!!!! November 26 at 5:02am

5 Alberta: infatti nn [*sic*] è verooooooo quell'obrobrio lo lascio a te! Novembre 26 alle 5:02
Alberta: in fact it isn't trueeeeee I'll leave that obrobrio [horrific tattoo] *to you! November 26 at 5:02 a.m.*

6 Silvia: grazie voglio l'esclusiva su quello stupendo tattoo!!! Novembre 26 alle 5:03
Silvia: thank you I want the copyrights for that marvelous tattoo!!! November 26 at 5:03 a.m.

7 Alberta: te lo lascio no problem! Novembre 26 alle 5:04
Alberta: I'll leave it to you no problem! November 26 at 5:04 a.m.

8 Silvia: yeeeeeeeeeeeeeeeeehhhhhh!!! November 26 at 5:04 a.m.

→ 9 Chiara: e non rubare nemmeno il mio [timestamp not available]
Chiara: and don't steal mine either

10 Alberta: cazzo a quello ci stavo pensando . . . uff e ora . . . mannaggia va bè cambierò!!! Novembre 26 alle 5:14
Alberta: shit I was thinking about it . . . drats and now . . . damn it what the heck I'll do something else!!! November 26 at 5:14 a.m.

11 Chiara: ahhahahahahha November 26 at 5:15 a.m.

12 Valeria: ooooook! November 26 at 6:49 a.m.

This comment thread is opened by Alberta's announcement in the comment at Post 1, which secures three different responses from Silvia, Chiara, and Valeria in the comments at Posts 2, 9, and 12. The actions performed in the comments at Posts 2 and 9 initiate two separate dyadic exchanges where Alberta and Silvia and then Alberta and Chiara publish a series of later comments which contain actions that explicitly orient to the actions performed in the most recent contributions of the other.

In the comment at Post 1 Alberta performs her first action in this interaction; she tells Friends that she is considering having a new tattoo and that on Sunday she wants to discuss it with Valeria (*Ho in mente un tatuaggio strafigo . . . . Valeria, domenica buttiamo giù qche idea . . .*). In the comment at Post 2 Silvia posts the *first pair part* of a question-answer sequence. Silvia asks Alberta what kind of tattoo she wants (*tipo???*). The action performed in this comment launches a dyadic exchange between Alberta and Silvia. In the comment at Post 3 Alberta responds to Silvia's question by mocking her and saying that she is considering having a tattoo that represents two married skulls (*due sposi teschi!!! ahahahahahah*). The way Silvia responds to this comment shows that this is a reference to a previous conversation she had with Alberta, and which probably was about a tattoo Silvia wanted. By saying in the comment at Post 4 that Alberta is stealing her own idea for a tattoo, Silvia shows that she has understood the joke in the comment at Post 3 (*nooooo copiona quello è il miooooo!!!!*).

In the comment at Post 5 Alberta explicitly tells Silvia that she was teasing her (*infatti nn è verooooooo quell'obrobrio lo lascio a te!*) and in the comment at Post 6 Silvia continues to play with the theme of "stolen" tattoos by telling Alberta that she owns the copyright for the tattoo mentioned in the comment at Post 3 (*grazie voglio l'esclusiva su quello stupendo tattoo!!!*). The humorous comment on the copyright at Post 6 is responded to by Alberta in the contribution at Post 7, where she says that she is happy to leave Silvia the copyright for her tattoo (*te lo lascio no problem!*). Then, in the comment at Post 8 Silvia performs another action in this comment thread; she expresses excitement for having "won" the battle for the tattoo (*yeeeeeeeeeeeeeeeeehhhhhh!!!*).

In the contributions at Posts 3, 4, 5, 6, 7, and 8 Alberta and Silvia have posted six later comments each of which contains an action that orients to the action performed in the most recent comment in this interaction and which creates a private dyadic exchange (the first) in this comment thread.

The same occurs in the contributions at Posts 10 and 11 where after the first contribution published by Chiara, she and Alberta begin another private dyadic exchange (the second) in this comment thread. Specifically, in the comment at Post 9 Chiara performs her first action in this comment thread; she posts a first contribution which refers to the topic of the stolen tattoo discussed by Alberta and Silvia in previous comments. Chiara warns Alberta to not try to steal her own tattoo (*e non rubare nemmeno il mio*). In the contribution at Post 10 Alberta posts a later comment which contains an action that clearly orients to the action performed by Chiara in her previous comment at Post 9; she mocks Chiara by saying that she was thinking about stealing her tattoo (*cazzo a quello ci stavo pensando . . . uff e ora . . . mannaggia va bè cambierò!!!*). In the comment at Post 11 Chiara shows that she has understood the facetious tone embedded in Alberta's previous comment at Post 10, and she responds with a representation of laughter (*ahhahahahahha*).

A private dyadic exchange may occur within an FB comment thread opened by an initial telling when the initial poster and a Friend publish several later comments which contain actions that explicitly orient to the actions performed in their most recent contributions in the comment thread.

Just as with the previous example, in this interaction participants utilize specific grammatical devices to indicate the private nature of their comments. This can be seen clearly in the comments at Posts 5, 7, and 9 where Alberta and Chiara use the second-person singular pronoun "*te*" (you) as well as the second-person singular of the imperative verb "*non rubare*" (do not steal) to explicitly select one person as the only recipient of their contributions in this comment thread.

Dyadic exchanges may occur within an FB comment thread when the person posting the original comment and a Friend are simultaneously online and therefore available to interact. The more precise timing of this extract shows this clearly. This example also suggests that a dyadic exchange may stop when a Friend who is not involved in the comment thread publishes his or her first comment in the interaction. The dyadic exchange between Alberta and Silvia stops when Chiara posts her first contribution, and then the interaction between Alberta and Chiara stops when Valeria publishes her first comment in this comment thread. However, it is not clear whether the comment from another Friend has stopped the interaction; the timing suggests that perhaps the dyadic interactions were already over in the contributions at Posts 8 and 11, respectively.

Similar dyadic exchanges occur between the person posting the original comment and a couple of Friends in Extract 8.9, where Claudio posts another photo of the tiramisù cake.

Extract 8.9 Tiramisù conversation

1 Claudio: Helping the poor tiramisu [*sic*] Yesterday at 6:03am
[Claudio publishes a photo which shows him eating the tiramisù cake]

A 4 persone piace questo

4 people like this

2 Auro: eggià lo stai aiutando a finire . . . Ieri alle 6:04
Auro: you're really helping it to finish . . . Yesterday at 6:04 a.m.

→ 3 Roger: Oh please no! Yesterday at 6:43 a.m.

4 Claudio: Oooh . . . here you are Roger ;) Yesterday at 6:43 a.m.

5 Roger: Ok, so Tuesdays and Thursdays are Mascarpone Days and Mondays, Wednesdays and Fridays are Tiramisù Days . . . and Saturday is Mascarpone-Tiramisù day ;) Yesterday at 6:46 a.m.

6 Claudio: Tiramisu [*sic*] is made with Mascarpone . . . so basically . . . a Mascarpone's week ;) Yesterday at 6:47 a.m.

7 Roger: Well I'm sure you'll vary things next week and have a Strutto week Yesterday at 6:48 a.m.

8 Claudio: when I finish the lube maybe :P Yesterday at 6:50 a.m.

→ 9 Yan: ahhhh ma beneeeee!! e [*sic*] poi mi chiedi come sviluppare gli addominali !!!! :-) Ieri alle 9:45
Yan: ahhhh well doneee!! and then you ask me how to strengthen your abdominals !!!! :-) Yesterday at 9:45 a.m.

10 Claudio: Cazzo mi ha sgamato anche Yan!!! Ma è . . . yogurt . . . O_O Ieri alle 9:47
Claudio: Fuck Yan caught me too!!! But it's . . . yogurt . . . O_O Yesterday at 9:47 a.m.

11 Yan: ahahahaah :-) Yesterday at 9:48 a.m.

12 Loris: il solito mangione -.- ahaha 13 ore fa
Loris: the same old glutton -.- ahaha 13 hours ago

This comment thread contains several later comments which create two separate dyadic exchanges between Claudio and Roger and between Claudio and Yan.

In the comment at Post 1 Claudio ironically comments on his photo-telling, which shows him eating the cake, by saying that he is helping the tiramisù by finishing it (*Helping the poor tiramisù*). After a contribution from Auro in the comment at Post 2, in the comment at Post 3 Roger performs his first action in this interaction. This contribution starts a dyadic exchange where he and Claudio publish a series of later comments which contain actions that explicitly orient to the actions performed in each other's most recent comments in this comment thread. In the comment at Post 3 Roger publishes an ironic negative evaluation of the photo-telling in the comment at Post 1. He tells Claudio to stop eating the cake (*Oh please no!*). This comment is responded to by Claudio in the contribution at Post 4, where he publishes his first later comment in this comment thread, explicitly naming Roger (*Oooh . . . here you are Roger ;)*).

In the contribution at Post 5 Roger posts his first later comment in the comment thread. After publishing the discourse marker "*ok*" which seems to summarize what he has seen and read in previous comment threads, Roger performs another action in this interaction; he mocks Claudio by saying that this week he has eaten only mascarpone cheese or tiramisù (*Ok, so Tuesdays and Thursdays are Mascarpone Days and Mondays, Wednesdays and Fridays are Tiramisù Days . . . and Saturday is Mascarpone-Tiramisù day ;)*). This comment explicitly refers to previous comment threads included within the tiramisù cake series, where Claudio has told Friends that he was eating lots of mascarpone cheese and tiramisù. In the comment at Post 6 Claudio posts another later comment which clearly orients to the action performed in the contribution at Post 5, the most recent comment in this comment thread, and continues the dyadic exchange started in the comment at Post 4. Claudio shows that he has understood the humorous tone embedded in the comment at Post 5; he tells Roger that since tiramisù is made with mascarpone he has eaten mascarpone for an entire week (*Tiramisu is made with Mascarpone . . . so basically . . . a Mascarpone's week ;)*).

In the contribution at Post 7 Roger continues the humorous dyadic exchange based on the theme of food by publishing another later comment in this comment thread where he suggests to Claudio that next week, he may vary his diet by having a "*strutto*" (lard) week (*Well I'm sure you'll vary things next week and have a Strutto week*). In the contribution at Post 8 Claudio publishes a later comment that contains an action which, even though unclear, directly orients to the action performed in the comment at Post 7. Claudio ironically says to Roger that he will change his diet when he will finish the "*lube*," which perhaps means fat in *Romagnolo* dialect (*when I finish the lube maybe :P*), or could just be a mistranslation for the Italian word *grasso* (fat).

In the contributions at Posts 4, 5, 6, 7, and 8 Claudio and Roger have posted five later comments which contain actions that orient to the actions performed in each other's most recent comments in this interaction and create a private dyadic exchange (the first) in this comment thread.

A second dyadic exchange occurs in the comments at Posts 9, 10, and 11. The action performed in the comment at Post 9 clearly orients to the comment at Post 1; Yan, who based on other comment threads, is Claudio's personal trainer, ironically congratulates Claudio for eating almost all the tiramisù cake, and then says that he has no right to ask him how to strengthen his abdominal muscles (*ahhhh ma beneeeee!! e poi mi chiedi come sviluppare gli addominali !!!! :-)*). After an initial expletive, in the comment at Post 10 Claudio performs an action that orients to the action performed by Yan in the comment at Post 9 by publishing an ironic justification for eating almost all the cake. Claudio tells Yan that it contains yogurt (*Cazzo mi ha sgamato anche Yan!!! Ma è . . . yogurt . . . O_O*). In the contribution at Post 11 Yan publishes his first later comment in this comment thread, which is a representation of laughter followed by a smiling emoticon (*ahahahaah :-)*). The action performed in this comment clearly orients to the action performed by Claudio in the comment at Post 10 and concludes the dyadic exchange.

In general, then, private dyadic exchanges may occur when the initial poster and a Friend publish several later comments which contain actions that explicitly orient to the actions performed in their most recent comments in the comment thread. Moreover, dyadic exchanges seem to start when the FB user initiating the interaction and a Friend are simultaneously online and available to interact. The time of publication of the comments at Posts 3, 4, 5, 6, 7, 8, 9, 10, and 11 clearly indicates that Claudio and Roger and then Claudio and Yan were simultaneously online when they published those contributions in this comment thread, with at most a couple of minutes between each comment in the dyadic interactions.

In addition, in the comments at Posts 4, 7, and 9, Claudio, Roger, and Yan utilize the second-person singular pronouns "you" and the second-person singular of the verb *chiedere* (ask) to explicitly select them as recipients of their comments while potentially excluding other Friends from these dyadic exchanges.

Further evidence of the private nature of dyadic exchanges which take place within FB comment threads comes from Extract 8.10, which has already been discussed earlier in Chapters 3 and 6 and is presented here in an abbreviated form. This is the only case in the data where a dyadic exchange occurs between two Friends who participate in a comment thread, rather than between a Friend and the original poster.

Extract 8.10 iPhone[4]

1 Renzo: non ce l'ho fatta . . . alla fine l'ho preso!!! il [*sic*] mio primo iphone!!!!
Ieri alle ore 5:35
Renzo: I couldn't resist . . . at the end I bought it!!! my first iphone!!!!
Yesterday at 5:35 a.m.

A Loris, Mauro e altre 4 persone piace questo elemento
Loris, Mauro, and other 4 people like this

[. . .]

5 Linda: auhaha noooo!! devi [*sic*] essere riposato . . . se no nn [*sic*] riesci as [*sic*] usarlo poi!!! Ieri alle ore 5:38
Linda: auhaha noooo!! You need to rest . . . otherwise, you won't be able to use it!!! *Yesterday at 5:38 a.m.*

6 Mauro: Ti abbiamo detto di aspettare! Ieri alle ore 6:05
Mauro: We told you to wait! *Yesterday at 6:05 a.m.*

→ 7 Alberto: renz [*sic*] non darlo in mano alla linda [*sic*] . . . ;) e nemmeno a ferrò che se no lo usa come sasso da far rimbalzare sull'acqua . . . Ieri alle ore 6:08
Alberto: renz don't give it to linda . . . ;) or to ferrò [probably the name of one of Renzo's Friends] *otherwise he'll use it as a stone to bounce on the water . . .* *Yesterday at 6:08 a.m.*

→ 8 Linda: ooohhh . . . Albe problemi!?!? Renz [*sic*] t [*sic*] capisco . . . avevi la scimmietta . . . Ieri alle ore 6:26
Linda: ooohhh . . . Albe do you have a problem!?!? Renz I understand you . . . you had to have it ["*scimmietta*" is a slang term which means to strongly desire something] . . . *Yesterday at 6:26 a.m.*

→ 9 Alberto: io no . . . l'iphone di renzo [*sic*] si se lo da in mano a te . . .! Ieri alle ore 6:27
Alberto: I don't . . . but renzo's iphone does, if he gives it to you . . .! *Yesterday at 6:27 a.m.*

10 Angela: spendaccione! ma [*sic*] fa bene coccolarsi a volte, no? io [*sic*] "invece" mi sa che ormai devo proprio decidermi a cambiare cell e a prenderne uno che almeno abbi [*sic*] la fotocamera, che dici? :) Ieri alle ore 6:29
Angela: spendthrift! but sometimes we have to spoil ourselves, don't we? Instead I reckon that I need to make up my mind and buy a new mobile with a camera, what do you reckon? :) *Yesterday at 6:29 a.m.*

→ 11 Linda: CANE!! Ieri alle ore 6:29
Linda: Dog!! *Yesterday at 6:29 a.m.*

→ 12 Alberto: a cuccia! Ieri alle ore 6:29
Alberto: sit! *Yesterday at 6:29 a.m.*

[. . .]

In the comments at Posts 7, 8, 9, 11, and 12, Alberto and Linda, two Friends who participate in this interaction, start a private dyadic exchange within the ongoing comment thread. In the comment at Post 7 Alberto publishes his first contribution in this interaction, which contains an action that also begins the dyadic exchange with Linda. The action performed in the initial unit of this comment clearly refers to Linda's joke in the comment at Post 5, where she asks Renzo to put down his phone and get some sleep (*auhaha noooo!! devi essere riposato . . . se no nn riesci as usarlo poi!!!*). Alberto suggests to Renzo that he should not leave his new phone in Linda's hands (*renz non darlo in mano alla linda . . . ;)*). Although the comment at Post 7 is phrased as an interaction with Renzo, the action performed by Linda in the comment at Post 8 shows that she has understood the humorous approach of Alberto's previous comment at Post 7, and in fact in the initial unit of the comment at Post 8 she asks him if he has a problem (*ooohhh . . . Albe problemi!?!?*), before explicitly returning to talk to Renzo (*Renz t capisco . . . avevi la scimmietta . . .*). In the comment at Post 9 Alberto continues the dyadic exchange with Linda by performing another action in this comment thread. He responds to her ironic question in the comment at Post 8 when he tells her that though he does not have any problems with her, Renzo's new phone might have a problem if Renzo gives it to her (*io no . . . l'iphone di renzo si se lo da in mano a te . . .!*). Even though in the comment at Post 10, Angela publishes her first contribution in this comment thread, Linda and Alberto explicitly ignore this comment while continuing their playful private dyadic exchange. In the comment at Post 11 Linda performs another action in this interaction when she jokingly offends Alberto by saying that he is a dog (*CANE!!*) and in the comment at Post 12 Alberto tells Linda to calm down and stay in her place (*a cuccia!*) (sit).

Therefore, it seems that even though almost all the dyadic exchanges included in the data generally involve the initial poster and a Friend, a dyadic exchange is also possible between two other Friends, although for the first few exchanges in this interaction both parties also explicitly perform actions that orient to the person initiating the thread (Renzo) in part of their comments, while clearly selecting the other Friend in another part of the contribution. Moreover, this comment thread has demonstrated the strength of dyadic exchanges, and in fact even though another Friend (Angela) has posted a contribution in the middle of this exchange, Alberto and Linda have ignored it while continuing with their private interaction.

Conclusions

This chapter has introduced the idea of a later comment and has argued that when an original poster or a Friend publishes a later comment in a comment thread opened by an initial telling, this regularly contains an action that orients to the action performed in the most recent contribution posted in the comment thread. As per first comments, this shows that the system has an impact on the structure of comment threads. In fact, when an FB user publishes a later comment in a comment thread, he or she does exactly what the system seems designed for him or her to do, responding to the most recent comment in the comment thread.

Furthermore, when an original poster and a Friend post a series of later comments which contain actions that orient to the actions performed in their most recent contributions, this may initiate a dyadic exchange within the comment thread. The private nature of these dyadic exchanges is shown by the use of specific grammatical devices, such as second-person singular pronouns and the imperative mood, which explicitly select participants as recipients of their comments, while potentially excluding other Friends from those exchanges. Moreover, those dyadic exchanges seem to occur only when the initial poster and a Friend are simultaneously online and therefore available to interact in a comment thread.

This chapter has thus focused on answering the second of the research questions of this book: *What is the sequence organization of FB comment threads?* This organization is very simple. Following an initial comment that contains a first-post telling, Friends' first comments contain actions that orient to either this initial comment or the action performed in the contribution immediately before their own; later comments from Friends or the original poster contain actions that orient to the action performed in the most recent comment. These patterns of organization align well with the affordances and limitations of the FB system.

9

Conclusion

Introduction

The aim of this book is to describe the organization of FB comment threads. More precisely, this book has applied the principles of conversation analysis to analyze interactions which occurred among speakers of Italian on the FB Home, and has attempted to address the following research questions:

- Are comments within FB comment threads organized in an identifiable structure?
- If so, what is the *sequence organization* of FB comment threads?

After summarizing the reasons which allow us to see that there is an organization in FB comment threads, this chapter gathers together some of the major findings of this book and it provides some suggestions for future research.

Evidence of *sequence organization* in FB comment threads

As mentioned in Chapter 1, one of the principal features of spoken conversation is that conversationalists perform actions when they produce turns at talk (Liddicoat, 2011; Sacks, 1992; Schegloff, 2007). This idea is used by researchers to explain the *sequence organization* of spoken conversation. Turns at talk come one after the other because of the actions they perform. In other words, the action accomplished in a first turn at talk makes the action performed in a second turn the relevant next, which may generate a third action and so on. Turns at talk are therefore organized in sequences, such as request-acceptance or decline, question-answer, greeting-greeting, and so on, because of the actions they perform (Liddicoat, 2011; Sacks, 1992; Schegloff, 2007). The idea of *sequence organization* is thus used by analysts to describe what normally happens in spoken conversation, which is that turns at talk are organized in sequences because of the actions they perform.

This idea can also be applied to FB comment threads and social media more generally. In fact, as shown by this book, FB users perform actions when they post comments in comment threads. For example, when an FB user publishes the first comment in a new comment thread, he or she accomplishes an action, and generally is responding to the system prompt *What's on your mind?* (see **Chapter 2**). On the other hand, when a Friend posts a first comment in an already existing comment thread, he or she performs another action, which is to respond to either the action performed in the initial or the most recent comment in the comment thread (see **Chapter 7**). FB users can also perform an action when they publish a later comment in a comment thread, generally responding to the action performed in the most recent comment in the interaction (see **Chapter 8** for more detail). Therefore, FB users perform actions when they publish comments in comment threads. This means that comments do not casually follow one after the other, but are organized in a coherent way. This is because of the actions performed by FB users in these contributions. This organization is referred to in this book as *sequence organization*.

Thus, although spoken conversation and FB comment threads are two different exchange systems, *sequence organization* is identifiable in both of them. More specifically, even though spoken conversation is oral, synchronous and normally takes place among copresent speakers, while FB comment threads are mainly written asynchronous, and generally among geographically dispersed users, contributions occurring in both these systems are not random, but organized in a meaningful way.

In summary, this book has found that FB users accomplish actions when they post comments in comment threads. In addition, these actions are not random, but they are organized in sequences, such as those that characterize turns at talk in spoken conversation (see **Chapter 3**).

Features of the *sequence organization* of FB comment threads

As mentioned above, this book has demonstrated that there is *sequence organization* in FB comment threads. Features of this organization are summarized below.

A typical feature which characterizes the *sequence organization* of FB comment threads is that comment threads are generally opened by first-post tellings (see **Chapter 4**). This finding confirms what has been hypothesized by previous research on FB status updates[1] (Bolander and Locher, 2010; Carr, Schrock, and Dauterman, 2012; Farina, 2015; Frobenius and Harper, 2015; Georgakopoulou, 2013b; Georgalou, 2015b; Giaxoglou, 2015a, 2015b; Lee, 2011; Page, 2010b, 2012; West, 2013). This literature noted that status updates generally consist of narratives; however, this book has not only confirmed this, but has also argued that FB users utilize tellings to open comment threads. This is because FB users know that by performing a telling they are more likely to secure responses from Friends.

Strong evidence that FB users are aiming to secure responses from Friends comes from the additional actions they perform in their first-post tellings (see **Chapter 5**). In some cases an FB user may select the recipients of a telling by explicitly naming them; for instance, by publishing the nicknames of the Friends he or she wants to respond to the telling. In other cases an FB user may provide Friends with an interactional framework to interpret a telling. That is, an FB user may post a textual message which introduces or assesses the telling in order to provide Friends with information on the way he or she wants them to respond to it. Finally, an FB user may use humor to help secure responses from Friends, as humor creates a sense of in-group understanding among Friends, which indeed stimulates their responses to the telling (see **Chapter 5** for more detail).

This book has also argued that first-post tellings can have five different formats: textual messages only, photos only, hyperlinks only, or combinations of textual messages with photos or hyperlink-tellings (see **Chapter 4**). This suggests that the resources of FB have an impact on the format of first-post tellings. In other words, this book indicates that the presence of a photo or a hyperlink in the opening comment of a comment thread depends on how an FB user utilizes the "tools" available on the Home and other webpages. Such tools include the *Add Photo/Video* and *Share* buttons. While the *Add Photo/Video* button allows an FB user to publish photos and videos on the Home, the *Share* button enables him or her to post news, videos, and contents from other websites directly on the Home, and if desired, to comment on them.

Results of this book have also demonstrated that while the *Add Photo/Video* and *Share* buttons impact on the format of tellings, these do not affect the *sequence organization* of FB comment threads. Friends respond in the same way to first-post tellings that consist of textual messages only, photos only, and hyperlinks only as well as to those which consist of combinations of textual messages with photos or hyperlinks. In other words, even though the occurrence of a telling in the opening comment of a comment thread impacts on its *sequence organization*, the format of the telling does not (see **Chapter 4**).

This book has then argued that tellings occurring in the opening comments of FB comment threads can be autobiographical or about a third-person event (see **Chapter 4**). However, this book has found that, like the format of first-post tellings, this classification does not impact on the *sequence organization* of comment threads. Whether a first-post telling is autobiographical or about a third-person event, this does not affect the way in which Friends respond to it, in sequential terms (see **Chapter 7** for a detailed discussion on the ways in which Friends respond to initial tellings).

In summary, this book has found that neither the format nor the content of a telling impacts on the *sequence organization* of a comment thread. Friends respond in the same way to textual, photo, and hyperlink-tellings as well as to tellings which consist of combinations of textual messages with photos or hyperlinks about autobiographical and third-person events.

Comments in response to a first-post telling

After finding that FB users may perform several actions to secure recipients for initial tellings (see **Chapter 5**), this book has analyzed comments that respond to first-post tellings.

In investigating responses to initial tellings, this book has argued that Friends respond to first-post tellings in several different ways, for instance with positive or negative evaluations and unlikely statements (see **Chapter 7** for more detail). Despite the different ways in which Friends may respond to a first-post telling, these responses contain an action that shows an understanding of, and orients to, the initial telling. This is similar to what happens in spoken conversation, where responses to a telling generally contain actions that orient to and show understanding of it (C. Goodwin, 1986; M. Goodwin, 1993; Jefferson, 1984; Liddicoat, 2011; Mandelbaum, 1989; Norrick, 1993, 1994; Pomerantz, 1984; Sacks, 1974, 1992; Terasaki, 2004). This means that despite the medium, that is, whether an interaction is oral, synchronous, and among copresent participants like in a spoken conversation or written, asynchronous, and among geographically dispersed users, as in FB comment threads, one of the fundamental ways in which human beings respond to a telling is by performing an action that shows an understanding of the telling and orients to it.

Another major finding identified in investigating comments that respond to first-post tellings is that the first comment posted by a Friend in a comment thread generally contains an action that orients to either the action performed in the first or the most recent comment in the comment thread (see **Chapter** 7). This finding is particularly important in understanding the organization of FB comment threads. When a Friend publishes a first comment in an already existing comment thread, he or she seems to ignore the actions performed by other Friends in the interaction, and instead he or she performs an action that orients to either the action accomplished in the first or the most recent comment in the comment thread. Thus, the first comment published by a Friend in a comment thread does not need to be adjacently positioned after the initial telling to respond to it.

This finding is particularly important because it makes FB comment threads different from spoken conversation. Publishing a comment which contains an action that orients to the action accomplished in a contribution which does not immediately precede it, contrasts with one of the fundamental principles of spoken conversation, which claims that "next turns are understood by co-participants to display their speaker's understanding of the just prior turn and to embody an action responsive to the just-prior turn so understood" (Schegloff, 2007, p. 15). In FB comment threads, there is a far less strong emphasis on the "just prior" comment, with a corresponding stronger focus on the first comment in a comment thread.

This focus on the action performed in the first comment in a comment thread, in addition to a focus on the action performed in the most recent comment, shows that the medium impacts on the way FB comment threads are organized. In fact, when a Friend publishes a first comment in a comment thread, he or she is following the guidance of the system, which positions the possible dialogue box and the button for publishing a contribution to a comment thread immediately following either the first comment or the most recent comment in a comment thread.

This alignment of the FB system options to the normal behavior of users posting comments is also reflected in the case of later comments in comment threads. This book has in fact found that when an initial teller or a Friend publishes a later comment in a comment thread, he or she does what the system encourages him or her to do, which is to perform an action that orients only to the action performed in the most recent comment in the comment thread.

This book has found that while there are some similarities between spoken conversation and FB comment threads, the affordances and constraints of the medium affect the way in which Friends respond in comment threads which are opened by first-post tellings.

Suggestions for future research

Since this book has investigated the *sequence organization* of FB comment threads by using Italian data only, it would be useful for future research to examine data in other languages, to see whether there are similarities or differences in the *sequence organization* of FB comment threads across different languages.

It would also be useful to conduct research to verify whether other variables, such as the gender or age of contributors, impact on the *sequence organization* of FB comment threads. A recent study undertaken by Page (2012) suggests that FB status updates published by female users contain more nonverbal displays of emotions, such as emoticons, kisses, and laughter, than those posted by male users. It is thus possible that the gender and age of contributors may affect the way they interact on FB.

Finally, it would be useful to study whether *Reactions*, the emojis which have been recently introduced on FB, have an impact on the *sequence organization* of comment threads. These features which consist of a heart, a happy face, an astonished face, a crying face, and an angry face are used by FB users to respond to comments posted in comment threads. In other words, the function of these emojis appears to be similar to the function of the *Like* button; they provide FB users with the opportunity to provide a minimal response to a comment in a comment thread. However, although they are available after every comment posted in a comment thread, it seems that FB users use *Reactions* mainly to respond to the initial comment of a comment thread. This supports what has been repeatedly claimed in this book, that the opening comment of a comment thread has a special status in FB comment threads.

In closing

This book has applied a conversation analytic approach to investigate FB comment threads, and it has shown that comments in these interactions do not occur at random, but are organized in a specific way. This is important because it demonstrates that there is *sequence organization* in FB comment threads. In other words, this book has provided evidence of the orderliness of FB communication, showing that this type of interaction, like spoken conversation and other forms of computer-mediated communication, is not random, but organized in a meaningful way. In general, therefore, this book has demonstrated that FB users perform actions when posting comments in comment threads. Comments can be examined to see what actions are being accomplished through them, what possible response may follow a previous comment, what comment is next, and, more importantly, what sequence is being constructed within comment threads. Overall, comments in comment threads have a clear organization, and this structure can be analyzed in relation to the actions that are performed through them.

In general, this book has added to previous linguistic research on social interaction. It has suggested that the affordances and constraints of the medium seem to affect the way in which the interaction is organized. In doing this it encourages further research to explore whether this is also the case for other types of computer-mediated communication, such as interactions that take place on Twitter and WhatsApp.

Appendix A

Extracts 3.5 and 5.19 Metroman

1 Mauro: Cmq [*sic*] ormai siamo arrivati ad un Livello Superiore. L'anno prossimo partecipa agli EMA's [Mauro publishes a hyperlink about Metroman] Lunedì alle 9:27

Mauro: by the way it's clear that he has reached a higher Level. Next year he will participate in the European Music Awards *Monday at 9:27 a.m.*

A 5 persone piace questo

5 people like this

2 Mauro: Parola d'ordine: SUBBBLIMARE [quote taken from the video contained in the hyperlink at post 1] Metroman . . . mannagia a te . . . Lunedì alle 9:27

Mauro: password: SUBBBLIMARE [term probably created by Metroman which is impossible to translate] *damn you Metroman . . .*

Monday at 9:27 a.m.

3 Mauro: Gianni Zaira Valeria Amelia Claudia Sara Aldo

Monday at 9:28 a.m.

4 Vanessa: hahahahhahahhahahaahahhahaahhaahhahhahaahhaah sto piangendo Lunedì alle 9:29

Vanessa: hahahahhahahhahahaahahhahaahhaahhahhahaahhaah I'm crying *Monday at 9:29 a.m.*

5 Mauro: Alessio Chiara Auron Monday at 9:29 a.m.

6 Vanessa: io sono un artista perchè mio padre da giovane era un'artista [*sic*] [quote taken from the video contained in the hyperlink at post 1]. Lunedì alle 9:30

Vanessa: I'm an artist because my father was an artist when he was young

Monday at 9:30 a.m.

7 Alessio: quella mattina a cascina gobba [*sic*] [metro station] mi ha cambiato la vita . . . lo ammetto . . . Lunedì alle 9:30

Alessio: that morning at Cascina Gobba he changed my life . . . I have to admit *Monday at 9:30 a.m.*

8 Mauro: [Mauro publishes a hyperlink containing another video about Metroman] Monday at 9:30 a.m.

9 Vanessa: ma . . . milano777 su utube [*sic*] è lui che si fa i video da solo sul suo canale suppongo ahahhah :D Lunedì alle 9:31
Vanessa: but . . . milano777 on utube I suppose that he shoots his own videos and then uploads them on his channel ahahhah :D Monday at 9:31 a.m.

10 Mauro: Parole Grosse che faranno tremate [*sic*] La Critica Musicale Internazionale: "IO SO [*sic*] MEGLIO DI BAGLIONI, IO Sò [*sic*] MEGLIO DI RENATO ZERO . . . IO sò [*sic*] MEGLIO DE GIORG MAIKOL [*sic*]" [quote probably taken from the video contained in the hyperlink at Post 1] Applausi. Lunedì alle 9:32
Mauro: Important words that will shake the International music critics: "I'M BETTER THAN BAGLIONI, I'M BETTER THAN RENATO ZERO [Italian singers] . . . *I'M BETTER THAN GIORG MAIKOL* [English musician]" *Applause. Monday at 9:32 a.m.*

11 Vanessa: AHHAHAHHAAH mio padre e [*sic*] di torino [*sic*] mia madre e [*sic*] siciliana e io ho origini romane [quote probably taken from the video contained in the hyperlink at Post 1] ODDDIOOOOOO Lunedì alle 9:32
Vanessa: AHHAHAHHAAH my father was from Turin and my mother was Sicilian and I have roman origins OH MY GODDDDDDDD Monday at 9:32 a.m.

12 Alessio: qua lagggente [*sic*] è tutta triste . . . io sono il punto di riferimento [quote taken from the video published within the hyperlink at Post 1] Lunedì alle 9:33
Alessio: everyone here is sad . . . I'm the point of reference Monday at 9:33 a.m.

13 Vanessa: AHAHAHHAHAHAHAHAHHAHAAHHHHA ODDDIO io lo amo. lui [*sic*] è un artista completo Lunedì alle 9:33
Vanessa: AHAHAHHAHAHAHAHAHHAHAAHHHHA O MY GOOD I love him. he's a complete artist Monday at 9:33 a.m.

14 Mauro: 3.33 IO SONO PURE PSPSSICOLOGO [*sic*] CAPITO [quote taken from the video published within the hyperlink at Post 1] Stangin [*sic*] Ovation Lunedì alle 9:33
Mauro: 3.33 I'M ALSO A PISYPSYCHOLOGIST Stangin Ovation Monday at 9:33 a.m.

15 Valeria: A livello di completezza io mi ritengo un artista completo [quote taken from the video published within the hyperlink at Post 1]. Lunedì alle 9:34
Valeria: As far as completeness is concerned I consider myself a complete artist. Monday at 9:34 a.m.

16 Vanessa: Valeria: il livello della mia arte . . . ehhhhh ahhhh mm cioè ad esempio eheheh ohhhh RENATO ZERO E' UN ATTORE [quote taken from the video published within the hyperlink at Post 1]. Lunedì alle 9:35
Vanessa: Valeria: the level of my art . . . ehhhhh ahhhh mm for example eheheh ohhhh RENATO ZERO [Italian singer] *IS AN ACTOR. Monday at 9:35 a.m.*

17 Alessio: volevo dedicare questa canzone a Jose Mourinho . . . un grande allenatore! [quote taken from the video published within the hyperlink at Post 1] basta [*sic*] Jose Mourinho qua io mi sciolgo Lunedì alle 9:35
Alessio: I would like to dedicate this song to Jose Mourinho [famous soccer coach] . . . *a great coach! at this point I melt down Monday at 9:35 a.m.*

18 Mauro: Minuto 2.30 "INQUADRAMI IL SALTO MORTALE" [quote taken from the video published within the hyperlink at Post 1] Lunedì alle 9:36
Mauro: Minute 2.30 "FRAME THE SOMERSAULT" Monday at 9:36 a.m.

19 Mauro: ahahahaAlessio [*sic*] Jose Mourinho . . . quello è il passpartout [*sic*] per il tuo cuore, da domani butterai via tutti i file musicali che hai . . . SOLO LUI. Lunedì alle 9:37
Mauro: ahahahaAlessio . . . that's the pass for your heart, starting from tomorrow you'll throw away all your audio files . . . ONLY HIM. Monday at 9:37 a.m.

20 Valeria: Eccoooooooooooooooooooooo, è il video in cui ci sono io! Lunedì alle 9:37
Valeria: Hereeeeeeeeeeeeeeeee, in this video you can see me! Monday at 9:37 a.m.

21 Vanessa: dove valeeeeee [*sic*] ahahahaha Lunedì alle 9:38
Vanessa: where are you valeeeeee ahahahaha Monday at 9:38 a.m.

22 Vanessa: ah ccotiiii [*sic*] seis eduta [*sic*] ahhahah Lunedì alle 9:38
Vanessa: ah I found youuuuu you're seated ahhahah Monday at 9:38 a.m.

23 Amelia:—gnahahahah ma infatti ti vedi mentre gli fai il video lì seduta o sbaglio? (il vecchio in imbarazzo in primo piano:voto [*sic*] mille) Lunedì alle 9:38
Amelia:—gnahahahah that's right you can see yourself seated while filming him or am I wrong? (the embarrassed old man on the video looks amazing) Monday at 9:38 a.m.

24 Mauro: Prima Seduta a Destra. Borsa Beige. Lunedì alle 9:38
Mauro: the First One Seated on the Right. Beige Bag. Monday at 9:38 a.m.

25 Vanessa ahhahahahahahahaha il saltooooooooooooooooooooo Lunedì alle 9:39
Vanessa ahhahahahahahahaha the jumppppppppppppp Monday at 9:39 a.m.

26 Amelia: ASPE [*sic*] CHE DEVO FARE IL SALTO [quote taken from the video published within the hyperlink at Post 18]. muoio [*sic*]. Lunedì alle 9:39
Amelia: WAIT BECAUSE I HAVE TO JUMP. I'm dying. Monday at 9:39 a.m.

27 Valeria: Ero in lacrime, giuro. Lunedì alle 9:39
Valeria: I swear I was crying. Monday at 9:39 a.m.

28 Mauro: UNO OSAVA TENERE SU LE CUFFIE . . . che Blasfemìa . . . Lunedì alle 9:40
Mauro: A MAN DARE TO HAVE HIS HEADPHONES ON . . . Blasphemy . . . Monday at 9:40 a.m.

29 Daniele: AHAHA vale [*sic*], dovevi alzarti e fargli il controcoro come fai con gli Into ;) Lunedì alle 9:41
Daniele: AHAHA Valeria, you should have stood up and sang harmonies as you generally do with the Into [probably the name of Valeria's band] *;) Monday at 9:41 a.m.*

30 Mauro: [Mauro publishes a fourth hyperlink containing another video about Metroman] Mario Pietro Pino Arturo questa è per Voi Lunedì alle 9:41
Mauro: Mario Pietro Pino Arturo [nicknames of Mauro's Friends] *this is for You Monday at 9:41 a.m.*

31 Mauro: Il Balletto con SMile [*sic*] che tira fuori la Lingua . . .OLA! Lunedì alle 9:42
Mauro: the Dance with the Smile pulling out its tongue . . . OLA! Monday at 9:42 a.m.

32 Vanda: faccio effetto solo [*sic*] Milano, capito?????? [quote taken from the video published within the hyperlink at Post 1] ero sulla banchina della metro e l'ho sentito da fuori. peccato [*sic*] che non ho fatto in tempo a entrare in quel vagone :) Lunedì alle 9:43
Vanda: I make sense only in Milan, do you understand????? I was waiting on the subway bench and I heard him from the outside. Such a shame I had no time to catch that carriage:) Monday at 9:43 a.m.

33 Zaira: io ho provato questa emozione e ne sono orgogliosa cazzo.
Zaira: I've experienced this emotion and fuck I'm proud of it. Timestamp not available

34 Zaira: e pensa che non la prendo quasi mai la metro io! . . . mi [*sic*] ha fatto "terra promessa" . . . ♥ Lunedì alle 9:45
Zaira: and to think that I hardly ever use the subway . . . he sang "terra promessa" [Italian song] *. . . for me ♥ Monday at 9:45 a.m.*

35 Mauro: Le Origini . . . il MOONWALKER di MM. [Mauro publishes a fifth hyperlink containing another video about Metroman] Lunedì alle 9:58
Mauro: the Origins . . . the MOONWALKER of MM. Monday at 9:58 a.m.

36 Giorgio: . . . mi vergogno di essere vissuto in quella citta! Lunedì alle 10:22
Giorgio: . . . I'm ashamed of having lived in that city! Monday at 10:22 a.m.

37 Riva: AHAHAHAHAHAHAHAAAAAAAAAAAAAHHHHHHHHHHH!!!!!!!!!
Monday at 10:43 a.m.

38 Aldo: Ha una nomination garantita x best underground artist 16 ore fa
Aldo: he will definitively receive a nomination for best underground artist 16 hours ago

39 Pietro: l'altro giorno l'ho beccato per la terza volta!!! 15 ore fa
Pietro: the other day I saw him for the third time!!! 15 hours ago

Extracts 3.7, 6.3, and 8.10 iPhone

1 Renzo: non ce l'ho fatta . . . alla fine l'ho preso!!! il [*sic*] mio primo iphone!!!!
Renzo: I couldn't resist . . . at the end I bought it!!! my first iphone!!!!

A Loris, Mauro e altre 4 persone piace questo elemento
Loris, Mauro, and other 4 people like this

2 Sara: io ancora resisto . . .
Sara: I still resist . . .

3 Linda: che emozione!!! domani [*sic*] smanettiamo!!!
Linda: how exciting!!! tomorrow we'll play with it!!!

4 Renzo: ssiiiiiiiIiiiiii!!! non [*sic*] so se riuscirò a dormire!!
Renzo: yeahahahahahha!!! I don't know, whether I'll be able to sleep!!

5 Linda: auhaha noooo!! devi [*sic*] essere riposato . . . se no nn [*sic*] riesci as [*sic*] usarlo poi!!!
Linda: auhaha noooo!! You need to rest . . . otherwise, you won't be able to use it!!!

6 Mauro: Ti abbiamo detto di aspettare!
Mauro: We told you to wait!

7 Alberto: renz [*sic*] non darlo in mano alla linda [*sic*] . . . ;) e nemmeno a ferrò che se no lo usa come sasso da far rimbalzare sull'acqua . . .
Alberto: renz don't give it to linda . . . ;) or to ferrò [probably the nickname of one of Renzo's Friends], *otherwise he'll use it as a stone to bounce on the water . . .*

8 Linda: ooohhh . . . Albe problemi!?!? Renz [*sic*] t [*sic*] capisco . . . avevi la scimmietta . . .
Linda: ooohhh . . . Albe do you have a problem!?!? Renz I understand you . . . you had to have it ["*scimmietta*" is a slang term which means to strongly desire something] . . .

9 Alberto: io no . . . l'iphone di renzo [*sic*] si se lo da in mano a te . . .!
Alberto: I don't . . . but renzo's iphone does, if he gives it to you . . .!

10 Angela: spendaccione! ma [*sic*] fa bene coccolarsi a volte, no? io [*sic*] "invece" mi sa che ormai devo proprio decidermi a cambiare cell e a prenderne uno che almeno abbi [*sic*] la fotocamera, che dici? :)
Angela: spendthrift! but sometimes we have to spoil ourselves, don't we? Instead I reckon that I need to make up my mind and buy a new mobile with a camera, what do you reckon? :)

11 Linda: CANE!!
Linda: Dog!!

12 Alberto: a cuccia!
Alberto: sit!

13 Renzo: In effetti l'intento era quello di aspettare a prenderlo ma . . . non ho resistito . . . mi farò regalare il 5 per natale in caso!!
Renzo: actually the idea was to wait before buying it but . . . I couldn't resist . . . I'll ask someone to buy me the 5 for Christmas just in case!!

14 Piera: ma non avevamo convinto salvo [*sic*] a prenderlo??????
Piera: but didn't we persuade salvo [probably the nickname of another of Renzo's Friends] *to buy it??????*

15 Fabiana: il mio primo?? ma [*sic*] perchè ci sarà un secondo eo [*sic*] un terzo? io [*sic*] posso prendere il tuo rottamato poi
Fabiana: my first?? does that mean that there'll be a second and a third one? So then I can have your old one

16 Giulia: mani bucate! ;P
Giulia: spendthrift! ;P

Extracts 3.8 and 7.4 Music discussion-Bancale

1 [Mauro publishes a hyperlink which contains a video of one of the songs of Bancale] 10:56

A 3 persone piace questo
3 people like this

2 Mauro: eccolo, questo è il nuovo Guru—Il Neubauten Italiano [*sic*] che sembra TufKad (e molti altri—meno che un cantante diciamo . . .) Alessia, Zaira, Claudia, Chiara, Bono, Cinzia 10:56
Mauro: here he is, the new Guru—The Italian Neubauten who looks like TufKad [names of two singers] *(and many others—apart from a singer shall we say . . .) Alessia, Zaira, Claudia, Chiara, Bono, Cinzia 10:56 a.m.*

3 Dario: sopra tutto [*sic*] . . . la cariola [*sic*]! 11:15
Dario: especially . . . the wheelbarrow! 11:15 a.m.

4 Gianni: E MI CHIEDI CHE COS'E' IL MIO VUOTO!?!?!? 19:41
Gianni: AND YOU ASK ME WHAT IS MY EMPTINESS!?!?!? 7:41 p.m.

5 Alessia: —oddio, ma è il numero uno O_ò 20:25

Alessia:—oh my god, but he is the best O_ò 8:25 p.m.

6 Claudia: Mi piace! Vorrei che mi parlasse di notte, seduto per terra accanto al mio letto.

Io lo so da che libro vengo. 22:00

Claudia: I like him!

I wish he would talk to me at night, sitting on the floor close to my bed.

I know from which book I come from. 10 p.m.

7 Mauro: io porto Torce 22:00

Mauro: I'll bring Torce [the term *Torce* could refer to the Human Torch, one of the characters of the comic book Fantastic Four] *10 p.m.*

8 Cinzia: tenerezza quando salutava con la manina, io cmq [*sic*] voglio dare loro una seconda chance. 3:13

Cinzia: how sweet when he waved goodbye with his little hand, in any case I want to give them a second chance. 3:13 a.m.

9 Sara: io no 3:13

Sara: I don't 3:13 a.m.

10 Cinzia: L'idea iniziale è quella di scrivere canzoni in cui il blues delle origini incontri le rispettive influenze dei tre componenti del gruppo per raccontare sia nei testi che nelle atmospfere [*sic*] dei brani la provincia bergamasca come luogo geografico, sociale ed esistenziale. 3:16

Cinzia: The initial idea was to write songs in which the original blues was mixed with the respective influences of the three members of the band in order to be able to tell of the province of Bergamo as a geographical, social and existential place in both the texts and the atmospheres of the songs. 3:16 a.m.

11 Cinzia: = non venite mai a bergamo [*sic*] 3:16

Cinzia: = don't ever come to bergamo 3:16 a.m.

12 Mauro: Poeta e Maniaco, Ragioniere e Muratore. Credo inizi ed essere perfetto. 3:18

Mauro: Poet and Maniac, Accountant and Bricklayer. I think that it/he/they [either the situation, the singer, or more members of the band] *is/are starting to be perfect. 3:18 a.m.*

13 Rosanna: dai che sti [*sic*] qua sono dei frantuma-cojones! 5:31

Rosanna: please these people are a pain in the arse! 5:31 a.m.

14 Mauro: questo di sicuro . . . anche a colpi di mazza! ☺ 5:57

Mauro: absolutely . . . a huge pain in the arse! [original play on words on the term "*rompere*" (to break) in the comment at post 13 which is not translatable]*!* ☺ *5:57 a.m.*

15 Rosanna: e a colpi di carriola! 6:25

Rosanna: a mega pain in the arse [another comment that refers to the play on words started in the comment at post 13]*!* *6:25 a.m.*

16 Mauro: e di cazzuola! 10:33
Mauro: a super mega pain in the arse [another comment that refers to the play on words in the comments at Posts 13, 14, and 15]*!* *10:33 a.m.*

17 Veronica: La R moscia non l'avevo notata! 11:07
Veronica: I hadn't previously noticed his French R! *11:07 a.m.*

18 Mauro: le tettine si però . . . 5 ore fa
Mauro: but you noticed the tits . . . *5 hours ago*

Extracts 4.8 and 5.12 The affair

1 Elisa: oh signur!!!
Elisa: oh my god!!!
[Elisa publishes a hyperlink which contains the news about the affair between Barbara D'Urso, an Italian TV personality, and Massimiliano Allegri, former coach of the soccer team A.C. Milan]

2 Franco: Nooooo . . . quella ce lo demotiva!!!! Salvatelo!!!
Franco: Nooooo . . . that [woman] *will have a negative impact on his motivation!!!! Save him!!!*

3 Elisa: esattoooooooooooooo!!!help [*sic*]!!!
Elisa: correcttttttttttttttttttt!!!help!!!

4 Franco: Speriamo non gli faccia una delle sue facce tristi ed indignate se no per lui è la fine . . . apace [*sic*] che rinunci al suo cognome per coerenza
Franco: We can only hope that she won't look at him with one of her sad and indignant facial expressions, because this [expression] *might be his end . . . to be coherent he may change his surname* [Allegri is the Italian translation for the English adjective "happy"]

5 Elisa: ahahahahahahaha . . . speriamo di no!!mi [*sic*] mette ansia quella donna . . . basta che nn [*sic*] se la porti in panchina ;-)
Elisa: ahahahahahahaha . . . let's hope not!! [that woman] *makes me anxious . . . I hope he won't allow her to sit on the coaching bench;-)*

6 Franco: io "invece" spero che la metta in panchina presto . . . definitivamente
Franco: indeed, I hope he will put her on the coaching bench [idiomatic expression that means "to dump" someone] *as soon as possible . . . forever*

7 Elisa: ☺
Elisa: ☺

8 Sandro: gran MILF bravo max
Sandro: great MILF well done max [Allegri's name]

9 Elisa: ci mancava solo lei . . . ahahahah
Elisa: she was the last thing we needed . . . ahahahah

Extracts 4.12, 5.16, and 7.7 Metroman-Carnevale

1 Mauro: ho Deciso . . . A CARNEVALE MI VESTO DA METROMAN [the busker that has already been mentioned in Extract 3.5]
Mauro: I have decided . . . . AT THE NEXT CARNEVALE PARTY I'LL DRESS UP AS METROMAN

A Elisa ed altre 12 persone piace questo
Elisa and other 12 people like this

2 Auro: non dormo più!
Auro: I can't sleep anymore

3 Filippo: io da banana
Filippo: and I will dress up like a banana

4 Aria:—ti prego fallo davvero, non illudermi/ci.
Aria:—please do it, don't let us down.

5 Mina: Oltre a vestirti come lui, però dovrai cantare tutta la sera sennò non vale!! ;D
Mina: If you dress up like him [Metroman], *you will have to sing all night long or otherwise it won't count!! ;D*

6 Mauro: sai bene quanto io sia serio in queste occasioni.
Mauro: you know how serious I am in these circumstances.

7 Mauro: Mina: OVVIO.
Mauro: Mina: OF COURSE.

8 Mauro: da domani dirò ogni volta che non potrò presienziare da qualche parte . . . "DOMANI NON CI SONO, ESCO CON UNA RAGAZZA, UNA CINESE . . ."
Mauro: starting from tomorrow, every time I won't be able to go to an appointment I'll tell people . . . "TOMORROW I'M UNAVAILABLE, I HAVE TO GO OUT WITH A GIRL, A CHINESE GIRL . . ." [this is likely to be a quote taken from one of Metroman's videos]

9 Mina: Lo so che è ovvio . . . purtroppo ti conosco :D
Mina: I know it's obvious . . . unfortunately I know you :D

10 Richard: sexy
Richard: sexy

11 Daniele: @Mina: purtroppo ti conosco è un insulto gravissimo . . . io non ti parlerei + a vita ;) @Mauro: io mi vesto da palo della metro, così puoi attaccarti al palo e girare!!!

Daniele: @Mina: unfortunately "I know you" is a terrible offence . . . I feel like not talking to you anymore;) @Mauro: I will dress up as an underground pole, so you can attach yourself to the pole and swing around me!!!

12 Mauro: e li salto! sicuro [*sic*]?
Mauro: and then I'll jump! Are you sure?

13 Roberta: UAHAHAHAHAHAHH SCUSA DANI ALLORA PASSERò IL TEMPO AD APPICCICARTI STICKERS ADDOSSO! E anche appendere annunci pubblicitari!!!!
Roberta: UAHAHAHAHAHAHH I'M SORRY DANY BUT I WILL SPEND MY TIME STICKING STICKERS ON YOU! And hang posters as well!!!!

14 Mina: @daniele [*sic*]: ??????????? che [*sic*] stai a di [*sic*] daniele [*sic*]? anche [*sic*] mauro [*sic*] purtroppo mi conosce!! ;) chiedigli [*sic*] del tamarro party a casa della nostra amica rita un paio di anni fa
Mina: @daniele: ??????????? what are you talking about daniele? even Mauro knows me unfortunately;) ask him about the "tamarro party" ["*tamarro*" is a term used to describe people who normally go to clubs] *we had a couple of years ago at our friend Rita*

15 Daniele: ecco . . . c'è stato un tamarro party e non sono stato invitato!!!tzè [*sic*] . . . gentaglia ;D ehehehe
Daniele: you see . . . there was a "tamarro party" and nobody invited me,!!! shame on you . . . bad people;D ehehehe

16 Mauro: eri ancora piccolo daniele [*sic*] . . .
Mauro: Daniele you were too young . . .

Extracts 4.14 and 5.17 It can't rain forever

1 Auro: "Non può piovere per sempre" [quote taken from the Italian version of the movie *The Crow*]
Auro: "It cannot rain forever"

A Claudio piace questo
Claudio like this

2 Alex: ma può smettere per un pò . . .
Alex: but it can stop for a while . . .

3 Matteo: però può continuare per un bel pò . . .
Matteo: or it can keep raining for a long time . . .

4 Alex: non ci sono più le mezze stagioni . . . eggià!!! [Italian proverb]
Alex: there is no Spring or Autumn anymore . . . that's for sure!!!

5 Auro: pioev pioev pioev là gallina là fà il oef [Italian proverb]
Auro: it rains rains rains and the hen lays an egg

6 Mauro: Don't say the cat is in the sac [quote taken from Giovanni Trapattoni the former coach of the Italian national soccer team]

7 Auro: io adoro Giovanni trapattoni
Auro: I love Giovanni trapattoni

8 Mauro: Idem [Mauro publishes a YouTube video containing a clip about Trapattoni]
Mauro: me too

Extracts 5.18 and 8.7 Fabio Volo's quote

1 Elisa: Forse c'è qualcosa di peggio dei sogni svaniti: la non voglia di sognare ancora. Fabio Volo [quote taken from a book of Fabio Volo, an Italian radio presenter] 10 ore fa
Elisa: Maybe there is something worst than vanished dreams: the desire to no longer dream. Fabio Volo *10 hours ago*

A 11 persone piace questo
11 people like this

2 Franco: Già . . . poveri interisti. 10 ore fa
Franco: yeah . . . poor interisti [nickname for F. C. Inter supporters]. *10 hours ago*

3 Elisa: :-) 10 ore fa
Elisa: :-) *10 hours ago*

4 Franco: Però anche tu infierisci . . . sei cattiva! 10 ore fa
Franco: but you like to rub salt into a wound . . . you're mean! *10 hours ago*

5 Elisa: ahhaha . . . si si cattivissima . . . ! 10 ore fa
Elisa: ahhaha . . . yeah yeah really mean . . . ! *10 hours ago*

6 Franco: Come una punizione di Carletto . . . violenta e spietata! 10 ore fa
Franco: Like a free kick of Carletto [probably the nickname of a former soccer player of the team A. C. Milan] . . . *violent and cruel!* *10 hours ago*

7 Francesca: mi piace!!! 7 ore fa
Francesca: I like it!!! *7 hours ago*

8 Elisa: l'ho copiata dall'ultimo libro . . . lo voglio!!!!:-) 6 ore fa
Elisa: I copied it from his latest book . . . I want it!!!!:-) *6 hours ago*

9 Francesca: ma ce l'ho!te [*sic*] lo passo se vuoi! 6 ore fa
Francesca: I have it! I can give it to you! *6 hours ago*

10 Elisa: già comprato?:-) 6 ore fa
Elisa: have you already bought it?:-) *6 hours ago*

11 Francesca: e già letto! 6 ore fa
Francesca: and I've already read it! 6 hours ago

12 Elisa: beneeee . . . si grazie,se [*sic*] me lo presti mi fai un favore!hi [*sic*] hi hi 6 ore fa
Elisa: well doneeee . . . yes please,if you can give it to me I'll really appreciate it!hi hi hi 6 hours ago

13 Antonia: bella! la [*sic*] copio subito! 6 ore fa
Antonia: nice! I'll copy it straight away! 6 hours ago

14 Elisa: copia pure cara! 6 ore fa
Elisa: you can copy it darling! 6 hours ago

15 Antonia: L'ho già comprato anche io il libro!! Non vedo l'ora di iniziarlo! 6 ore fa
Antonia: I have already bought it too!! I can't wait to start reading it! 6 hours ago

16 Elisa: bene!!!mi [*sic*] piace un sacco 6 ore fa
Elisa: well done!!!I love him so much 6 hours ago

Extracts 7.5 and 8.6 Music discussion- The Smashing Pumpkins

1 Mauro: Zero Compromessi
[Mauro publishes a hyperlink containing a video of the band The Smashing Pumpkins] 21 ore fa
Mauro: Zero Compromises 21 hours ago

A 3 persone piace questo
3 people like this

2 Mauro: o quasi. 21 ore fa
Mauro: or almost. 21 hours ago

3 Claudio: piaciuto? A me no . . . 21 ore fa
Claudio: did you like it? I didn't . . . 21 hours ago

4 Auro: piaciuto :)? 21 ore fa
Auro: liked it :)? 21 hours ago

5 Petra: Mauro non deludermi 21 ore fa
Petra: Mauro please don't disappoint me 21 hours ago

6 Mauro: mi sa che è piaciuto a pochi amici . . . sono tra quei pochi. 21 ore fa
Mauro: I think that few friends liked it . . . and I'm one of them. 21 hours ago

7 Petra: ok m'hai delus [*sic*]! 21 ore fa
Petra: ok you've disappointed me! 21 hours ago

8 Mauro: c'eri Petra? 21 ore fa
Mauro: Petra did you go? 21 hours ago

9 Petra: appunto perchè non c'ero 21 ore fa
Petra: exactly because I didn't go 21 hours ago

10 Mauro: ah ok, ma non so se ti sarebbe piaciuto . . . poche canzoni conosciute, acidissimo, assoli lunghi . . . io parto già sapendo che quello che sto vedendo non sono gli Smashing Pumpkins ma Corgan con american idol [*sic*] . . . eppure adoro la sua testardaggine e devozione a sè stesso . . . 21 ore fa
Mauro: ah ok, but I don't know whether you would have liked it . . . a few famous songs, hateful, long solos . . . I already knew that I was going to watch not The Smashing Pumpkins but Corgan with american idol . . . and yet I love his stubbornness and devotion to himself . . . 21 hours ago

11 Petra: allora è un altro discorso e posso capire se ti è piaciuto . . . (sospettavo di una tua teoria mauriana).ma [*sic*] come direbbe qualcuno,"chi vuole andare in gita,non [*sic*] sa non sa non sa!" (il mio billy [*sic*] resta il mio billy [*sic*],solo [*sic*] nella mia testa,ora [*sic*] su quel palco c'è un fuori di testa che cerca ancora di "vendere musica") 21 ore fa
Petra: in this case it's a different story and I can understand why you liked it . . . (I suspected a maurian theory).but as someone would say, "who ever wants to go on tour, doesn't know doesn't know doesn't know!" (my billy remains my billy,only in my head, on that stage right now there's a fool who's still trying to "sell music") 21 hours ago

12 Roberta: e il fatto che non gliene frena nulla di compiacere gli altri lo rende un vero artista . . . 21 ore fa
Roberta: and it's the fact that he couldn't care less about gratifying others that makes him a real artist . . . 21 hours ago

13 Petra: si ma roberta [*sic*] fare musica di merda al giorno d'oggi solo per andare ancora in giro in tour a suonare zero ai pochi fan accaniti e nostalgici che veramente ci stanno sotto è un offesa [*sic*] nel profono [*sic*] anche a quello [*sic*] che fu l'era dei GRANDi 1 [possibly the name of one of the songs of The Smashing Pumpkins or a typo] 21 ore fa
Petra: ok roberta but to make crappy music nowadays just because you want to go on tour to play nothing for a few nostalgic, obstinate fans is a deep offence to what used to be the era of the GREAT ONES 1 21 hours ago

14 Auro: concordo con roberta [*sic*].a [*sic*] anche qui a londra [*sic*], fatte salve le aspettative, è stato dal punto di vista musicale molto bello!però [*sic*] concorderei anche col malumore di quelli che avrebbero voluto vedere e sentire QUEI pezzi di QUEGLI smashing [*sic*] . . . !insomma [*sic*] un po' d'amaro a me lo ha lasciato comunque. 21 ore fa
Auro: I agree with roberta.even here in london, apart from the exceptions, from a musical point of view it was fantastic!but I agree with the discontent

of those who were hoping to see and hear songs from THOSE smashing . . . !actually the concert left me with a bitter-taste in any case. *21 hours ago*

15 Mauro: non credo che voglia per forza vendere, tanto è vero che non fa nemmeno musica di facile presa . . . penso sia l'unica cosa che gli rimane . . . e nella musica che fa penso ci metta proprio la rabbia e la sfida del o mi ami o mi odi, gli Smashing Pumpkins sono sempre stato io ecc . . . ecc . . . senza Sacralizzarlo [*sic*] e sapendo cosa sarebbe un concerto con 1979, Perfect,Ava [*sic*] Adore [names of some of the songs of The Smashing Pumpkins] ecc ecc ecc . . . credo però di preferire che sia così, se facesse un concerto di singoloni con questa bandnonband, risulterebbe caricaturale e ridicolo. Preferisco che sia acido e sincero e mandi a fanculo la buon costume ed il [*sic*] Greatest hits. 21 ore fa

Mauro: I don't think that he necessarily wants to sell, in fact he's not making music which is popular . . . I reckon this is the only thing that he has left . . . and in his music he is putting the rage and the challenge of either love me or hate me, The Smashing Pumpkins have always been me etc . . . etc . . . without I idolizing him and knowing what a concert would have been like with 1979, Perfect,Ava Adore etc etc etc . . . yet I think that it is better this way, if he gave a concert of huge singles with this bandnoband, he would seem ridiculous and a caricature. I prefer him to be brutal and honest and that he tells the police and the Greatest hits to fuck off. *21 hours ago*

16 Mauro: ah lo capisco Auro . . . davvero. basta [*sic*] l'inizio di Tonight per aprire una voragine . . . forse è bello rimaner con l'Utopia, piuttosto che con l'edulcorazione [*sic*] del prodotto originale, boh, mi piglia così. Ovvio se ci penso a cosa sarebbe averli visti 12 anni fa . . . ciao . . . 21 ore fa

Mauro: ah Auro I understand you . . . really. The opening of Tonight is enough to open an abyss . . . maybe it's better to stick to Utopia, rather than sugar coating the original product, well, that's what I think. Obviously I wonder what it would have been like to see them 12 years ago . . . bye . . . *21 hours ago*

17 Mauro: Petra come intitolavi . . . ai nostalgici regala un cazzo. Zero Compromessi . . . e di questo ne andre [*sic*] fiero. 21 ore fa

Mauro: Petra as you said . . . he doesn't give shit to nostalgic people. Zero Compromises . . . and he should be proud of this. *21 hours ago*

18 Petra: per me un artista deve capire dove fermarsi,se [*sic*] a cominciare da d'arcy [*sic*],pure [*sic*] james [*sic*] e jimmy [*sic*] [three of the original members of The Smashing Pumpkins] hanno deciso di andarsene c'è un motivo.Che [*sic*] bOlly [*sic*] sia egocentrico si sa,lo [*sic*] è sempre stato,ma [*sic*] era così già da Gish [first album of The Smashing Pumpkins].Non [*sic*] è una scusa per continuare ad andarsene in giro con una band di minorenne [*sic*] spacciandoli per "smashing pumpkins" [*sic*] . . . a me pisces

iscariot [*sic*] [one of the albums of The Smashing Pumpkins] non me lo da più indietro nessuno e il fatto che lui ancora ostenti qualcosa mi fa na [*sic*] tristezza . . . se proprio vuole fare roba nuova smettesse di suonare col nome di una band che non tornerà mai più e di tentare di cantare invano tonight tonight [*sic*] [one of the songs of The Smashing Pumpkins] 21 ore fa

Petra: in my opinon an artist has to understand where to stop,if starting from d'arcy, james and jimmy also decided to quit there must be a reason. Everyone knows that bOlly is egocentric,is well-known he's always been like this and he was like this since Gish.This isn't an excuse to go on tour with a band of minors selling them as "smashing pumpkins" . . . nobody will give me back pisces iscariot and the fact that he's still showing off something makes me so sad . . . if he really wants to produce new stuff, he needs to stop using the name of a band that won't come back anymore and trying to sing tonight tonight in vain 21 hours ago

19 Mauro: credo sia proprio l'opposto di questo che ho scritto di aver visto stasera ma ormai sei partita per la tangente e capisco :D! 21 ore fa

Mauro: I think that it's exactly the opposite of this that I wrote about tonight's concert but at this point you're overeacting and I understand:D! 21 hours ago

20 Petra: mauro [*sic*],non [*sic*] ti preoccupare,capisco [*sic*] e rispetto il tuo punto di vista,credo [*sic*] abbia fondamento aldilà di tutto,e [*sic*] sulla soggettività della musica non metto bocca,però [*sic*] se mi infervoro è perchè ci sono cose almeno pè [*sic*] mmia [*sic*] non esistono.Sono [*sic*] troppo pumpkiniana vecchia scuola! ♥ 21 ore fa

Petra: mauro,don't worry, I understand and respect your point of view,I think it's basically right despite everything,and I don't dare discuss the subjectivity of the music,however if I get carried away it's because there are things that at least for me are unacceptable.I'm a very old school The Smashing Pumpkins fan! ♥ 21 hours ago

21 Mauro: il finale di [*sic*] sarebbe piaciuto comunque . . . Tonight Tonight [one of the songs of The Smashing Pumpkins] ok, ma l'accoppiata Zero-Bullet [another of the songs of The Smashing Pumpkins] da brividi comunque . . . 20 ore fa

Mauro: anyway you would have loved the final song . . . Tonight Tonight is fine, but Zero-Bullet is always thrilling . . . 20 hours ago

22 Petra: ci pogai forte nel 2007,lì [*sic*] ero in veste di nostalgica anch'io ;) 20 ore fa

Petra: I jumped at the rhythm of those songs in 2007,in those days I was a nostalgic too ;) 20 hours ago

23 Mauro: e nella tua immagine sei molto d'arcy [*sic*] . . .:D 20 ore fa

Mauro: and in your image you're really d'arcy . . .:D! 20 hours ago

24 Petra: bravo,comprai [*sic*] il jazz proprio perchè mi ci fece appassionare lei ♥ e pensare che ora ha le labbra a canotto e spala il letame dei suoi cavalli . . . aaaaah! 20 ore fa
Petra: true,I bought jazz because she got me into it ♥ and to think that now she's got bottox in her lips and she cleans after her horses . . . aaaaah! 20 hours ago

25 Mauro: Claudia non mi dire che ti sei persa il finale . . . 11 ore fa
Mauro: Claudia don't tell me that you've missed the final song . . . 11 hours ago

26 Claudia: c'eravamo, dietro. poi [*sic*] la nebbia. 9 ore fa
Claudia: we were there, at the back, and then the fog. 9 hours ago

Notes

Chapter 1

1 A *Like* is a "contentless" message posted by an FB user using the *Like* button available under every message posted in a comment thread.

2 A social interaction is an interaction which takes place between people (C. Goodwin and Heritage, 1990).

Chapter 2

1 This is unless these users have customized their profiles to be public and not only accessible to Friends. In this case any FB user can see the comment threads that A and B started.

2 The prompts in the dialogue boxes in Figure 2.1 are in Italian because this was the language in which I set up the FB account utilized to collect data for this book.

3 This button, as well as the *Reactions* button which will be described later on in this section, was not available at the time data were collected for this work. Therefore, it will not be discussed in this book.

4 If a comment thread includes many comments, the system of FB does not present all of them. It only shows the first and the four or five most recent comments published in a comment thread. If an FB user wants to see all the contributions published in an interaction, he or she has to click on the *Visualizza altri commenti* (View more comments) button.

5 A translation into English is only provided when a comment is in Italian or in another language that is not English.

Chapter 3

1 As will be discussed in Chapter 4, this book claims that comments within comment threads might consist of textual messages only, photos only, hyperlinks only as well as combinations of textual messages with photos or hyperlinks. This means that FB users can type, upload, or publish a comment in a comment thread.

2 As already mentioned in Chapter 2, in this book information in square brackets and italics have different functions. Information in square brackets describes non-textual materials added by FB users using the *Add Photo/Video* and *Share* buttons, syntactic and other errors that appear in the original data, and information I added to clarify the meaning of specific comments. Italic, on the other hand, is used to mark when an FB user utilizes the *Like* button (that is available under every comment posted on the Home) to respond to a contribution in a comment thread. Italic is also used to provide a fairly literal translation into English of the comments posted in comment threads. For example, in Extract 3.1 the text in square brackets indicates the information I added to clarify the meaning of the comments at Posts 1 and 3, and two grammar mistakes at Posts 1 and 3. On the other hand, italic indicates that three Friends have read Guido's comment and used the *Like* button to respond to it. This is in addition to anyone else who may have read the comment at Post 1 and not responded to it, and potentially in addition to Giorgio, Silvio, and Ruggero who responded through the dialogue box *Write a comment*. It is in fact possible that the Friends who clicked on the *Like* button to respond to the comment at Post 1 were Giorgio, Silvio, and Ruggero.

3 At the time data were collected for this study, FB did not provide the exact timing in which comments were posted in comment threads. Nowadays, this information seems to be available to FB users in comment threads.

4 In this book some comment threads will be discussed in more than one chapter and through different analytical perspectives. Only the contributions that are relevant to the analysis will be presented in chapters, while the entire comment threads will be available in Appendix A.

5 At the time data were collected for this study FB did not notify when a Friend was typing a comment in a comment thread. However, it seems that nowadays a feature that informs when a Friend is typing a comment in a comment thread is available on FB.

6 A full version of this comment thread is available in Appendix A.

7 Allocation can also be achieved by typing and then selecting the name of a Friend in a comment within a comment thread. In this case FB automatically notifies the selected Friend that he or she has been named in a comment. There are no cases in the data where participants in this study have used this feature to select recipients for their comments.

8 A full version of this comment thread is available in Appendix A.

Chapter 4

1 In this book the term *first-post tellings* refers to the tellings that occur in the very first comments that open FB comment threads. However, it also refers to a few tellings

where a poster uses both the comments at Posts 1 and 2 to construct a single telling, as in Extract 3.8 in Chapter 3.

2 This is the only example in the data where a first-post teller uses the feature *Tagga persone nel tuo post* (Tag people in your post) in a comment thread. When an FB user launches a comment thread by using the dialogue box *What's on your mind?* he or she may take advantage of the feature *Con chi sei?* (Who are you with?) to add the names of Friends he or she is with at the time of publication of a first comment in a comment thread. Therefore, it seems that Alberta has used the tagging feature *Tag people in your post* to suggest to Friends that she was with Eleonora at the time she published the comment at Post 1. In addition, this feature has probably triggered the response at Post 2. In other words, it appears that Eleonora has responded to the comment at Post 1 because she was selected by Alberta as the intended recipient of this contribution.

3 Even though it is possible to upload videos other than hyperlinks on FB, for example, videos made by Friends using their mobiles, there are no examples of such cases in the data. Therefore, they have not been discussed in this book.

4 A full version of this comment thread is available in Appendix A.

5 As per Extract 4.8, a full version of this extract is available in Appendix A.

6 As per previous examples, a full version of this comment thread is available in Appendix A.

Chapter 5

1 Note that in this example, unlike the following ones, one Friend has clicked the *Like* button. Although the actions performed by Friends using the *Like* button may have a role in comment threads, they in fact could be a type of response or acknowledgment directed at the first-post tellers, it is impossible to establish this from the data. Therefore, the number of *Likes* received by first-post tellings has not been considered in the analysis. In addition, the data show that Friends who use the *Like* button are generally those who participate more fully in a comment thread. In other words, they also often post textual messages that respond to the initial tellings, thus suggesting that Friends use the *Like* button to acknowledge that they read the comments of first-post tellers, while using textual messages to respond to them. This is not always the case, however, as can be seen in the current example.

2 The action of naming described in this chapter was not performed by FB users using the *Tag friend* feature available in the dialogue box *What's on your mind?* which automatically notifies users who have been named in a comment, and thus stimulates their responses. Rather it refers to FB users typing the names of the Friends they want to select as recipients of their tellings.

3 The action performed by Lucia in her response in the comment at Post 4 (*mi hanno detto che non scendi D:*) does not seem to relate to the topic at all, but rather refers to how Claudio is unfortunately not returning (to Italy). This is not taken up here as a topic at all.
4 A full version of this comment thread is available in Appendix A.
5 A complete version of this comment thread is available in Appendix A.

Chapter 6

1 As will be discussed in Chapter 7, first-post tellings are normally responded to with comments, evaluations, or assessments.

Chapter 7

1 As discussed in Chapter 4, in some cases original posters may make their "first" comments over two contributions, but these are treated here as a single comment.
2 A detailed comparison between spoken conversation and FB comment threads is included in Chapter 1.
3 This interaction is in English therefore it does not need to be translated.
4 One Friend in the comment at Post 9 posts a first comment which responds instead to the comment at Post 8; this will be discussed in the following section.
5 As discussed in Chapter 4, in this book the term *initial telling* refers to tellings which occur within a single comment, such as those in the comments at Posts 1 in Extracts 7.1 to 7.3 as well as those that occur across the comments at Posts 1 and 2, such as that in Extract 7.4. Thus, the comments at Posts 1 and 2 in Extract 7.4 jointly constitute the initial telling.
6 The Italian translation for Human Torch is *Torcia Umana*. Therefore, it is possible that Mauro is telling Claudia that he will bring the Human Torch to light her while in company of the lead singer of Bancale.
7 A complete version of this comment thread can be found in Appendix A.

Chapter 8

1 We claim that in the comment at Post 3 Elisa changes topic because she works from Monday to Friday. The initial unit of the comment at Post 1 therefore refers to what Elisa did on Sunday (yesterday), while the final unit of this comment

refers to the problem with the heating system that she had at work on Monday. An alternative interpretation of this comment, which makes no difference to the analysis, would be that Elisa, in the final unit of the comment at Post 3, says that the day before she did not see Claudia because of the chaos generated by the problem with the heating system.

2 Dyadic interactions occurring within FB comment threads opened by a first-post telling will be discussed later in this chapter.

3 A full version of this comment thread has already been presented in Chapter 2 on page 22.

4 A full version of this comment thread can be found in Chapter 6 on page 110 as well as in Appendix A.

Chapter 9

1 In these studies the term *status updates* refers to comments posted by FB users on either the Home or their personal profiles.

References

Adetunji, A. (2013). The Interactional Context of Humor in Nigerian Stand-up Comedy. *Pragmatics, 23*(1), 1–22.

Androutsopoulos, J. (2010). Localizing the Global on the Participatory Web. In N. Coupland (ed.), *The Handbook of Language and Globalization* (pp. 203–31). Chichester, UK: Wiley-Blackwell.

Androutsopoulos, J. (2014a). Languaging when Contexts Collapse: Audience Design in Social Networking. *Discourse, Context & Media, 4–5*, 62–73.

Androutsopoulos, J. (2014b). Moments of Sharing: Entextualization and Linguistic Repertoires in Social Networking. *Journal of Pragmatics, 73*, 4–18.

Androutsopoulos, J. (2015). Networked Multilingualism: Some Language Practices on Facebook and their Implications. *International Journal of Bilingualism, 19*(2), 185–205.

Antaki, C., Ardévol, E., Núñez, F., and Vayreda, A. (2005). "For She Who Knows Who She is": Managing Accountability in Online Forum Messages. *Journal of Computer-Mediated Communication, 11*(1), 114–32.

Bamberg, M. and Georgakopoulou, A. (2008). Small Stories as a New Perspective in Narrative and Identity Analysis. *Text & Talk, 28*(3), 377–96.

Barbulet, G. (2013). Social Media-A Pragmatic Approach: Contexts & Implicatures. *Procedia—Social and Behavioral Sciences, 83*, 422–26.

Baron, N. S. (2013). Instant Messaging. In D. Stein, T. Virtanen and S. Herring (eds.), *Pragmatics of Computer-Mediated Communication* (pp. 135–62). Berlin and Boston: De Gruyter Mouton.

Barton, D. and Lee, C. (2013). *Language Online Investigating Digital Texts and Practices.* New York: Taylor and Francis.

Baym, N. (1995). The Performance of Humor in Computer-Mediated Communication. *Journal of Computer-Mediated Communication, 1* (2).

Baym, N. (2015). *Personal Connections in the Digital Age.* New York: John Wiley & Sons.

Bistarelli, A. (2014). L'interferenza dell'inglese sull'italiano. Un'analisi quantitativa e qualitativa. *inTRAlinea, 16.* http://www.intralinea.org/archive/article/Linterferenza_dellinglese_sullitaliano

Blattner, G. and Fiori, M. (2009). Facebook in the Language Classroom: Promises and Possibilities. *International Journal of Instructional Technology and Distance Learning, 6*(1), 17–28.

Bolander, B. and Locher, M. (2010). Constructing Identity on Facebook: Report on a Pilot Study. *SPELL: Swiss Papers in English Language and Literature, 24*, 165–87.

Boyd, M. D. (2006). Friends, Friendsters, and Top 8: Writing Community Into Being on Social Network Sites. *First Monday, 11*(12).

Boyd, M. D. and Ellison, B. N. (2007). Social Network Sites: Definition, History, and Scholarship. *Journal of Computer-Mediated Communication, 13*(1), 210–30.

Bugeja, M. J. (2006). Facing the Facebook. *The Chronicle of Higher Education, 52*(21), C1.

Carr, T. C., Schrock, D. B., and Dauterman, P. (2012). Speech Acts Within Facebook Status Messages. *Journal of Language and Social Psychology, 31*(2), 176–96.

Castells, M. (2013). *Communication Power*. Oxford: Oxford University Press Ed..

Cerruti, M. (2011). Regional Varieties of Italian in the Linguistic Repertoire. *International Journal of the Sociology of Language, 210*, 9–29.

Cheung, C. M. K., Chiu, P.-Y., and Lee, M. K. O. (2011). Online Social Networks: Why do Students use Facebook? *Computers in Human Behavior, 27*(4), 1337–43.

Crystal, D. (2006). *Language and the Internet* (second ed.). Cambridge: New York Cambridge University Press.

Dabrowska, M. (2012). "HAPPY B'DAY BHAIYA." Characteristics of Facebook Indian English. *Studia Linguistica Universitatis Lagellonicae Cracoviensis, 129*(1), 61–89.

Davies, J. (2011). Facebook on Facebook as a New Literacy Practice. *Computers & Education 59*(1), 19–29.

Dong, Q. (2008). Explaining Why Young Adults Use MySpace and Facebook Through Uses & Gratification Theory. *Human Communication, 12*(2), 215–29.

Facebook. (2017). Company Info. Retrieved May 23, 2017, from http://newsroom.fb.com/company-info/

Farina, M. (2015). Facebook First Post Telling. *Journal of Pragmatics, 90*, 1–11.

Farman, J. (2012). *Mobile Interface Theory: Embodied Space and Locative Media*. London: Routledge.

Frobenius, M. and Harper, R. (2015). Tying in Comment Sections: The Production of Meaning and Sense on Facebook. The Self-explicative Organization of Communication Acts on and Through Facebook. *Semiotica, 204*, 121–43.

Garcia, C. A. and Jacobs, B. J. (1998). The Interactional Organization of Computer Mediated Communication in the College Classroom. *Qualitative Sociology, 21*(3), 299–317.

Garcia, C. A. and Jacobs, B. J. (1999). The Eyes of the Beholder: Understanding the *Turn-taking System* in Quasi-Synchronous Computer-Mediated Communication. *Research on Language and Social Interaction, 33*(4), 337–67.

Gennaro, C. and Dutton, W. (2007). Reconfiguring Friendships: Social Relationships and the Internet. *Information, Communication and Society, 10*(5), 591–618.

Georgakopoulou, A. (2002). Narrative and Identity Management: Discourse and Social Identities in a Tale of Tomorrow. *Research on Language and Social Interaction, 35*(4), 427–51.

Georgakopoulou, A. (2007a). *Small Stories, Interaction and Identities*. Amsterdam: John Benjamins Publishing Company.

Georgakopoulou, A. (2007b). Thinking Big with Small Stories in Narrative and Identity Analysis. In M. Bamberg (ed.), *Narrative—State of the Art* (pp. 145–55). Amsterdam: John Benjamins.

Georgakopoulou, A. (2013a). Narrative Analysis and Computer-mediated Communication. In C. S. Herring, D. Stein, and T. Virtanen (eds.), *Pragmatics of Computer-Mediated Communication* (pp. 695–716). Berlin: De Gruyter Mouton.

Georgakopoulou, A. (2013b). Storytelling on the go: Breaking News Stories as a Travelling Narrative Genre. In L.-C. Hydén, M. Hatavara, and M. Hyvarinen (eds.), *The Travelling Concepts of Narrative* (pp. 201–24). Amsterdam: John Benjamins.

Georgakopoulou, A. (2014). Small Stories Transposition and Social Media: A Micro-perspective on the "Greek Crisis." *Discourse & Society, 25*, (4).

Georgakopoulou, A. (2016). From Narrating the Self to Posting Self(Ies): A Small Stories Approach to Selfies. *Open Linguistics, 2*(1), 300–17.

Georgalou, M. (2015a). Beyond the Timeline: Constructing Time and Age Identities on Facebook. *Discourse, Context & Media, 9*, 24–33.

Georgalou, M. (2015b). Small Stories of the Greek Crisis on Facebook. *Social Media + Society*, 1–15.

Georgalou, M. (2016). "This Is a Wall of Memories": Time and Age Identity in Facebook Discourse. In S. Leppänen, E. Westinen, and S. Kytola (eds.), *Social Media Discourse, (Dis)identifications and Diversities* (pp. 242–71): Milton Park: Taylor & Francis.

Gèorlach, M. (2003). *Terminology and Lexicography Research and Practice : English Words Abroad.* Amsterdam and Philadelphia: John Benjamins Publishing Company.

Gerolimos, M. (2011). Academic Libraries on Facebook: An Analysis of Users' Comments. *D-Lib Magazine, 17*(11).

Giaxoglou, K. (2015a). Entextualising Mourning on Facebook: Stories of Grief as Acts of Sharing. *New Review of Hypermedia and Multimedia, 21*(1), 87–105.

Giaxoglou, K. (2015b). "Everywhere I go, you're Going with me": Time and Space Deixis as Affective Positioning Resources in Shared Moments of Digital Mourning. *Discourse, Context & Media, 9*, 55–63.

Gibson, W. (2009a). Intercultural Communication Online: Conversation Analysis and the Investigation of Asynchronous Written Discourse. *Forum: Qualitative Social Research, 10*(1).

Gibson, W. (2009b). Negotiating Textual Talk: Conversation Analysis, Pedagogy and the Organisation of Online Asynchronous Discourse. *British Educational Research Journal, 35*(5), 705–21.

Giles, D., Stommel, W., and Paulus, T. M. (2017). The Microanalysis of Online Data: The Next Stage. *Introduction/Journal of Pragmatics, 115*, 37–41.

Giles, D., Stommel, W., Paulus, T., Lester, J., and Reed, D. (2015). Microanalysis of Online Data: The Methodological Development of "Digital CA." *Discourse, Context & Media*, 7, 45–51.

Godwin-Jones, R. (2008). Mobile Computing Technologies: Lighter, Faster, Smarter. *Language Learning & Technology, 12*(3), 3–9.

Golder, S., Wilkinson, D., and Huberman, B. (2007). Rhythms of Social Interaction: Messaging within a Massive Online Network. In C. Steinfield, B. T. Pentland, M. Ackerman, and N. Contractor (eds.), *Communities and Technologies* (pp. 41–66). London: Springer.

Goodwin, C. (1984). Notes on Story Structure and the Organization of Participation. In M. Atkinson and J. Heritage (eds.), *Structures of Social Action* (pp. 225–46). Cambridge: Cambridge University Press.

Goodwin, C. (1986). Audience Diversity, Participation and Interpretation. *Text*, *6*(3), 283–316.

Goodwin, C. (1989). Turn Construction in Conversational Organization. In B. Dervin, L. Grossberg, B. O'Keefe, and E. Wartella (eds.), *Rethinking Communication: Paradigm Exemplars* (pp. 88–102). Newbury Park, CA: Sage.

Goodwin, C. and Heritage, J. (1990). Conversation Analysis. *Annual Review of Anthropology*, *19*, 283–307.

Goodwin, C. and Goodwin, M. (1992). Assessments and the Construction of Context. In A. Duranti and C. Goodwin (eds.), *Rethinking Context* (pp. 147–90). Cambridge: Cambridge University Press.

Goodwin, M. (1982). "Instigating": Storytelling as a Social Process. *American Ethnologist*, *9*, 799–819.

Goodwin, M. (1990). *He-Said-She-Said Talk as Social Organization among Black Children*. Bloomington and Indianapolis: Indiana University Press.

Goodwin, M. (1991). Retellings, Pretellings and Hypothetical Stories. *Research on Language and Social Interaction*, *224*, 261–74.

Goodwin, M. (1993). Tactical Uses of Stories: Participation Frameworks within Girls' and Boys' Disputes. In D. Tannen (ed.), *Gender and Conversational Interaction* (pp. 110–42). New York: Oxford University Press.

Harper, R. (2011). *Texture: Human Expression in the Age of Communications Overload*. Cambridge, MA: MIT Press.

Heritage, J. (1984). *Garfinkel and Ethnomethodology*. Cambridge: Polity Press.

Heritage, J. (1988). Explanations as Accounts: A Conversation Analytic Perspective. In C. Antaki (ed.), *Analysing Everyday Explanation: A Casebook of Methods* (pp. 127–44): London: SAGE Publications.

Heritage, J. (1997). Conversation Analysis and Institutional Talk: Analyzing Data. In D. Silvermann (ed.), *Qualitative Research: Theory, Method and Practice* (pp. 161–82). London: Sage.

Herring, C. S. (1999). Interactional Coherence in CMC. *Journal of Computer-Mediated Communication, 4,* (4).

Hew, K. F. (2011). Students' and Teachers' Use of Facebook. *Computer in Human Behavior*, *27*(2), 662–76.

Hille, S. and Bakker, P. (2014). Engaging the Social News User. *Journalism Practice*, *8*(5), 563–72.

Hsu, C. C., Chen, H. C., Huang, K. K., and Huang, Y. M. (2012). A Personalized Auxiliary Material Recommendation System Based on Learning Style on Facebook Applying an Artificial bee Colony Algorithm. *Computer and Mathematics with Applications, 65*(3), 1506–13.

Jefferson, G. (1978). Sequential Aspects of Storytelling in Conversation. In J. Schenkein (ed.), *Studies in the Organization of Conversational Interaction* (pp. 219–48). New York, San Francisco and London: Academic Press.

Jefferson, G. (1979). A Technique for Inviting Laughter and its Subsequent Acceptance/Declination. In G. Psathas (ed.), *Everyday Language: Studies in Ethnomethodology* (pp. 79–96). New York: Irvington Publishers.

Jefferson, G. (1984). On Stepwise Transition from Talk About a Trouble to Inappropriately Next-positioned Matters. In *Structures of Social Action: Studies in Conversation Analysis* (pp. 191–222). Paris: Editions de la Maison des sciences de l'homme.

Kabilan, M. K., Ahmad, N., and Abidin, M. J. Z. (2010). Facebook: An Online Environment for Learning of English in Institutions of Higher Education? *The Internet and Higher Education, 13*, 179–87.

Karrebæk, S. M., Stæhr, A., and Varis, P. (2015). Punjabi at Heart: Language, Legitimacy, and Authenticity on Social Media. *Discourse, Context & Media, 8*, 20–29.

Kasper, G. (2006). Conversation Analysis as an Approach to SLA. *AILA Review, 19*, 83–99.

Kitsis, S. M. (2008). The Facebook Generation: Homework as Social Networking. *English Journal, 98*(2), 7.

Kristeva, J. (1980). *Desire in Language: A Semiotic Approach to Literature and Art.* New York: Columbia University Press.

Labov, W. and Waletzky, J. (1997). Narrative Analysis: Oral Versions of Personal Experience. *Journal of Narrative and Life History, 7*(1–4), 3–38.

Lambiase, J. (2010). Hanging by a Thread: Topic Development and Death in an Online Discussion of Breaking News. *Language@Internet, 7*.

Lampe, C., Ellison, N. B., and Steinfield, C. (2006). *A Face (book) in the Crowd: Social Searching vs. Social Browsing.* Paper presented at the Computer supported cooperative work, New York, NY, USA.

Larrue, J. and Trognon, A. (1993). Organization of Turn-taking and Mechanisms for Turn-taking Repairs in a Chaired Meeting. *Journal of Pragmatics, 19*(2), 177–96.

Lee, C. (2011). Micro-blogging and Status Updates on Facebook: Texts and Practices. In C. Thurlow and K. Mroczek (eds.), *Digital Discourse Language in the New Media* (pp. 110–28). Oxford and New York: Oxford University Press.

Lenihan, A. (2011). "Join Our Community of Translators": Language Ideologies and/in Facebook. In K. Mroczek & C. Thurlow (eds.), *Digital Discourse: Language in the New Media* (pp. 48–64): Oxford University Press.

Leonardi, M. (2009). *Narrative as Self Performance: The Rhetorical Construction of Identities on Facebook Profiles.* Albuquerque: The University of Nex Mexico.

Liddicoat, A. J. (2011). *An Introduction to Conversation Analysis*. London: Continuum International Publishing Group.

Lomicka, L. and Lord, G. (2012). A Tale of Tweets: Analysing Microblogging Among Language Learners. *System, 40*(1), 48–63.

Maíz-Arévalo, C. (2013). "Just Click 'Like'": Computer-mediated Responses to Spanish Compliments. *Journal of Pragmatics, 51*, 47–67.

Mandelbaum, J. (1989). Interpersonal Activities in Conversational Storytelling. *Western Journal of Speech Communication, 53*, 114–26.

Markee, N. (2000). *Conversation Analysis*. London: Lawrence Erlbaum Associates, Publishers.

Maynard, D. (2006). The News Delivery Sequence: Bad News and Good News in Conversational Interaction. In P. Drew and J. Heritage (eds.), *Conversation Analysis* (Vol. II, pp. 203–39). London, Thousand Oaks and New Delhi: SAGE Publications.

Miller, D. (2011). *Tales from Facebook*. Polity.

Mills, N. A. (2009). *Facebook and the use of Social Networking Tools to Enhance Language Learner Motivation and Engagement*. Paper presented at the Northeast Association for Language Learning Technology (NEALLT).

Mondada, L. (2012). The Dynamics of Embodied Participation and Language Choice in Multilingual Meetings. *Language in Society, 41*(2), 213–35.

Mondada, L. (2013a). The Conversation Analytic Approach to Data Collection. In J. Sidnell and T. Stivers (eds.), *The Handbook of Conversation Analysis* (pp. 32–56). Hoboken: Blackwell Publishing.

Mondada, L. (2013b). Embodied and Spatial Resources for Turn-taking in Institutional Multi-party Interactions: Participatory Democracy Debates. *Journal of Pragmatics, 46*(1), 39–68.

Negretti, R. (1999). Web-based Activities and SLA: A Conversation Analysis Research Approach. *Language Learning & Technology, 3*(1), 75–87.

Norrick, N. (1993). *Conversational Joking Humor in Everyday Talk*. Bloomington and Indianapolis: Indiana University Press.

Norrick, N. (1994). Involvement and Joking in Conversation. *Journal of Pragmatics, 22*, 409–30.

Norrick, N. (2000). *Conversational Narrative. Storytelling in Everyday Talk*. Philadelphia: John Benjamins Publishing Company.

Oxford English Dictionary Online. (2017) (Vols. 2017). Great Britain: Oxford University Press.

Page, R. E. (2010a). *New Perspectives on Narrative and Multimodality*. London: Routledge.

Page, R. E. (2010b). Re-examining Narrativity: Small Stories in Status Updates. *Text & Talk, 30*(4), 423–44.

Page, R. E. (2012). *Stories and Social Media: Identities and Interaction*. New York and London: Routledge.

Page, R. E., Harper, R., and Frobenius, M. (2013). From Small Stories to Networked Narrative: The Evolution of Personal Narratives in Facebook Status Updates. *Narrative Inquiry, 23*(1), 192–213.

Papacharissi, Z. (2010). *A Networked Self: Identity, Community, and Culture on Social Network Sites.* London: Routledge.

Papacharissi, Z. and Mendelson, A. (2010). Media Perspectives for the 21st Century. In S. Papathanassopoulos (ed.), *12 Toward a New (er) Sociability: Uses, Gratifications and Social Capital on Facebook.* London and New York: Routledge.

Pérez-Sabater, C. (2013). The Linguistics of Social Networking: A Study of Writing Conventions on Facebook. *Linguistik Online, 56*(6).

Placencia, M. E. and Lower, A. (2013). Your Kids are so Stinkin' Cute! :-): Complimenting Behavior on Facebook Among Family and Friends. *Intercultural Pragmatics, 10*(4), 617–46.

Pomerantz, A. (1984). Agreeing and Disagreeing with Assessments: Some Features of Preferred/Dispreferred Turn Shapes. In M. J. Atkinson and J. Heritage (eds.), *Structures of Social Interaction* (pp. 57–101). Cambridge: Cambridge University Press.

Psathas, G. (1995). The Methodological Perspective of Conversation Analysis. In G. Psathas (ed.), *Conversation Analysis* (pp. 45–54). Thousand Oaks: SAGE Publications.

Rando, G. (1970). The Assimilation of English Loan—Words in Italian. *Italica, 47*(2), 129–42.

Reed, D. (2001). *"Making Conversation": Sequential Integrity and the Local Management of Interaction on Internet Newsgroups.* Paper presented at the Proceedings of the 34th Hawaii International Conference on System Sciences, Maui, Hawaii.

Rendle-Short, J. (2003). "So What Does this Show us?": Analysis of the Discourse Marker "so" in Seminar Talk. *Australian Review of Applied Linguistics, 26*(2), 46–62.

Sacks, H. (1974). An Analysis of the Course of a Joke's Telling in Conversation. In R. Bauman and J. Sherzer (eds.), *Explorations in the Ethnography of Speaking* (pp. 337–53). London and New York: Cambridge University Press.

Sacks, H. (1975). Everyone Has to Lie. In M. Sanches and B. G. Blount (eds.), *Sociocultural Dimensions of Language Use* (pp. 57–80). New York: Academic Press.

Sacks, H. (1978). Some Technical Considerations of a Dirty Joke. In J. Schenkein (ed.), *Studies in the Organization of Conversational Interaction* (pp. 249–69). New York, San Francisco, and London: Academic Press.

Sacks, H. (1986). Some Considerations of a Story Told in Ordinary Conversations. *Poetics, 15*, 127–38.

Sacks, H. (1992). *Lectures on Conversation* (Vol. II). Cambridge: Blackwell Publishers.

Sacks, H. (2004). An Initial Characterization of the Organization of Speaker Turn-taking in Conversation. In G. H. Lerner (ed.), *Conversation Analysis. Studies from the First Generation* (pp. 45–53). Philadelphia: John Benjamins.

Sacks, H., Schegloff, E. A., and Jefferson, G. (1974). A Simplest Systematics for the Organization of Turn-Taking for Conversation. *Language, 50*(4), 696–735.

Schegloff, E. A. (1972). Notes on a Conversational Practice: Formulating Place. In D. Sudnow (ed.), *Studies in Social Interaction* (pp. 75–119). New York: The Free Press.

Schegloff, E. A. (1987a). Analyzing Single Episodes of Interaction: An Exercise in Conversation Analysis. *Social Psychology Quarterly*, *50*(2), 101–14.

Schegloff, E. A. (1987b). Some Sources of Misunderstanding in Talk-in-interaction. *Linguistics*, *25*, 201–18.

Schegloff, E. A. (1993). Reflections on Quantification in the Study of Conversation. *Research on Language and Social Interaction*, *26*(1), 99–128.

Schegloff, E. A. (2006). Interaction: The Infrastructure for Social Institutions, the Natural Ecological Niche for Language, and the Arena in Which Culture is Enacted. In N. J. Enfield and S. C. Levinson (eds.), *Roots of Human Sociality: Culture, Cognition and Interaction* (pp. 70–96): Oxford: Berg.

Schegloff, E. A. (2007). *Sequence Organization in Interaction* (Vol. *1*). Cambridge: Cambridge University Press.

Schegloff, E. A. and Sacks, H. (1973). Opening up Closings. *Semiotica*, *8*(4), 289–327.

Schiffrin, D. (1987). *Discourse Markers*. Cambridge: Cambridge University Press.

Schönfeldt, J. and Golato, A. (2003). Repair in Chats: A Conversation Analytic Approach. *Research on Language and Social Interaction*, *36*(3), 241–84.

Seargeant, P., Tagg, C., and Ngampramuan, W. (2012). Language Choice and Addressivity Strategies in Thai-English Social Network Interactions. *Journal of Sociolinguistics*, *16*(4), 510–31.

Sharma, B. K. (2012). Beyond Social Networking: Performing Global Englishes in Facebook by College Youth in Nepal. *Journal of Sociolinguistics*, *16*(4), 483–509.

Sheldon, P. (2008a). The Relationship Between Unwillingness-to-communicate and Students' Facebook Use. *Journal of Media Psychology*, *20*(2), 67–75.

Sheldon, P. (2008b). Student Favorite: Facebook and Motives for its Use. *Southwestern Mass Communication Journal*, *23*(2), 39–53.

Sheldon, P. (2009). "I'll Poke you. You will Poke me!" Self Disclosure, Social Attraction, Predictability and Trust as Important Predictors of Facebook Relationships. *Journal of Psychosocial Research on Cyberspace*, *3*(2).

Sherman, T. and Švelch, J. (2015). "Grammar Nazis Never Sleep": Facebook Humor and the Management of Standard Written Language. *Language Policy*, *14*(4), 315–34.

Stæhr, A. (2015). Reflexivity in Facebook Interaction—Enregisterment Across Written and Spoken Language Practices. *Discourse, Context & Media*, *8*, 30–45.

Stern, L. A. and Taylor, K. (2007). Social Networking on Facebook. *Journal of the Communication, Speech & Theatre Association of North Dakota*, *20*, 9–20.

Stommel, W. (2008). Conversation Analysis and Community of Practice as Approaches to Studying Online Community. *Language@Internet*, *5*(5), 1–22.

Stutzman, F. (2006). An Evaluation of Identity-Sharing Behavior in Social Network Communities. *The Journal of The International Digital Media and Arts Association*, *3*, (1).

Taecharungroj, V. and Nueangjamnong, P. (2015). Humour 2.0: Styles and Types of Humour and Virality of Memes on Facebook. *Journal of Creative Communications, 10*(3), 288–302.

Tagg, C. (2015). *Exploring Digital Communication Language in Action*. Milton Park: Taylor & Francis.

Tagg, C. and Seargeant, P. (2012). Writing Systems at Play in Thai-English Online Interactions. *Writing Systems Research, 4*(2), 195–213.

ten Have, P. (1999). *Doing Conversation Analysis A Practical Guide*. London: SAGE Publications.

Terasaki, A. K. (2004). Pre-announcement Sequences in Conversation. In G. H. Lerner (ed.), *Conversation Analysis: Studies from the First Generation* (pp. 171–233). Amsterdam: John Benjamins.

Tudini, V. (2004). Virtual Immersion: Native Speaker Chats as a Bridge to Conversational Italian. *Australian Review of Applied Linguistics, 18*, 63–80.

Tudini, V. (2007). Negotiation and Intercultural Learning in Italian Native Speaker Chat Rooms. *The Modern Language Journal, 91*(4), 577–601.

Tudini, V. (2010). *Online Second Language Acquisition Conversation Analysis of Online Chat*. London: Continuum International Publishing Group.

Tudini, V. (2013). Form-focused Social Repertoires in an Online Language Learning Partnership. *Journal of Pragmatics, 50*, 187–202.

Tufekci, Z. (2008). Can you see me now? Audience and Disclosure Regulation in Online Social Network Sites. *Bulletin of Science, Technology & Society, 28*(1), 20–36.

Vàsquez, C. (2015). Intertextuality and Interdiscursivity in Online Consumer Reviews. In R. H. Jones, A. Chik, and C. A. Hafner (eds.), *Discourse and Digital Practices: Doing Discourse Analysis in the Digital Age*. London: Routledge.

Wang, Y.-C., Burke, M., and Kraut, R. (2013). *Gender, Topic, and Audience Response: An Analysis of User-Generated Content on Facebook*. Paper presented at the Proceedings of the SIGCHI Conference on Human Factors in Computing Systems.

West, L. (2013). Facebook Sharing: A Sociolinguistic Analysis of Computer-mediated Storytelling. *Discourse, Context & Media, 2*(1), 1–13.

West, L. (2015). *Responding (or not) on Facebook: A Sociolinguistic Study of Liking, Commenting, and other Reactions to Posts*. (Doctoral Dissertetion), Georgetown University.

West, L. and Trester, A. M. (2013). Facework on Facebook: Conversations on Social Media. In D. Tannen and A. M. Trester (eds.), *Discourse 2.0 Language and New Media* (pp. 133–54). Washington, DC: Georgetown University Press.

Westlake, E. J. (2008). Friend Me if You Facebook Generation Y and Performative Surveillance. *TDR: The Drama Review, 52*(4), 21–40.

Wooffitt, R. (2005). *Conversation Analysis and Discourse Analysis: A Comparative and Critical Introduction*. London: Sage.

Zemel, A. and Çakir, M. (1999). Reading's Work in VMT. In G. Stahl (ed.), *Studying Virtual Math Teams* (pp. 261–76). New York, Dordrecht, Heidelberg and London: Springer.

Zhao, S., Grasmuck, S., and Martin, J. (2008). Identity Construction on Facebook: Digital Empowerment in Anchored Relationships. *Computers in Human Behavior*, *24*, 1816–36.

Index